The LINDBERGH KIDNAPPING CASE

A CRITICAL ANALYSIS
OF THE TRIAL OF
BRUNO RICHARD HAUPTMANN

The LINDBERGH KIDNAPPING CASE

A CRITICAL ANALYSIS OF THE TRIAL OF BRUNO RICHARD HAUPTMANN

JAMES M. DEDMAN III &
GEORGE R. DEKLE, SR.

TALBOT
PUBLISHING
Clark, New Jersey

ISBN 978-1-61619-533-5

TALBOT PUBLISHING

AN IMPRINT OF

THE LAWBOOK EXCHANGE, LTD.

33 Terminal Avenue

Clark, New Jersey 07066-1321

Please see our website for a selection of our other publications and fine facsimile reprints of classic works of legal history:
www.lawbookexchange.com

Library of Congress Cataloging-in-Publication Data

Names: Dedman, James M., III, author. | Dekle, George R., 1948- author.
Title: The Lindbergh kidnapping case : a critical analysis of the trial of Bruno Richard Hauptmann / James M. Dedman III and George R. Dekle, Sr.
Description: Clark, NJ : Talbot Publishing An Imprint of The Lawbook Exchange, Ltd., 2016. | Includes bibliographical references and index.
Identifiers: LCCN 2016031411| ISBN 9781616195335 (hardcover : alk. paper) | ISBN 1616195339 (hardcover : alk. paper)
Subjects: LCSH: Hauptmann, Bruno Richard, 1899-1936--Trials, litigation, etc. | Lindbergh, Charles Augustus, 1930-1932--Kidnapping, 1932. | Trials (Kidnapping)--New Jersey. | Trials (Murder)--New Jersey.
Classification: LCC KF223.L53 D43 2016 | DDC 345.749/02533--dc23
LC record available at https://lccn.loc.gov/2016031411

Printed in the United States of America on acid-free paper

To my loving wife Pat—just me and you

Jim Dedman

To the memory of my paternal grandfather, John Ervin Dekle, Sheriff of Union County, Florida around the time of the Lindbergh Kidnapping Case, a man of great physical strength, courage, and sharp intellect, against whom I had many a spirited debate; and to the memory of my maternal grandmother, Jewel Smith Coleman, who introduced me to the wonder of books and reading.

Bob Dekle

Contents

Introduction

When the media received the first reports of the Lindbergh kidnapping, a mighty river of ink began to flow as reporters, writers, and public figures of all stripes weighed in on the circumstances and the significance of the event. With the possible exception of the O.J. Simpson case, the Lindbergh case received the most extensive media coverage of the Twentieth Century. The international interest became so intense that a special New Jersey to London transatlantic wire was set up so that Europe could receive news of the trial without delay.[1] The river of ink has slowed since March 1, 1932, but it continues to this day. In 2012 at least four new books on the trial saw publication,[2] at least one in 2013,[3] and at least two more in 2014.[4] The second guessing began

---

[1] "Direct wire to London set up for trial news," *The New York Times*, January 4, 1935, NYT Archive, http://www.nytimes.com/ref/member center/nytarchive.html (accessed July 8, 2012), hereafter cited *NYT*.

[2] Robert Zorn, *Cemetery John: The Undiscovered Mastermind of the Lindbergh Kidnapping* (New York: The Overlook Press, 2012); Mark W. Falzini and James Davidson, *New Jersey's Lindbergh Kidnapping and Trial* (Mount Pleasant, SC: Arcadia Publishing, 2012); Michael Foldes, Diana Bean, and Chuck Haupt, *Sleeping Dogs: A True Story of the Lindbergh Baby Kidnapping* (Amazon Digital Services, Inc.: Michael Foldes, 2012); Henry M. Holden, *Famous Cases of the FBI: The Lindbergh Baby Kidnapping* (Amazon Digital Services, Inc.: Blackhawk Publishing, 2012).

[3] Adam Schrager, *The Sixteenth Rail: The Evidence, the Scientist, and the Lindbergh Kidnapping* (Golden, CO: Fulcrum Publishing, 2013).

[4] Richard T. Cahill Jr., *Hauptmann's Ladder: A Step-by-Step Analysis of the Lindbergh Kidnapping* (Kent, Ohio: Kent State University Press, 2014); William A. Cook, *The Lindbergh Baby Kidnapping* (Mechanicsburg, Pa.: Sunbury Press, 2014).

almost immediately upon the conviction of Bruno Richard Hauptmann for the murder of the Lindbergh baby, and the ensuing eight decades have seen the publication of a plethora of books accusing almost everyone connected to the case with either killing the child or framing Hauptmann or both.

It seems to be a law of nature that the more intensely the press covers a criminal case, the more surreal the case becomes. As if the case itself were not bizarre enough, petty criminals, con men, hucksters, "psychics," envious lawmen, and even Al Capone all became involved on the periphery of the case. The shenanigans of these figures added to the circus atmosphere of the trial, impeded the orderly administration of justice, and provided pundits and critics with a wealth of material for comment and critique.

With so much ink already spilled on the case, the reader is justified in asking "Hasn't every aspect of the case been hashed and rehashed multiple times already? Why another book?" As a matter of fact, at least one aspect of the case has gone unexamined. The actual trial itself has never been subjected to a comprehensive forensic analysis. The prosecution and defense of a complex criminal case can be viewed as partly art, partly science, and largely technique, and much can be learned from an intensive analysis of a major case. As retired criminal trial advocates with a combined 64 years' experience prosecuting and defending criminal cases, we feel we can make a unique contribution to the literature on the Lindbergh case by looking at the case through a lens which no other author has used—the lens of the veteran prosecutor. Readers of this critique should keep in mind the comment made by Carl von Clausewitz when he critiqued the performance of other military leaders:

> If therefore a critic points out an error made by a Frederick or a Bonaparte, that does not mean that he who makes the criticism would not have committed

> the same error; he may even be ready to grant that had he been in the place of these great Generals he might have made much greater mistakes.[5]

Taking Clausewitz as our guide, we do not claim to have greater wisdom than the lawyers who actually tried the case, nor do we claim superior talent. We readily admit we may have made even more egregious errors than the prosecution and defense teams. We do, however, claim to have near 20/20 hindsight, and we feel that our experience, coupled with that hindsight gives us a singular opportunity to contribute to the understanding of the trial.

We do not intend to give a full account of all the facts and circumstances surrounding the case, especially those bizarre aspects which do not bear directly on the actual evidence relating to the question of guilt or innocence. We do intend to give a full analysis of the relevant evidence which was or could have been presented at trial. We will not seek to prove Hauptmann either guilty or innocent. We will seek to show how the advocates analyzed and presented the evidence for and against Hauptmann's guilt. We will not undertake to malign the character of any of the lawyers involved in the trial or to accuse them of any sort of unethical behavior. We will seek to critique the performance of the lawyers involved in the trial, indicating what they did well, what they did poorly, and what they left undone. By the end of the book, readers should be able to decide for themselves whether justice was done in the case.

---

[5] Carl von Clausewitz, *On War*. Translated by J.J. Graham (London: N. Trubner and Company, 1873), 76.

Dramatis Personae

Cemetery John
Shadowy figure who received the ransom payment from John F. Condon. May or may not have been Hauptmann.

Condon, John F.
Eccentric septuagenarian educator who interjected himself into the ransom negotiations.

Fawcett, James M.
Attorney who represented Hauptmann during the extradition proceedings in New York.

Fisch, Isidore
Business associate of Hauptmann. Hauptmann testified that Fisch gave him the ransom money.

Fisher, C. Lloyd
Associate defense counsel at the trial who became lead counsel during the post-conviction litigation.

Fredericksen, Christian
Bronx bakery owner who gave Hauptmann an alibi for the night of the kidnapping.

Fredericksen, Kate
Wife of Christian Fredericksen who corroborated Frederickson's alibi for Hauptmann.

Freeman, Allyne
Political ally of Harold G. Hoffman and foreman of the Mercer County Grand Jury who obtained a delay of Hauptmann's execution to investigate the possibility that Paul Wendel committed the kidnapping.

Gow, Bessie (Betty) Mowat
The child's nurse.

Hammer, Ernest E.L.
Bronx Supreme Court Justice who presided over extradition proceedings.

Haring, J. Vreeland
Examiner of questioned documents held for rebuttal but not called. Wrote a book entitled *The Hand of Hauptmann.*

Hauck, Anthony M.
Local prosecutor who called upon the Attorney General for help in prosecuting the case.

Hauptmann, Anna
Wife of the defendant who stood by him to the bitter end.

Hauptmann, Bruno Richard
Defendant. Accused kidnapper and killer of Charles A. Lindbergh, Jr.

Hoffman, Harold G.
Governor of New Jersey who became active in post-conviction phase of the case.

Hudson, Erastus Meade
Fingerprint expert called in by the New Jersey State Police. Eventually testified for the defense.

Keith, Stanley R.
Metallurgist who matched nails in the ladder to a keg of nails found in Hauptmann's garage. Did not testify to his findings at trial but did testify to the ladder's chain of custody.

Kimberling, Mark O.
Warden of the state penitentiary at Trenton who oversaw Hauptmann's execution.

Kloppenburg, Hans
Friend of Hauptmann who gave him an alibi for the night of the ransom delivery.

Koehler, Arthur
Wood expert who connected Hauptmann to the ladder found at the scene of the crime.

Lanigan, Joseph
Assistant Attorney General and member of the prosecution team.

Large, George K.
A former judge who lived in Flemington. Associated with the prosecution team.

Leibowitz, Samuel
Attorney brought in by the defense team during the post-conviction phase. Leibowitz unsuccessfully tried to persuade Hauptmann to confess and avoid the death penalty.

Lindbergh, Anne Morrow
Author. Wife of Charles A. Lindbergh and mother of murdered child.

Lindbergh, Charles A., Sr.
National hero. Father of the child victim, Charles A. Lindbergh, Jr.

Loney, Arch W.
Wood expert and potential defense witness at trial. Not called during the trial but became prominent during post-conviction attempts to impeach Arthur Koehler's testimony.

Morrow, Elizabeth
Grandmother of the child and widow of U.S. Senator Dwight W. Morrow. Testified as last rebuttal witness to alibi Violet Sharpe.

Osborn, Albert S.
Nationally famous examiner of questioned documents who first identified Hauptmann as the author of the ransom letters.

Parker, Ellis
"The American Sherlock Holmes." His offer to assist investigation of the kidnapping was rebuffed by Schwarzkopf. Procured confession of Paul Wendel to kidnapping of baby. Later sentenced to prison for kidnapping Wendel.

Peacock, Robert
Assistant Attorney General and member of the prosecution team.

Pope, Fred A.
Attorney and member of the Hauptmann defense team.

Reilly, Edward J.
Prominent criminal defense attorney who led the defense team at the trial of Hauptmann.

Rosecrans, Egbert
Attorney and member of the Hauptmann defense team.

Schwarzkopf, H. Norman
Director of New Jersey State Police who oversaw the investigation. Father of Norman Schwarzkopf, Jr., leader of coalition forces in the Persian Gulf War.

Sellers, Clark
Examiner of questioned documents who testified as the last of eight handwriting experts at the trial.

Sharpe, Violet
Maid to Elizabeth Morrow. Committed suicide rather than undergo further questioning as a suspect in the kidnapping.

Stock, Robert
Assistant Attorney General and member of the prosecution team.

Trenchard, Thomas W.
Supreme Court Justice who presided over the Hauptmann trial.

Trendly, John M.
Handwriting examiner who testified in defense of Hauptmann.

Walton, Charles
Foreman of the trial jury.

Wendel, Paul
Disbarred attorney who confessed to kidnapping the child but later recanted and claimed he confessed under duress.

Whateley, Elsie
The Lindberghs' maid.

Whateley, Oliver
The Lindberghs' butler. Died before the case came to trial.

Wilentz, David T.
Attorney General of New Jersey who, despite his opposition to the death penalty, served as lead prosecutor in the case.

1

The Kidnapping

The evening of Tuesday March 1, 1932 was cold and wet in Hunterdon County, New Jersey. At the newly-built home of Charles and Anne Lindbergh, the household routine was not going according to schedule. The Lindberghs customarily spent weeknights in Englewood at the estate of Anne's mother, Elizabeth Morrow, and the weekends at their not-quite-finished home in Hopewell. On this particular week, though, they decided to stay a few extra days in Hopewell to accommodate the illness of their infant child, Charles Jr. Anne Lindbergh called her mother's home and asked Bessie Gow, the nurse who kept little Charles on weekdays, to come to the new home and help her with him. Bessie had a date with a young man named Red Johnson, but she telephoned him and broke it. Mrs. Morrow's chauffer gave her a ride to the new home, and when she arrived she took over the care of little Charles.

That evening the Lindberghs shuttered their windows against the weather, but one shutter in the nursery on the second floor had warped and would not lock. Anne Lindbergh and the baby's nurse, Bessie Gow, put little Charles to bed at 8:00 p.m. They rubbed his chest with Vick's Salve, and Gow sewed a makeshift shirt to put on the child under his sleeping suit. They fitted his hands with thumb guards to keep him from sucking his thumbs and tucked him into bed, pinning the covers down to keep him from kicking them off in the night. According to the custom of the house they would let him sleep undisturbed until 10:00 p.m., when Bessie Gow would return to the nursery to check on him.

Charles Lindbergh, Sr. arrived home around 8:30 from New York City, and the couple ate supper. After supper, Anne went upstairs to her bedroom and Charles went to his study. While in the study, situated directly under the nursery, Lindbergh heard a crashing sound but thought nothing of it. At 10:00 p.m. Bessie Gow went to the baby's nursery to check on him. She could not find him in his crib. Gow immediately told Lindbergh, who was still in his study beneath the nursery. They roused the other occupants in the house and searched high and low. Little Charles was nowhere to be found.

Lindbergh armed himself with a Springfield rifle and searched the grounds of his home to no avail. Sometime during the excitement he told his butler Oliver Whateley to call the police. Before the police arrived, Lindbergh went back into the nursery and found something—an envelope on the window sill under the warped shutter and muddy footprints leading away from the windowsill towards the crib. He ordered that no one should touch the envelope until the police arrived. When the police got to the Lindbergh home, they opened the envelope and found a note. It said:

> Dear Sir!
>
> Have 50.000$ redy 25 000$ in 20$ bills 15000$ in 10$ bills and 10000$ in 5$ bills After 2–4 days we will inform you were to deliver the mony.
>
> We warn you for making anyding public or for notify the Police Little Charles is in gut care.
>
> Indication for all letters are
> Singnature [Symbol]
> and three hohls.

The symbol consisted of a red circle inscribed in two intersecting blue circles. Three holes completed the symbol—one of them in the red circle and the other two flanking the blue circles.

Upon searching the grounds around the house, the police found a three-piece homemade ladder which appeared to have been broken, a chisel, and markings under the nursery window suggesting that the ladder had been placed against the house in that location. Based on these observations, the police theorized that the kidnapper had used the ladder to get into the second floor nursery through the window. The ladder had supported the kidnapper's weight going up, but when the kidnapper came down with the additional weight of the baby, it broke and the kidnapper abandoned it. After little Charles was found dead, the police theorized that he had died from a blow to the head suffered when he fell to the ground after the ladder broke.

The kidnapping touched off a massive manhunt and criminal investigation under the supervision of Colonel H. Norman Schwarzkopf, the director of the New Jersey State Police. Bad news travels like wildfire, and it wasn't long before the Lindbergh estate was swamped with reporters trying to learn anything they could about the case.

In the days immediately following the abduction the Lindberghs made a public plea for the return of their child and asked that while in captivity he be fed according to a special diet.[1] Soon after the publication of the diet, Charles Lindbergh received a second note which read:

> Dear Sir. We have warned you note to make anything public also notify the police now you have to take consequences—means we will have to hold the baby until everything is quite. We can note make any

---

1 "Sleepless Father Persists in Search," *NYT*, March 3, 1932.

> appointmant just now. We know very well what it means to us. It is realy necessary to make a world affair out of this, or to get your baby back as soon as possible to settle those affair in a quick way will be better for both—don't by afraid about the baby—keeping care of us day and night. We also will feed him according to the diet. We are interested to send him back in gut health. And ransom was made aus for 50000 $ but now we have to take another person to it and probably have to keep the baby for a longer time as we expected. So the amount will be 70000 20000 in 50$ bills 25000 $ in 20$ bill 15000 $ in 10$ bills and 10000 in 5$ bills Don't mark any bills or take them from one serial nomer. We will form you latter were to deliver the money. But we will note do so until the Police is out of the cace and the pappers are qute. The kidnaping we prepared in years so we are prepared for everyding.

And Lindbergh's close friend and attorney, Henry Breckenridge, received a third note addressed to Lindbergh in his care. The note said:

> Dear Sir: Did you receive ouer letter from March 4. we sent the mail on one off the letter—near Boro Hall, Brooklyn. We know Police interfer with your privat-mail. How can we come to any arrangements this way. in the future we will send our letters to Mr. Breckenbridge at 25 Broadway. We believe polise captured two letter and let not forwarded to you. We will not accept any go-between from your sent. We will arrangh theas latter. There is no worry about the boy. He is very well and will be feed according to the diet. Best dank for information about it. We are interested to send your boy back in gut health. It is necessary to make a world-affair out of it, or to get your boy back as soon as possible. Why did you ignore oue letter which we left in the room the baby would be back long ago. You would not get any result from Polise becauce our kinaping was pland for a year allredy. But we were afraid the boy

> would not be strong enough. Ouer ransom was made out for 50000$ but now we have to put another to it as propperly have to hold the baby longer as we expected so it will be 70000$ 20000 in 50$ bills 25000 in 25$ 12000$ in 10$ bills and 10000 in 5$ bills. We warn you again not to mark any bills or take them for one ser. No. We will inform you latter how to deliver the mony but not before the polise is out of this cace and the pappers are quite.

Both notes contained additional demand information and the curious symbol at the bottom. Both bore New York City area postmarks.

As can be expected, reports that the only son of the most famous man in America had gone missing touched off a media firestorm. A number of people, including Al Capone and other underworld figures, offered to assist in the recovery of little Charles. A high profile case like the Lindbergh case inevitably attracts crooks, crackpots, and con men, and the Lindbergh kidnapping case had its share of them. Usually, dealings with people of this ilk prove to be nothing but a waste of time, as demonstrated by Lindbergh's dealing with a gentleman by the name of John Hughes Curtis, whom we will meet a little later in this narrative. One eccentric old gentleman, however, stepped forward with what proved to be genuine assistance. Dr. John F. Condon, a resident of the Bronx, wrote a letter to the *Bronx Home News* offering to act as a go-between in any ransom negotiations, and also offering $1,000 of his own money as part of an exchange. The newspaper published the letter, and an extortionist soon replied to it.

On March 12, as Joe Perrone drove his taxi down Gun Hill Road in the Bronx, someone flagged him down and gave him a dollar to deliver an envelope to Dr. Condon. Perrone would eventually identify Bruno Richard Hauptmann as the man who gave him the envelope. He delivered the letter, and Condon opened it. It read:

> Mr. Dr. John Condon 2974 Decatur Ave. New York, NY
>
> dear Sir: If you are willing to act as go-between in the Lindbergh case please follow strictly instruction. Handel incloced letter personaly to Mr. Lindbergh. It will explain everything. don't tell anyone about it as soon we find out the press or Police is notified everything are cancell and it will be a further delay. After you get the money from Mr. Lindbergh put these 3 words in the New-York American.
>
> Mony is redy After notise we will give you further instruction. don't be affraid we are not out for your 1000$ keep it. Only act stricly. Be at home every night between 6–12 by this time you will hear from us.
>
> dear Sir. please handel incloced letter to Col. Lindbergh. It is in Mr. Lindbergergh interest not to notify the Police.

The enclosed letter read:

> dear Sir, Mr. Condon may act as go-between. You may give him the 70000$. make one packet the size will bee about....(sketch of a box) we have notify your already in what kind of bills. We warn you not to set any trapp in any way. If you or someone els will notify the Police ther will be a further delay After we have the mony in hand we will tell you where to find your boy You may have a airplain redy it is about 150 mil awy. But befor telling you the odr. a delay of 8 houers will be between.

Condon took the note to Lindbergh, and Lindbergh chose to permit Condon to act on his behalf as an intermediary in the ransom negotiations. Condon conducted the remaining negotiations, placing cryptic ads in the newspaper and receiving several additional handwritten notes containing the curious symbol. On March 13, almost two weeks after the abduction, Condon met with the purported author of the notes at Woodlawn Cemetery in the Bronx. The extortionist refused to give Condon a name, so Condon referred to him as "Cemetery John." Condon demanded to see little Charles, but Cemetery John refused. He did agree to send Condon proof of his *bona fides*. Shortly after this first meeting, Cemetery John sent a package to Condon. It contained a baby's sleeping suit which the Lindberghs identified as the one little Charles was wearing the night he disappeared.

After much negotiation, Cemetery John agreed to a ransom amount ($70,000) and a meeting date. Lindbergh, fearing that the kidnappers might kill his son, insisted that the authorities not be involved in any way in the delivery of the ransom money. The authorities reluctantly acceded to Lindbergh's demand, but they persuaded him to let them record the serial numbers of the bills used for the payoff. With Lindbergh's consent they carefully prepared the ransom money, recording the serial numbers of each bill. In order to help with later identification of the notes, they included a large number of Series 1928 gold notes, including a $20,000 packet of easily identifiable fifty dollar gold notes. On April 2, 1932, the day appointed for the delivery of the ransom, Lindbergh met with Condon at Condon's home in the Bronx. They received a note giving them instructions where to go, and Lindbergh drove Condon to a location near St. Raymond's Cemetery in the Bronx. They heard Cemetery John call out "Hey, Doctor," and Condon went to meet with him while Lindbergh waited in the car with the money. After a brief negotiation, Condon persuaded Cemetery John to take $50,000 instead of the agreed-upon $70,000. He returned to Lindbergh in the car to retrieve the money, the two men removed the package containing the easily identifiable packet of fifty dollar gold certificates, and Condon delivered the ransom. Cemetery John then gave Condon the last ransom note, which read:

> The boy is on the Boad Nelly. It is a small boad 28 feet long. Two persons are on the boad. The are innosent. you will find the Boad between Horseneck Beach and gay Head near Elizabeth Island.

Condon went with Lindbergh to the area described, and they exhausted themselves with a fruitless aerial search for the Boad Nelly. Condon published several pleas in the paper asking for better directions, but he never heard from Cemetery John again. At this point John Hughes Curtis inserted himself into the case. He claimed to be in communication with the kidnappers and claimed he could find out where the child was being held. Lindbergh placed more confidence in Condon than in Curtis, but he was desperate enough to try any avenue that might save his child. After several "meetings" with the kidnappers, Hughes claimed he had arranged for Lindbergh to meet the kidnappers on a schooner off the coast of Block Island, Massachusetts. Hughes led Lindbergh on a merry chase as they sailed the seas off Block Island searching for the nonexistent schooner.

Finally, on May 12, Lindbergh abandoned the fruitless search for the schooner, and as he returned home, two workmen found the decomposed body of a child in a shallow grave just a few miles from the Lindbergh house. Charles Lindbergh and Bessie Gow identified the body as Charles A. Lindbergh, Jr., and Gow also identified the clothing on the body as the garment she had made for little Charles to wear under his sleeping suit the night he disappeared. This shirt was later matched to remnants of cloth still in the home.

The medical examiner determined that little Charles had died from blunt force trauma to the head.

Curtis eventually confessed that he had duped Lindbergh, and Anthony Hauck, the Prosecutor of the Pleas for Hunterdon County, filed criminal charges against him. C. Lloyd Fisher, who later served on the Hauptmann defense team, defended Curtis, who was convicted and sentenced to prison. Interestingly, the only way to convict Curtis was to allege that he was actually in contact with a gang of kidnappers. When Hauptmann stood trial, the prosecution presented a theory that he acted alone. (He certainly didn't have any contact with Curtis). Fisher believed that the conviction of Curtis validated the theory that the kidnapping was the work of a gang. Fisher argued that the prosecution could not have it both ways. If Curtis was guilty, Hauptmann was innocent; and if Hauptmann was guilty, Curtis was innocent.

After the payment of the ransom, the police sent a list of serial numbers to all banks in the New York area asking them to be on the lookout for bills bearing those numbers. Over the next few years the authorities dutifully traced the origin of each bill which the banks identified as bearing the correct serial numbers. Most of the bills were found to have been passed in the vicinity of New York City. The authorities traced one of those bills to the Sheridan Theater on the corner of 12th Street and 7th Avenue in New York. Cecile Barr, the ticket taker, noticed the man who passed the bill because she wasn't busy at the time "and he threw a five-dollar bill in at me, which was folded three times in eight parts." [2] On September 15, 1934, a man purchased a small quantity of

---

[2] Transcript of Trial, *State of New Jersey v. Bruno Richard Hauptmann* (Hunterdon County Oyer and Terminer Court, 1934), 4360, hereafter cited as "Transcript."

gasoline in the Bronx and paid with a $10 gold certificate. The gas station attendant was suspicious of gold certificates since they had been recalled by the United States government in 1933. He recorded the man's license tag number on the edge of the $10 bill. When the bill was deposited at the bank, bank personnel identified it as ransom money. Bank officials called the police, and the police traced the tag number on the bill to Bruno Richard Hauptmann, who lived in the Bronx near the two cemeteries where the negotiations had occurred. The gas station attendant later identified Hauptmann as the man who passed the $10 gold certificate.

The police set up surveillance on Hauptmann's house, and they didn't have long to wait. As he left home on the morning of September 19, they stopped his car. He had a $20 gold certificate in his wallet. The bill's serial number identified it as part of the ransom payment. Hauptmann initially said he had $300 more in gold certificates at his home. The police returned to Hauptmann's home and asked Hauptmann to show them the $300 in gold certificates. Hauptmann showed them $120 in gold coins and said there were no more gold certificates. The authorities searched Hauptmann's garage and found $13,760 in gold certificates. Hauptmann said there were no more. They decided to take the garage apart board by board, and during the demolition found another $850 in gold certificates. All the gold certificates were Lindbergh ransom money. Hauptmann was charged in New York with the offense of extortion, and New Jersey indicted him for the murder of the Lindbergh child. The Trial of the Century was under way.

2

Extraditing Hauptmann

After his arrest on September 19, 1934, Hauptmann made several statements to the police and to the Bronx District Attorney's Office, but he steadfastly refused to confess. Hauptmann's statements to the authorities were self-serving but contradictory, and the police became so frustrated with him that they resorted to beating him in an effort to get him to confess. This was a blunder on several levels. Had they maintained their composure and continued to question him, his stories would likely have become even more contradictory and implausible. Sometimes when a suspect tells a horrendous lie, this fact persuades jurors of his guilt just as much as if he had made a full confession. The beating itself caused problems, but not of the type that one might imagine. In order for a beating to render a defendant's statement inadmissible, it must precede the statement. Hauptmann's contradictory statements were therefore admissible against him in evidence. The beating accomplished only three things: It ended Hauptmann's willingness to cooperate, it robbed the police of the opportunity to entangle him further in lies and implausibility, and it was an embarrassing fact which the defense used to discredit law enforcement.

The governor of New Jersey sent a request to the governor of New York asking that Hauptmann be surrendered to New Jersey authorities so he could be returned to New Jersey to face the charge of murder. The New York Governor signed an extradition warrant, and

Hauptmann's New York attorney, James M. Fawcett, filed a petition for writ of habeas corpus alleging that Hauptmann's confinement in New York on the extradition warrant was illegal. If he could get a judge to agree with him, Hauptmann would stay in New York facing only charges of extortion. Because Fawcett filed the petition, he bore the burden of proving that Hauptmann's confinement on the extradition warrant was illegal. The filing would also require that Fawcett go first in offering proof, and he did not have a lot of time to prepare the case.

Fawcett's petition came on to be heard before Justice Ernest E.L. Hammer in the Supreme Court for Bronx County on October 15, 1934. Because the petition alleged that Hauptmann was being illegally detained, the petition named his jailer, John Hanley, Sheriff of Bronx County, as the defendant. In addition to having little time to prepare and bearing the burden of proof, Fawcett had a third problem—he would have to disclose a lot of defense information in the hearing.

The habeas corpus hearing would not decide the issue of whether Hauptmann was guilty of the murder. Fawcett could not contend his client was innocent. He could only offer evidence that Hauptmann was not in New Jersey when the crime occurred, and he had to prove that fact conclusively.[1] Justice Hammer laid out the issues in the following language:

> [Hauptman]'s evidence must be clear and convincing. He must show by uncontradicted facts that he was not in the demanding State. If the evidence is conflicting and reasonable inference can be drawn that [he] was

---

[1] People *ex rel.* Hauptmann v. Hanley, 153 Misc. 61, 274 N.Y.S. 813 (New York Sup.Ct., Bronx County), *affirmed* 242 App Div. 257 (New York Ct. App., 1934).

> within the demanding State, he should be delivered up for trial.[2] …
>
> The question of alibi or any question of the guilt or innocence of the accused may not properly be considered on a habeas corpus proceeding, but must wait trial for determination.... When it is conceded, or when it is so conclusively proved that no question can be made that the person was not within the demanding State when the crime is said to have been committed, … then the court will discharge the defendant.[3]

When Hammer said he wouldn't consider alibi evidence, he meant that Hauptmann would be prevented from proving that he was somewhere else within the state of New Jersey. Evidence that Hauptmann was somewhere else outside the state of New Jersey would, of course, be considered alibi evidence at his trial, but in the habeas corpus hearing it would be proof that New Jersey did not have the jurisdiction to try Hauptmann.

At the request of Bronx District Attorney Samuel Foley, Justice Hammer permitted David Wilentz, the Attorney General of New Jersey, to represent Foley's office in contesting the petition.[4] Wilentz would later serve as the lead prosecutor at the trial in New Jersey. Fawcett revealed his lack of preparation at the very beginning of the hearing when Wilentz offered Hauptmann's employment records to Fawcett. Fawcett offered them into evidence, not realizing that they contradicted Hauptmann's claim that he worked on the day of March 1.[5] The records showed that Hauptmann did not begin

---

[2] *Id* at 817.

[3] *Id* at 818.

[4] Transcript of Hearing on Petition for Writ of Habeas Corpus, *People ex rel Hauptmann v. Hanley* (New York Sup.Ct., Bronx County, 1934), 2, hereafter cited as "Hearing."

[5] Hearing, 5.

working for Reliance Property Management until after the middle of March. Throughout the hearing it did not appear that Fawcett realized what he had done or what the records reflected.

To prove his petition, Fawcett called five witnesses to the stand, four of whom testified that Hauptmann was in New York State on the evening of Tuesday, March 1, 1932. Christian Fredericksen, Kate Fredericksen, Anna Hauptmann, and Richard Hauptmann all swore that Hauptmann had been at the Fredericksen's bakery in the Bronx on the evening of the abduction, miles away from the Lindbergh estate. All David Wilentz had to do to defeat the petition was to offer enough contradictory evidence to show that their testimony was inconclusive. If he could do so, New York would honor New Jersey's request and deliver Hauptmann up for trial in New Jersey.

Fawcett contended that Anna Hauptmann, a regular employee of the bakery, worked late on Tuesday nights because Fredericksen's wife did not work Tuesday evenings. Hauptmann would arrive at the bakery around 8:00 p.m. to drive Anna home from work at the end of her shift, and he did so on the night of the kidnapping. The claim was easy to make but hard to prove. When asked whether Hauptmann came to the bakery to get his wife on the evening of March 1, Christian Fredericksen could only say, "To the best of my knowledge. I cannot swear to it, to the best of my knowledge he must have called for her that night."[6] Although Fredericksen said Hauptmann customarily picked up his wife on Tuesday nights, he conceded, "I cannot swear he was there every week."[7] On cross-examination Wilentz weakened Fredericksen's testimony even more by referring to Fredericksen's statement to Bronx Assistant District Attorney Breslin.

---

[6] Hearing, 11.

[7] Hearing, 11.

Q: Do you remember being asked the question, referring to Anna, "Do you remember whether her husband was there that Tuesday night?"

A: Yes.

Q: And you answered "no."

A: I cannot say for sure.

Q: Did you not answer that question just as I have given it to you?

A: Yes.[8]

Fredericksen's concession that he could not provide Hauptmann an absolute alibi for Tuesday night, March 1, was now a matter of record, and came back to haunt him when he testified at the trial in New Jersey.

Fawcett then called Kate Fredericksen to establish that Anna worked for Kate when Kate was away on Tuesday and Friday nights. Kate's testimony that she was away from the bakery that night provided the basis for drawing a series of inferences. If Kate was not at the bakery that night, then Anna must have worked. If Anna worked that night, Hauptmann must have picked her up. If Hauptmann picked her up, he was not in New Jersey when the crime occurred. Fawcett asked about March 1.

Q: Now do you remember that Anna Hauptmann was working at the store during the day time on that day.

A: Yes, that I am sure of.[9]

When it came time for Wilentz to cross-examine, he asked her no questions. It was obvious from her testimony on direct that she had no personal knowledge of Hauptmann's whereabouts on the night of the abduction.

---

[8] Hearing, 13.
[9] Hearing, 17.

Fawcett next called Anna Hauptmann. Given the weakness of the Fredericksens' testimony, it was up to Anna to establish that her husband was at the bakery the evening of March 1. Anna testified that when Kate Fredericksen was not at the bakery she worked from 7:00 a.m. to 8:00 p.m.[10] Fawcett asked if Hauptmann picked her up at the bakery the evening of March 1, and Anna answered, "Yes, he did."[11] When asked what made her remember the first of March, 1932, Anna testified, "Well, I found out it was on a Tuesday that 1st of March, and there was not a day he would miss on Tuesday—he had to call for me, and Fridays, because it was late for me to go home and he was there every Tuesday."[12] Anna didn't know that Hauptmann came to the bakery on the evening of the abduction, she merely assumed that he did because that was what he usually did. Anna had testified to a routine practice rather than specific recollection of a specific night more than two years earlier. Wilentz had to establish that there were exceptions to the routine practice. Wilentz asked Anna, "You do not, of course, remember Tuesday night, March 1st by itself, do you?" Anna had to reply that she did not.[13] She also had to admit that there were times when Hauptmann was away from home for days at a time, possibly Tuesdays. Having shown that there were exceptions to the routine practice, Wilentz directed Anna's attention to her statements to the police after Hauptmann was arrested.

> **Q:** And did you not tell Inspector Bruckman and others who were there present at the time, that you had no recollection at all of what happened March

---

[10] Hearing, 19.
[11] Hearing, 21.
[12] Hearing, 22–23.
[13] Hearing, 23.

1st, and that it was too far back, that you don't know whether your husband was with you or not?

A: I did tell him that.[14]

Now locked into her concession, Anna would be forced to say "usually" instead of "always" when she testified later at trial. After calling three witnesses, Fawcett had merely proven that Hauptmann might have gone to the bakery that evening. He had fallen far short of conclusively proving Hauptmann was in New York. If he was going to carry his burden of proof, he had to do it with Hauptmann's testimony.

Fawcett called Hauptmann. Fawcett directed his client's attention to March 1, 1932. "Now do you recollect the 1st day of March 1932, do you remember that day?" Hauptmann answered, "Yes, I do."[15] Hauptmann testified that he remembered a day over two years earlier when he did not appear to have a memory marker occurring that day to cause him to remember it. Fawcett needed Hauptmann to give an explanation for why he could remember that specific day so long ago. Since Wilentz had established breaks in the routine practice of Hauptmann picking his wife up at the bakery on Tuesday evenings,[16] Hauptmann had to give more definite testimony.

Q: And then, on that morning, did you work for the Reliance Property Management, Inc.?

A: Well, that is one thing I cannot exactly remember.[17]

Fawcett had suggested a memory marker to Hauptmann, but his client had refused to take it. Fawcett tried to repair the damage.

---

[14] Hearing, 26.
[15] Hearing, 44.
[16] Now codified in the Federal Rules of Evidence, Rule 406.
[17] Hearing, 45.

Q: Well, you did some work for the Reliance Property Management Inc. before the 1st of March, 1932, did you not?

A: If I worked at the Majestic Hotel before March 1st, then I was working March 1st and 2nd at the Majestic Hotel. Of that I am positively sure.[18]

The biggest word in Hauptmann's answer had only two letters—"if." Fawcett tried to erase that "if" with the payroll checks he had introduced into evidence.

Q: Well, do you remember getting from the Reliance Property Management, Inc. this check of $36.67 marked exhibit 7?

A: Yes, I do.[19]

Fawcett handed Hauptmann the second payroll check which Hauptmann testified he had received. The checks were dated March 31 and April 15, 1932. What Fawcett failed to realize that the checks did not prove Hauptmann had worked the first half of March. They represented work done beginning with the pay period for the middle of March.

Fawcett's questioning returned to whether Hauptmann worked on March 1, and again Hauptmann responded conditionally. "That I cannot exactly remember, if I worked for the Majestic Hotel, but as far as I can remember I took the subway and went down—I don't know if I went down to 6th Avenue looking for a job, or I went to the Majestic Hotel."[20] Qualifications like "I cannot exactly remember," "if," and "I don't know" did not provide conclusive proof. Hauptmann had locked himself into this conditional testimony about any alibi for

---

[18] Hearing, 45.
[19] Hearing, 46.
[20] Hearing, 50–51.

the day of March 1. Fawcett next tried for the evening of March 1. "You remember seeing her at the bakery on that evening, do you not?" Hauptmann answered, "Yes, I do."[21] Fawcett asked a few more questions about the bakery before ending his questioning of his client.

Wilentz immediately focused on the work alibi.

> **Q:** So that you don't know now whether you were working on March 1st or whether you were looking for a job, you don't know?"
>
> **A:** I don't know exactly.[22]

Wilentz reminded Hauptmann that he had told the police after his arrest that he had been working at the Majestic Hotel on March 1 and asked Hauptmann why his answer was different now. "They did not give me any chance to think at all,"[23] Hauptmann replied. Hauptmann would later testify that he went to the Majestic Hotel for work "but I am not positive sure about that."[24]

Wilentz next began asking questions which were not only beyond the scope of the direct examination, they were irrelevant to the issues being tried on the habeas corpus petition. Fawcett failed to object.

> **Q:** Do you know how to build a ladder?
>
> **A:** Well, I guess everybody—every carpenter does know it.[25]

Wilentz then connected Hauptmann with the National Lumber Yard where he had worked and purchased lumber. Wilentz had scored a major point because he had

---

[21] Hearing, 55.
[22] Hearing, 57.
[23] Hearing, 58.
[24] Hearing, 60.
[25] Hearing, 62.

proof that part of the ladder had come from the National Lumber Yard. Fawcett did not object. He didn't seem to appreciate why Wilentz was asking these questions. Wilentz then explored Hauptmann's possession of Lindbergh ransom money and asked Hauptmann about the twenty dollar bill in his possession at his arrest.

> **Q:** You replied did you not, that that twenty dollar bill was a part of three hundred dollars that you had saved up in gold certificates, is that so?
>
> **A:** Yes.[26]

Wilentz then had Hauptmann concede that he had lied about the money.

> **Q:** So that your story at the time was that you had got this twenty dollar bill as a part of three hundred dollars that had been paid from time to time in the form of gold certificates, and that this money came from people who happened to have gold certificates, or from the bank, is that so?
>
> **A:** Yes.
>
> **Q:** Is that your story?
>
> **A:** Yes.
>
> **Q:** Was that the truth?
>
> **A:** No, it was not the truth.[27]

Wilentz moments later asked Hauptmann why he had not told the truth about the money. Hauptmann answered that he was trying to hide the money. Hauptmann admitted he had lied again to the police when they found money in his garage by telling them it was all the money.

---

[26] Hearing, 64.
[27] Hearing, 64–65.

Q: So that when you told them that was all the money there was, you told them, that you were not telling them the truth?

A: Yes, that is right.[28]

Wilentz then produced a piece of lumber which the police had removed from Hauptmann's closet. It had handwriting on it, and the handwriting included Dr. John Condon's address and 1932 phone number. Hauptmann equivocated on whether he had told the Bronx District Attorney's Office that all the handwriting was his. Wilentz wanted to lock Hauptmann in on the equivocation.

Q: You would not say it was not your handwriting, would you?

A: Would not say exactly, no.[29]

This testimony, beyond the scope of Fawcett's direct and irrelevant to the habeas corpus, came into evidence without a single objection from Fawcett. It later proved damaging to Hauptmann at the New Jersey trial.

Since a witness' credibility may be impeached by his criminal record, Wilentz led Hauptmann through his criminal convictions in Germany. Hauptmann admitted to being convicted in 1919 of grand larceny and sixteen days later being convicted of robbery with a gun.[30] Wilentz would return to the criminal record later asking Hauptmann about the robbery with a gun only to have Hauptmann not answer or reply that he didn't like to answer the questions.[31]

Satisfied that Hauptmann had conceded his criminal past, Wilentz returned to the board with the handwriting.

---

[28] Hearing, 67.

[29] Hearing, 68.

[30] Hearing, 77.

[31] Hearing, 87.

He asked Hauptmann about the statement he gave to the Bronx District Attorney's office after his arrest.

> **Q:** Were you asked this question on the same day at the same session of questioning, "Hauptmann, yesterday I showed you a piece of wood from your roof with Condon's address and phone number on it, is that correct? Answer Yes." Do you remember that?
>
> **A:** Yes.
>
> **Q:** The next question: "Do you remember that you wrote that on the board? Answer yes." Do you remember that?
>
> **A:** Yes.[32]

Fawcett tried to rehabilitate Hauptmann on redirect examination by having him testify that he found the money in a shoe box in his closet; that he had been given the box without knowing its contents; that he was afraid to take the money to a bank or tell anyone about it because he was in the United States illegally; and that he did not know it was Lindbergh ransom money.[33]

Both Fawcett and Wilentz asked a few more questions before releasing Hauptmann from the witness stand. Fawcett next called Howard James Knapp, assistant treasurer of the Reliance Property Management, Incorporated. Knapp handed Fawcett the records for Majestic showing Hauptmann's employment during March and April, 1932. Knapp could not testify whether the eleven days Hauptmann worked in March were eleven straight or eleven non-consecutive days. Fawcett wanted that clarified. "It does not show, does it?" Knapp replied, "It does not show."[34] However, Knapp testified that the

---

[32] Hearing, 99.
[33] Hearing, 101–107.
[34] Hearing, 114.

March records only reflected the second half of March—adding that the Reliance records for the first half of March did not appear to exist.[35] Knapp's records for the April 15 payroll showed that Hauptmann was paid $6.67 and that he resigned during that pay period.[36]

Wilentz asked Knapp about a card index system Reliance had showing when employees began work. Knapp acknowledged such a system, and Wilentz asked, "Take a look at that card and see if it refreshes your recollection in regard to when this man Hauptmann started to work for this company?" Knapp looked at the card and answered, "That record indicates he started work March 21, 1932."[37] The two Reliance payroll checks that Fawcett introduced at the beginning of the hearing were consistent with Hauptmann beginning work on March 21, working eleven days in March and working two days in April before resigning. The ransom was paid on April 2, 1932.

Having offered some not very compelling evidence, Fawcett rested his case. All Wilentz had to do was establish some conflict or contradiction in the evidence. If he could do this, he could force New York to send Hauptmann to New Jersey to face trial. Wilentz called Frank A. Kelly of the New Jersey State Police who had recovered the ransom note in the Lindbergh nursery after the abduction. Kelly authenticated and introduced the nursery note into evidence.[38] Fawcett asked no questions.

James M. Phelan next testified that he was employed by Col. Breckenridge in 1932 and that his secretary,

---

[35] Hearing, 114. The payroll records for the period March 1–March 15 were discovered among the evidence collection in the possession of the New Jersey State Police at the museum and archives in Trenton, N.J. The March 1–15 records do not include the name of Bruno Richard Hauptmann.

[36] Hearing, 115–116.

[37] Hearing, 117.

[38] Hearing, 121.

Lillian Ragdl, had opened a letter in his office and handed it to him. Upon reading the letter, Phelan called Col. Breckenridge at the Lindbergh estate and was told to bring the letter there. The letter, one of the ransom correspondence notes, was introduced into evidence.[39] Fawcett attempted to discredit the authentication of the letter without much luck and then released Phelan.

Wilentz then put Albert S. Osborn, a questioned document examiner, on the stand to establish that Hauptmann had written both of these notes. Although Wilentz had experience in civil trials, this hearing was his introduction to criminal practice. He had trouble establishing Osborn's credentials. Wilentz finally asked, "Mr. Osborn state your qualifications fully as you know them?"[40] In reply Osborn explained his experience such that he was permitted to give his opinion on who had written the notes. Wilentz had earlier introduced automobile registrations known to have been written by Hauptmann, and he asked Osborn to compare the ransom notes to the registration forms. Osborn testified that, "In my opinion, they were written by the same hand."[41] Fawcett offered a series of objections to the testimony without success. This testimony gave no direct proof of Hauptmann's presence in New Jersey, but it did form the basis for a chain of inferences: Hauptmann wrote the first ransom note. The kidnapper put the first ransom note in the nursery. The nursery was in New Jersey. The kidnapper was in New Jersey at the time of the crime. Hauptmann was the kidnapper. Hauptmann was in New Jersey at the time of the crime.

Osborn returned to the stand on the morning of the second day of the hearing and was provided more

---

[39] Hearing, 124.
[40] Hearing, 130.
[41] Hearing, 131.

documents including other ransom correspondence and writing Hauptmann made at the request of the police. Fawcett vigorously cross-examined Osborn on the science of questioned document examination, but the judge allowed Osborn to offer further opinions. Osborn testified that "the same hand"[42] had written all the documents. Osborn then offered a lengthy explanation of his opinion pointing out examples of the basis for his conclusion. Fawcett vigorously cross-examined Osborn on his methods and opinion, but Osborn proved a tough witness with considerable courtroom experience.

The prosecution established an important point with the testimony of Osborn. When he testified that in his opinion Hauptmann had written the note left in the nursery the night of the abduction, he placed Hauptmann in the crime prior to the actual abduction. If the nursery note had been written by Hauptmann, then he wrote the demand for the ransom in specific denominations. He would have also written the threat "We warn you for making anyding public or for notify the Police." And finally he would have knowledge about the child being involved by saying "The child is in gut care." Osborn provided the first solid step toward establishing that Hauptmann was involved early and had guilty knowledge about the crime and its particulars.

James Petrosino of the New York Police Department testified about finding the money hidden in Hauptmann's garage. Fawcett made an effort to exclude the testimony as not being relevant to the events of March 1, 1932, but failed. Petrosino testified that he and others had checked the serial numbers of the garage money against a list of serial numbers of the ransom bills and identified $13,760 in ransom bills.

---

[42] Hearing, 148.

John A. Lyons of the New York Police Department followed Petrosino to the stand to recount Hauptmann's explanation for the money. He testified Hauptmann had said "that Isidor Fisch, about three weeks before last Christmas left for Germany and prior to leaving, he gave him two dress suit cases filled with personal belongings and a cardboard package containing something that he did not know what it contained at the time, and that Fisch said to him "Put these two grips in the garage but don't put the money there." [43] Fawcett got Lyons to concede that Hauptmann had told him that he didn't discover that the money was in the package until about three weeks before his arrest.[44] Wilentz next called Henry Bruckman, Inspector with the New York police, who discovered the board with the handwriting in Hauptmann's closet. Wilentz asked if Hauptmann said anything when shown the board, and Bruckman replied, "Yes, he said he wrote it."[45]

With the testimony about the investigation completed, Wilentz wanted to present direct evidence that Hauptmann had been in New Jersey. He called Millard Whited to the stand. Wilentz wanted Whited to establish that he had seen Hauptmann in the vicinity of the Lindbergh estate in February, 1932, but he had trouble with the proper form of the question. After several attempts he was able to ask if Whited had seen "some man in the vicinity of the Lindbergh home, whom you have since identified and whom you see now?" Fawcett objected again but was overruled. Whited responded that he did. "Do you see him in the court room?" Whited responded, "Yes, sir," and pointed out Hauptmann. [46]

---

[43] Hearing, 188.
[44] Hearing, 191.
[45] Hearing, 195.
[46] Hearing, 202–203.

Fawcett asked a battery of cross-examination questions, but Whited stood his ground.

At the conclusion of Whited's testimony and the proof for New Jersey, Fawcett succeeded in having the court strike out the testimony of James Petrosino about finding the ransom money. Even with Petrosino's testimony stricken, Wilentz had produced enough evidence to create the contradiction necessary for the extradition of Hauptmann. Fawcett decided to offer rebuttal evidence to weaken the extradition request and keep Hauptmann in New York. Fawcett began attacking the evidence of Hauptmann's physical presence in New Jersey by calling William Diltz Whitehead, William Diehl, and George K.J. Lenz, neighbors of Millard Whited, to attack Whited's veracity as a witness.[47] If successful, Fawcett might be able to negate the testimony of Hauptmann's physical presence in New Jersey near the time of the abduction.

When a witness is called to attack the credibility of another witness, the attacking witness cannot testify to his personal opinion of the other witness's truthfulness. All the witness can testify to is the reputation of the other witness for truthfulness. Before the witness can testify to reputation, he must be shown to know the other witness's reputation. Fawcett asked Whitehead if he knew other people living in Hopewell who knew Whited and if he had spoken with them about Whited's reputation as to truth and veracity. Referring to Whited, Fawcett asked, "What is the last witness' reputation in the community of Hopewell, New Jersey, with regard to veracity and honesty." Whitehead replied, "Not much". Fawcett wanted clarification.

---

[47] During this rebuttal testimony, Fawcett used the name "Whitehead" when referring to Whited.

Q: Well, is it good or bad?
A: Bad.[48]

Fawcett had trouble establishing a foundation for the reputation question with Diehl. Directing Diehl to the people of Hopewell, he asked, "Have you discussed with them the reputation for veracity and honesty of Millard Whited"? Diehl said "No," failing to establish the predicate for Fawcett's next question. He proceeded anyway. "Do you know whether the reputation of Millard [Whited] in the neighborhood of Hopewell, New Jersey, as to veracity and honesty is good or bad?" Diehl answered "Bad, yes", but without the proper predicate it was only Diehl's opinion and not the community reputation necessary. Wilentz moved to strike Diehl's testimony.[49] Wilentz did not pursue his motion to strike and offered no cross-examination to either Whitehead or Diehl.

George Lenz testified that he knew many people in Hopewell, "the whole town," [50] who knew Millard Whited. When asked whether Whited's reputation for veracity and honesty was good or bad, Lenz replied, "Bad."[51] Fawcett asked Lenz if Whited had ever talked about the kidnapping, but Wilentz' objection to that was sustained. Wilentz showed that there were problems between Lenz and Whited that might influence the witness's testimony. "You and Mr. [Whited] had some controversy about a lumber bill, did you not." Lenz admitted that was true.[52]

---

[48] Hearing, 233.
[49] Hearing, 233.
[50] Hearing, 234.
[51] Hearing, 234.
[52] Hearing, 236.

Fawcett re-called Frank Kelly for further questioning. He wanted to establish that Kelly had little personal knowledge of when the crime had occurred, when the note had been left on the nursery window sill, had not talked to Bessie Gow, did not know Violet Sharpe, and had not seen Millard Whited on March 1, 1932. Kelly said that he had not gotten to the Lindbergh estate until March 2. On cross-examination Kelly said he found the note on the second floor of the house and that the ladder had been brought inside the house while he was there.[53] Fawcett's decision to recall Kelly had not accomplished much.

Fawcett attempted to finish the hearing with a flourish by re-calling his client. Hauptmann denied it was his handwriting on the ransom correspondence; denied being in New Jersey in January, February, or March of 1932, and claimed to have seen Millard Whited for the first time in the Bronx jail.[54] Wilentz had no questions. With the testimony closed, Wilentz asked that Fawcett's writ be dismissed, and Fawcett asked that it be sustained. The court recessed until 8:00 p.m. When court reconvened, Justice Hammer announced his ruling:

> I have considered all of the evidence adduced at the hearing upon the return of the writ of habeas corpus herein. My conclusion is that [Hauptman] has not conclusively established that he was not in the demanding state at the time that the crime alleged was committed. The writ is dismissed, and [Hauptman] is remanded to custody.[55]

---

[53] Hearing, 239.
[54] Hearing, 239–240.
[55] Hearing, 241.

Hammer later reduced his ruling to a formal, written opinion.[56] Fawcett appealed Hammer's ruling to the Appellate Division[57] which affirmed Hammer's decision and vacated the stay that held Hauptmann in New York. Hauptmann was on his way to New Jersey to face charges of murder.

Trial lawyers may question Fawcett's decision to contest extradition. Had Hauptmann been counseled by Fawcett to waive extradition, he would have been sent to New Jersey to face trial for murder, but no defense evidence or theories beyond what Hauptmann had already told the police would have been exposed to the prosecution. The hearing on Fawcett's petition had seriously compromised Hauptmann's work and bakery alibis for March 1. Hauptmann's New Jersey defense team was stuck with the concessions made by Hauptmann, Anna Hauptmann, and Christian Fredericksen. It may be that these witnesses could have been impeached by their statements to the police, but now Wilentz could also impeach them with their sworn testimony at the hearing. The New Jersey defense team had their work cut out for them in shoring up Hauptmann's alibi.

In addition to giving the prosecution a preview of the defense and providing them with more impeachment material for the trial[58] Fawcett did one other thing to hamstring the New Jersey defense team. Fawcett refused to turn over his files to them until he got paid, and they actually had to litigate a protracted lawsuit against him to force him to turn the files over. On December 31, 1934, Justice Frank F. Adel ruled that Fawcett could keep

---

[56] People *ex rel.* Hauptmann v. Hanley, 153 Misc. 61, 274 N.Y.S. 813, *affirmed* 242 App Div. 257 (New York Sup.Ct., Bronx County, 1934).
[57] People *ex rel.* Hauptmann v. Hanley, 242 A.D. 257, 274 N.Y.S. 824 (New York Ct.App., 1934).
[58] E.g., Transcripts of the testimony given by the witnesses at the extradition hearing.

possession of the files until his bill for $4,221.57 was paid in full.[59] The defense team immediately took an appeal of the court's decision, but the defense team could not get its hands on Fawcett's files until January 18, 1935. At that time the appellate court ordered Fawcett to turn the documents over to the defense team. In ruling that Fawcett had to turn the documents over, the court recognized that Fawcett had the right to a lien on the files until his fees were paid, but then went on to write:

> The respondent, however, is an officer of this court, and, under the circumstances here disclosed, to wit, that the appellant is now on trial upon an indictment for murder in the first degree in the state of New Jersey, the court is of the opinion that if the respondent has papers which would be of value to the defendant in his defense, the latter should not be deprived of the use thereof.[60]

By January 18, of course, the trial had been going on for two weeks, and the prosecution was very close to resting its case. There is no real way of telling how badly the New Jersey defense was hamstrung by this belated disclosure. It is fair to speculate, however, that had the defense gotten Fawcett's files before the trial began, they would have performed much better-prepared cross-examinations of the state's witnesses.

---

[59] "Prisoner Penniless Court Here is Told," *NYT*, December 31, 1934.

[60] Hauptmann v. Fawcett, 243 A.D. 613, 276 N.Y.S. 523, *modified* 243 A.D. 616, 277 N.Y.S. 631 (Sup.Ct., App.Div., 1935).

3

Preparing the Prosecution Case

With Hauptmann's arrest, the case entered a new phase, and the investigation shifted from crime detection to prosecution. The authorities no longer concerned themselves with identifying the killer and developing sufficient probable cause to arrest; the task at hand now involved marshalling sufficient evidence to ensure a conviction. When law enforcement officials conclude a lengthy and complex investigation and refer the case for prosecution, they usually present the prosecutor with a massive amount of information, much of which is not helpful. They have run down blind alleys; followed false leads; investigated and eliminated numerous suspects; collected large amounts of tangible evidence; and they have thoroughly documented all these activities. The prosecutor must separate the wheat of the useful from the chaff of the irrelevant, decide upon a charge, and then organize the evidence to make a cogent and compelling presentation to the judge and jury. Leadership of the law enforcement effort transferred from Colonel Schwarzkopf to Anthony M. Hauk, Jr., the Hunterton County prosecutor. Hauk, deciding that he had insufficient resources to handle the prosecution himself, called upon the recently appointed Attorney General of New Jersey, David Wilentz. Wilentz had the resources of a state agency behind him, while Hauk was merely the prosecutor in a small rural county. Hauk assumed a subordinate role as Wilentz, who had never before tried a criminal case,[1] took charge of the prosecution. The other members of the prosecution team were George K. Large, a former judge who practiced in Flemington, and three Assistant Attorneys General—Joseph Lanigan, Robert Peacock, and Robert Stock.

Wilentz first had to assimilate the available evidence and thoroughly learn both the facts of the case and the materials available to prove those facts. He then had to assess the facts and evidence in order to determine the best charge available to serve the ends of justice. His first step would be to devise a factual theory—an easily understandable statement of the case which logically described the wrong committed by the defendant. Then he would have to devise a legal theory which fit the facts. The legal theory is simply the crime or crimes charged. In crafting a charge, Wilentz wanted to achieve three objectives. The charge must (1) reflect the seriousness and extent of the offense, (2) give the court adequate powers to sentence and impose appropriate sanctions, and (3) enable him to present the case clearly and simply. We could state the Attorney General's factual theory in the following language:

> Bruno Richard Hauptmann used a home-made ladder to climb through Charles Lindbergh, Jr.'s bedroom window. He took the child from the house and left a ransom note. While he was climbing back out of the window, his ladder broke and he dropped the child, killing it.

From this factual theory, Wilentz wanted to devise a legal theory that adequately addressed the criminality, provided an appropriate punishment for the culpability,

---

[1] Transcript, 1917.

and maximized Hauptmann's convictability. Of the three objectives, Wilentz felt that punishing the culpability was the most important, and as we shall see, he willingly pursued a charge which was more difficult to prove in order to achieve the desired punishment.

The most obvious charges would be kidnapping and murder, and the most desirable punishment would be death. Wilentz could easily prove unlawful homicide, but he would find it difficult to prove capital murder. To all appearances, Hauptmann accidentally killed the child. An accidental killing is not capital murder and does not warrant the death penalty. Wilentz faced the task of devising a legal theory which would transform an accidental killing into a capital murder.

In New Jersey at that time, murder punishable by death could take two forms—premeditated murder or felony murder. A murder is premeditated when the offender kills after consciously deciding to do so. The intent to kill must have been formed before the killing and must be present in the mind of the offender at the time of the killing. First degree felony murder occurs when the offender kills during the course of committing certain statutorily enumerated felonies, regardless of whether he killed intentionally or accidentally. Most felony murder statutes will include at least the following crimes—arson, rape, robbery, burglary, and kidnapping. It is felt that anyone who decides to commit one of these felonies knows that the commission of the felony carries with it a high risk that someone might be killed. Deciding to commit such a dangerous crime with so great a risk of death shows that the offender has sufficient disregard for human life as to be equivalent to premeditation.[2] Unfortunately for Wilentz, kidnapping was not an enumerated felony in New Jersey's felony murder statute. Although

---

[2] State v. Branning, 271 Kan. 877, 887, 26 P.3d 673, 680 (2001).

kidnapping was punishable by a term of 30 years in prison, it wasn't even a felony—it was a "high misdemeanor." The New Jersey legislature quickly added kidnapping to the felony murder statute, but it could not be applied retroactively to transform an already-committed killing into capital murder.

Wilentz had to find another felony to enhance the killing to felony murder in the first degree. He decided upon burglary, but in so doing he complicated the proof required for a conviction. New Jersey had a broad burglary statute, but under New Jersey's felony murder statute only common law burglary would support a felony murder conviction. The common law of England defined burglary as the breaking and entering of a dwelling during the night time with intent to commit a felony inside the dwelling. Hauptmann *broke* when he opened the window; he *entered* when he crawled through the window; he did this during the nighttime; and the house was unquestionably the dwelling of Charles and Anne Lindbergh. But Wilentz needed to prove that Hauptmann intended to commit a felony inside the dwelling. What felony? It couldn't be kidnapping.

The baby was wearing bedclothes when he was kidnapped. Hauptman took and carried away the clothing with the baby. He stole the clothes. Depending on the value of the property stolen, larceny can be either grand or petit. Grand larceny is a felony and petit larceny is a misdemeanor. The clothes weren't worth enough to raise the crime to felony grand larceny. If Hauptmann committed no felony, he committed no burglary and he wasn't going to get the death penalty. Wilentz had an interpretation which could make petit larceny a felony. He was dealing with common law burglary, not modern burglary, and under the common law petit larceny was a felony. Wilentz strained at a gnat and swallowed a camel when he made such a tortured application of the law to the facts of the case. He certainly made his case more difficult to prove by advancing such a convoluted interpretation, but he wasn't going to get the death penalty any other way. Hauptmann was indicted accordingly. The indictment read:

> The grand inquest for the State of New Jersey in and for the body of the County of Hunterdon upon their respective oaths present that Bruno Richard Hauptmann on the first day of March in the year of Our Lord One Thousand Nine Hundred and Thirty-Two, with force and arms, at the Township of East Amwell, in the County of Hunterdon aforesaid, and within the jurisdiction of this court did willfully, feloniously and of his malice aforethought kill and murder Charles A. Lindbergh Junior, contrary to the form of the statute in such case made and provided and against the peace of the State, the Government and the dignity of the same.[3]

Some might criticize Wilentz for working so hard to charge capital murder for an accidental killing, but he did nothing wrong by working so hard to make the punishment fit the crime. The defense complained about the Attorney General's creativity on appeal, but the New Jersey Court of Errors and Appeals found his interpretation to be perfectly legal and proper.[4]

It might appear that Wilentz was now ready to go forward with his prosecution, but he still had more to do. He had to take his factual and legal theories and design a presentation which would forcefully persuade the jury to convict. The first step in designing any forensic presentation should be to devise a case theory—a simple statement of the factual and legal

---

[3] "Text of Indictment Accusing Hauptmann of 'Willful Murder' of Lindbergh Baby," *NYT*, October 9, 1934.

[4] State v. Hauptmann, 115 N.J.L. 412, 180 A. 809 (Ct.Err. & App. 1935) *cert.denied*, 296 U.S. 649 (1935).

theories which moves the jury to find a particular verdict. By design or default, every case has a case theory. Sometimes it is voiced by the advocate, sometimes it is implicit in the presentation. Wilentz never, either in opening statement or in final argument, articulated his case theory, but we can reconstruct it from the way he presented the case to the jury.

If we were to articulate the prosecution theory, our statement might go something like this:

> Bruno Richard Hauptmann kidnapped and killed Charles Augustus Lindbergh, Jr. and then conned the boy's parents out of $50,000 by telling them the child was healthy and unharmed and promising to return the child upon payment of the ransom. But before he could become a kidnapper, a killer, and a con man, he had to become a burglar and steal the child and his clothing out of his bedroom. We will prove all this with a tight web of circumstantial evidence which includes three important items—the ladder Hauptmann built and used to climb into the child's second story bedroom window; the letters Hauptmann wrote to demand the ransom; and the $14,590 in gold certificates found in Hauptmann's garage,[5] the only part of the ransom money he hadn't spent by the time of his arrest.

Wilentz had formulated his factual and legal theories: Hauptmann killed Charles A. Lindbergh, Jr. during the course of committing common law burglary and was therefore guilty of capital murder. Wilentz had to prove these ultimate facts in order to get the death penalty. Now how was he going to prove them? In order to prove these ultimate facts, he had to identify the preliminary facts which, taken as a whole, show that the ultimate facts are

---

[5] Jim Fisher, *The Lindbergh Case* (New Brunswick, N.J.: Rutgers University Press, 1994), 230.

true. For example, you could prove the ultimate fact that the New York Giants won the NFL Championship in Super Bowl XLVI by showing the preliminary facts that:

(1) The Giants played against the New England Patriots in Super Bowl XLVI.
(2) The Giants scored 21 points.
(3) The Patriots scored 17 points.
(4) At the conclusion of the game, the Giants were presented with the Vince Lombardi Trophy.

Proving that Bruno Richard Hauptmann murdered Charles A. Lindbergh, Jr. in the course of committing a common law burglary was a little more involved than that.

In proving the ultimate fact of Hauptmann's guilt, Wilentz would have to prove:

(1) That the victim was Charles A. Lindbergh, Jr.
(2) That the victim was dead.
(3) That the death resulted from the criminal agency of another human being.[6]
(4) That the killing occurred on March 1, 1932.
(5) That the killing occurred in Hunterdon County, New Jersey.
(6) That the killer was committing a common law burglary when he caused the death of the victim.

In order to prove the commission of a common law burglary, Wilentz had to prove that the killer

(7) broke and entered
(8) the dwelling of Charles A. Lindbergh, Sr.
(9) at night
(10) with intent to commit petit larceny of the child's sleeping suit.

---

[6] Judge Trenchard characterized the criminal agency as a "felonious stroke." Transcript, 4499, 4500.

The best way to prove intent to commit petit larceny is to prove the actual commission of a petit larceny. This meant Wilentz also had to prove

(11) The killer took, stole, and carried away
(12) the property of another
(13) of some value
(14) with intent to permanently deprive the owner of the property.

Finally, Wilentz would have to prove that

(15) Bruno Richard Hauptmann was the killer.

Prosecutors should draft an elements checklist and the checklist should include a description of the evidence the prosecutor expects to use in order to prove each of the elements of the crime charged. The best time to draft such a checklist is at the time the charge is filed. This serves as a failsafe to make sure that you can actually prove every element of the crime you have charged. The checklist should in any event be drafted as a part of trial preparation. Using the checklist, the prosecutor can mark off each element of the crime as it is proven, and can refer back to the checklist to make sure that all elements have been proven before resting. The checklist for the Hauptmann case would have looked something like the checklist reproduced in Figure 3–1. Wilentz obviously did not make or use such a checklist, otherwise he would never have rested his case until he had proven every essential element of the crime of larceny. Value is an essential element of every larceny. In order to prove a larceny, Wilentz had to prove that the baby's sleeping suit had some monetary value. This he did not do, and it caused problems on appeal. On appeal the defense argued that (1) the state's failure to prove value meant that the state failed to prove Hauptmann committed larceny; (2) the state's failure to prove Hauptmann committed larceny meant that the state failed to prove intent to commit larceny; (3) the state's failure to prove intent to commit larceny meant that the state failed to prove Hauptmann committed a burglary; (4) the state's failure to prove Hauptmann committed a burglary meant that the state failed to prove Hauptmann guilty of felony murder in the first degree. Taking their cue from the old rhyme "For Want of a Nail," the defense tried to take this small omission and snowball it into a major disaster for the prosecution.[7] The Court of Appeals

FIGURE 3-1

ELEMENTS WORKSHEET: FELONY MURDER

ELEMENT		PROOF
1.	Date	Charles A. Lindbergh, Sr.
2.	Venue	Circumstances
3.	Identity of victim	Charles A. Lindbergh, Sr.
4.	Fact of death	Medical Examiner
5.	Cause of death	Medical Examiner
6.	Killed during common law burglary	Ladder, ransom note
7.	Breaking and entering	Ransom note, muddy footprints in bedroom
8.	Of dwelling	Charles A. Lindbergh, Sr.
9.	At night	Charles A. Lindbergh, Sr.
10.	Intent to commit petit larceny	Commission of theft
11.	Take, steal, carry away	Clothing missing
12.	Property of another	Charles A. Lindbergh, Sr.
13.	Value of property	Charles A. Lindbergh, Sr.
14.	Intent to permanently deprive	Circumstances
15.	Identity of burglar/killer	Ladder; ransom notes, ransom money

[7] C. Lloyd Fisher, "Brief for Plaintiff in Error," State v. Hauptmann, 64–70 (1935).

rejected the argument,[8] but clearly Wilentz could have avoided the issue entirely by asking a simple question about the value of the sleeping suit.

Although Wilentz overlooked the issue of value, his plan for proof of Hauptmann's guilt shows his analysis of the evidence was sound. It is clear from a reading of the trial transcript that Wilentz saw three figures which had to be tied together and three cords which could bind them together—the figures were Bruno Richard Hauptmann, Cemetery John, and Charles A. Lindbergh, Jr., and the three cords were the ladder, the ransom letters, and the ransom money. Wilentz analyzed the evidence like this:

I. Bruno Richard Hauptmann—Ladder—Charles A. Lindbergh, Jr.

1. The person who took Charles Lindbergh, Jr. on March 1, 1932, killed the baby.
2. The killer had to enter the baby's bedroom to take him.
3. The killer entered the bedroom through the window from which the muddy foot tracks came. The killer needed a ladder to get through the window.
4. Investigators found a strange ladder near the house.
5. The killer used that ladder to get through the window.
6. The ladder was home-made rather than store-bought.
7. The killer built the ladder.
8. Prove who built the ladder, and you have proved who killed Charles Lindbergh, Jr.

---

[8] State v. Hauptmann, 115 N.J.L. 412, 424, 425, 180 A. 809, 818 (Ct.Err. & App. 1935).

9. Plane marks on the rails of the ladder match marks made by the plane found in Hauptmann's garage.
10. Hauptmann made the plane marks on the ladder with his plane.
11. North Carolina pine boards used as parts of the ladder came from a Bronx lumberyard near Hauptmann's home. Hauptmann had worked at the lumber yard. Hauptmann had bought lumber from the lumber yard.
12. Hauptmann bought the North Carolina pine boards at the lumber yard and later used them to build the ladder.
13. Nails used to build the ladder and nails from a keg in Hauptmann's barn came from the same batch of nails made in the same steel mill in Monessen, Pennsylvania.
14. The nails used to build the ladder came from the keg of nails in Hauptmann's garage. Hauptmann used the nails to build the ladder.
15. Handwriting examination of the ransom note in the nursery proves that Hauptmann wrote the nursery note.
16. Hauptmann used the ladder to climb into the Lindbergh bedroom and leave the ransom note.
17. Hauptmann is the killer.

II. Cemetery John—Ransom Correspondence — Charles A. Lindbergh, Jr.

1. The baby was not taken far from the house before it was buried in a shallow grave.
2. Before burying the baby, the killer removed the baby's sleeping suit.
3. Cemetery John had the baby's sleeping suit.
4. Cemetery John removed the sleeping suit from the baby.
5. Cemetery John identified the safety pins from the baby's crib.

6. Only someone who had been inside the baby's bedroom could have identified the safety pins.
7. Cemetery John was inside the baby's bedroom.
8. Cemetery John is the killer.

III. Bruno Richard Hauptmann—Ransom Money —Cemetery John

1. Cemetery John sent the later ransom notes to John Condon.
2. Handwriting examination proves Hauptmann wrote the later ransom notes.
3. John Condon identifies Hauptmann as Cemetery John.
4. Charles A. Lindbergh, Sr. identifies Hauptmann as Cemetery John.
5. John Condon gave Cemetery John $50,000 in traceable ransom money.
6. Hauptmann had very little money before Cemetery John received the ransom.
7. Hauptmann quit his job immediately after Cemetery John got the ransom money.
8. Hauptmann began spending extravagantly after Cemetery John got the ransom money.
9. Much of the ransom money was passed in the Bronx where Hauptmann lived.
10. Cecile Barr identified Hauptmann as passing a five dollar bill from the ransom money. Hauptmann used a ten dollar bill from the ransom money to buy gasoline at the Warner-Quinlan gas station in the Bronx.
11. When arrested, Hauptmann had a twenty dollar bill from the ransom money on his person.
12. Detectives found $14,590 in ransom money in Hauptmann's garage.
13. Hauptmann is Cemetery John.
14. Hauptmann is the killer.

Wilentz intended to use the ladder, the ransom notes, and the ransom money to make three indestructible cables securely binding Hauptmann to Cemetery John, Cemetery John to the killer, and the killer to Hauptmann. He could have used the mnemonic device Ladder, Letters, and Loot to diagram the three cornered relationship as shown in Figure 3–2. The durability of these cables depended entirely upon the credibility of a group of expert witnesses—Stanley R. Keith, the metallurgist who examined the nails; Arthur Koehler, the expert who examined the wood from the ladder; and twelve handwriting examiners led by Albert S. Osborn, Clark Sellers, and J. Vreeland Haring.

FIGURE 3-2

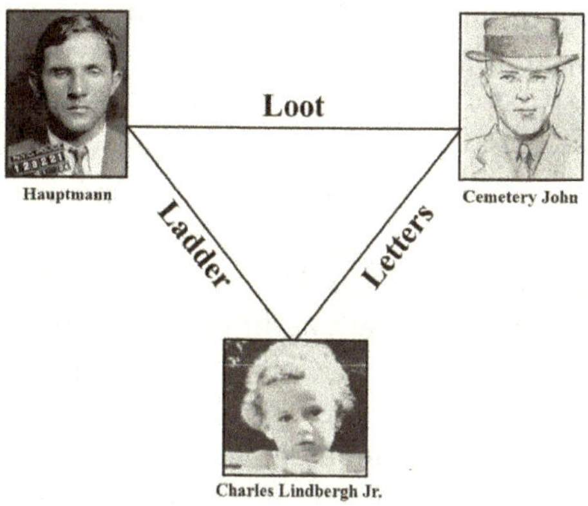

In order to present a case as large and complex as the Hauptmann case the prosecutor should break it down into a number of modules or "proof packages." Each module should address one specific aspect of the case, and in the ideal situation, you would present all the evidence as to each module before moving to proof of the next. Given the need to accommodate witnesses' schedules, the need to lay evidentiary foundations [9] for certain types of

---

[9] An evidentiary foundation is a preliminary showing which must be made to render evidence admissible. For example, the evidentiary

evidence, and the fact that one witness usually has information concerning more than one module, prosecutors find it next to impossible to neatly present each module as a unified whole. Study of the transcript suggests that Wilentz had a modular concept for presenting the evidence. Although we cannot know precisely how Wilentz subdivided his presentation, we can infer approximately nine modules. Let us set these modules forth in alphabetical order:

1. ARREST (ARR): The facts and circumstances surrounding Hauptmann's arrest and interrogation, and the search of his home and garage.
2. AUTOPSY (AUT): The discovery of the body of Charles Lindbergh, Jr., his identification, and the autopsy of his body.
3. CORRESPONDENCE (COR): The correspondence between the kidnapper and Charles Lindbergh, Sr., and the entry of John Condon as the go-between.
4. DELIVERY (DEL): The delivery of the ransom money and the resulting futile search for the child.
5. DISAPPEARANCE (DIS): The disappearance of Charles A. Lindbergh, Jr., and the collection of evidence at the Lindbergh home.
6. FINANCES (FIN): Evidence relating to Hauptmann's finances before and after the delivery of the ransom.
7. HANDWRITING (HAN): The examination of the ransom notes by the various handwriting examiners.
8. LADDER (LAD): The investigation of the ladder found at the scene.
9. RANSOM (RAN): Tracing the ransom money. Tying it to Hauptmann.

---

foundation for a confession to a crime is proof that the crime has been committed.

To these nine prosecution modules we can add a defense module and a responsive prosecution module:

10. DEFENSE (DEF): Those witnesses called on behalf of Hauptmann; and
11. REBUTTAL (REB): Those witnesses called by Wilentz to respond to the defense witnesses.

Wilentz could anticipate a four-pronged attack on his case: The defense would attempt to (1) undermine the truth value of some modules by casting doubt on the testimony of the lay witnesses and suggesting that many of the important witnesses actually participated in the kidnapping; (2) mitigate some of the modules by explaining or reinterpreting the facts; (3) offer facts directly contradicting the prosecution's case theory; (4) vigorously challenge the veracity of the expert testimony on all fronts.

There was very little discovery[10] in criminal cases during the first half of the Twentieth Century, and lawyers on both sides sought to ambush their opponents with surprise witnesses and evidence. The prosecution often had no idea what sort of defense might be mounted until the defense witnesses actually testified. This lack of knowledge by the prosecutor could prove a powerful weapon in the hands of skillful defense counsel, but the extradition hearing held in New York City had largely deprived Hauptmann's defense team of this resource.

The defense, which Hauptmann could have kept shrouded in mystery until his lawyers unveiled it at trial, had been broadcast to the world at the New York extradition hearing. Wilentz knew Hauptmann intended to claim an alibi for the dates of the kidnapping and the

---

[10] Discovery is the process whereby the parties to a lawsuit can "discover" the other side's evidence.

ransom exchange, and knew he intended to explain his possession of the ransom money by saying that Isidor Fisch had given him the money for safekeeping before returning to Germany. Having previewed these defenses at the hearing in New York, Wilentz could prepare to answer them even before the trial began.

Two of the nine modules contributed little to identifying Hauptmann as the killer—the Disappearance module only weakly connected Hauptmann to the crime and the Autopsy did not implicate Hauptmann at all, but Wilentz needed them to show that a homicide had occurred and that it occurred during the course of a burglary. Each of the remaining prosecution modules tended to show Hauptmann guilty to a greater or lesser degree. Despite the fact that the first two modules did not directly incriminate Hauptmann, Wilentz could expect vigorous attacks on both. The defense could use the Disappearance module to strongly suggest that one or more members of the Lindbergh household took part in the kidnapping. They could also try to show that the officers called to the Lindbergh home on the night of the kidnapping bungled the crime scene investigation. The Autopsy module was vulnerable to attack as well. The defense could contend that (1) the body found in the shallow grave was not adequately identified as the Lindbergh baby; (2) the medical examiner was mistaken as to the manner and cause of death; and (3) the evidence failed to prove that the death occurred in Hunterdon County.

Wilentz could anticipate his greatest difficulties would come with the Correspondence and Delivery modules because they relied so heavily upon the testimony of the eccentric publicity hound, John F. Condon. Condon had inserted himself into the ransom negotiations with the bizarre offer to act as an intermediary which he published in the *Bronx Home News*, had botched the ransom delivery by not giving Cemetery John the most easily identifiable bills (the fifty dollar gold certificates), had steadfastly refused to identify Hauptmann as Cemetery John before the trial in Hunterdon County, and had repeatedly engaged in all manner of odd behavior between delivery of the ransom and the beginning of the trial. Wilentz could not be sure that Condon would say that Hauptmann even resembled the kidnapper, much less that Hauptmann was the kidnapper. Even if he unequivocally identified Hauptmann, he might completely destroy his own credibility with weird behavior from the witness stand.

The Arrest module presented its own difficulties. In that module Wilentz would set forth the circumstances of the seizure of much of the most inculpatory evidence. It included the actual arrest of Hauptmann, the search of his home and garage, and the seizure of much evidence essential to proving guilt. No matter how well the police perform in the arrest stage of any criminal investigation, resourceful defense counsel can always find something to criticize. Critical thinking texts describe a certain form of defective analytical thinking as the "perfectionist fallacy."[11] Since no human has ever performed any task with absolute perfection, critics can always declare that because the action is imperfect it is unacceptable. The police had supplied the defense with an array of imperfections for use in manufacturing reasonable doubt.

The Finances module was consistent with a theory of Hauptmann's guilt but was not conclusive. This module would show that Hauptmann was near bankrupt before the delivery of the ransom money and had so much money afterward that he could immediately quit his job as a carpenter and never work at that trade again. Wilentz could state this fact with a simple sentence: proving it called for a complex presentation of Hauptmann's

---

[11] Brooke Noel Moore and Richard Parker, *Critical Thinking*, 7th ed. (New York: McGraw Hill, 2003), 191.

financial dealings with banks and stockbrokers capped off by testimony from an expert summarizing Hauptmann's finances. The jury could never decipher the convoluted financial evidence without the summary testimony. Although it could be considered somewhat novel at the time of the trial, today the use of summary testimony is recognized by the Federal Rules of Evidence and also by many state evidence codes.[12] If the defense held the Attorney General's feet to the fire and required strict proof, they could force him to make a complex and confusing presentation identifying and authenticating each set of records from each financial institution, showing that the records were regularly kept in the course of business, and showing that the entries as to each transaction were made at or near the time of the transaction by someone with personal knowledge of the transaction. He would have to do this by calling the official custodian of the records of each bank and each brokerage to establish these facts. He then needed to have the records interpreted and explained by either the custodian of records or someone else with knowledge of the concern's bookkeeping methods. After doing this with each set of records for each account, Wilentz would then have to call William Frank, the Department of the Treasury expert who analyzed Hauptmann's finances, and have Frank explain how those records showed Hauptmann's inexplicable wealth after the delivery of the ransom money. All this meant that Wilentz would have to make a lengthy, complex, and soporific presentation which was almost guaranteed to confuse the jury. Instead of insisting on strict proof, however, the defense stipulated the records into evidence.

---

[12] Rule 1006, Federal Rules of Evidence; Fla.Stat. § 90.956; Rule 1006, Mississippi Rules of Evidence.

Given this huge assist from the defense, Frank could state his findings simply: Hauptmann was broke the day before the ransom was paid and had plenty of money almost immediately afterward. At the time he quit his job, he had a stock portfolio worth $100 and $203.90 in the bank. Between the time he quit his job and the time he got arrested, he put $9,073.25 into the bank, $16,942.75 into his brokerage accounts, $3,750 into the purchase of a mortgage, lost $5,728.29 on the stock market, financed several expensive trips, and made lavish purchases. Hauptmann wasn't working as a carpenter, and he was losing money in the stock market. Where did the money come from? Interestingly, when you combine the money he put into banks, brokerage accounts, and mortgages with the Lindbergh ransom money in his garage and his $120 in gold coins, you get a total of $44,486, very close to the sum of $50,000 given to Cemetery John.[13]

The Ransom module rested on undeniable proof that Hauptmann had a large number of ransom bills in his possession. This fact naturally gave rise to an inference that he had the money because he was the one who extorted it from Condon and Lindbergh, but Hauptmann had an explanation—he got the money from Isidor Fisch. This type of presentation is sometimes called the "mysterious disappearing benefactor" defense—a rather common defense to possession of stolen property. The heart and soul of such a defense is the claim that some unknown or unavailable person gave the defendant the property. Although the claim is easily made and hard to disprove, it is often weakened because of inherent implausibility. In Hauptmann's case the story was so plagued by implausibility that it was called "the Fisch story."[14] In assessing the Fisch story, we would do well to

---

[13] Transcript, 1810–1815.

[14] Fisher, *The Lindbergh Case*, 201–208.

remember that one defense theory can be true but implausible just as easily as another can be untrue but plausible. Ideally, the defense wants to present a case theory which is both true and plausible.

Because the Handwriting module could be expected to come under vociferous attack both on cross-examination and also during the defense case, the prosecution would do well to devise a plan for protecting it. Wilentz had such a plan. Since he had a total of twelve experts for the Handwriting module, he divided his forces. He would call some to testify during the state's case in chief and save the remaining experts to testify on rebuttal. At first he planned on calling only a few experts during the case in chief, but the jury seemed so captivated by the testimony that he wound up calling eight experts and saving only four for rebuttal.

The defense could also be expected to mount a vigorous attack on the Ladder module. Wilentz again divided his forces. Arthur Koehler, a xylotomist (wood expert), would testify during the case in chief; and Stanley Keith, a metallurgist, would testify on rebuttal. When Reilly rested, however, Wilentz was so confident of his case that he called neither Keith nor the four reserve handwriting experts. Let us look at the testimony that Wilentz decided not to use.

The prosecution recruited Keith, a metallurgist with the A.P. Smith Manufacturing Company of East Orange, New Jersey, to study the nails used in the ladder. Keith determined that the nails used to build the ladder came from a keg of nails that the police had found in Hauptmann's garage. As with the financial evidence, the conclusion that the ladder's nails came from the keg could be stated simply enough, but proving it involved a lot of explaining. Keith first noticed that the nails from Hauptmann's home and the nails from the ladder were all eight penny nails, and each one of them had been stamped with a "P." Using the "P" as a guide, Keith was able to identify the Pittsburgh Steel plant in Monessen, Pennsylvania, as the manufacturer of the nails. At the plant, Keith learned that of the approximately 2,000,000 kegs of eight penny nails manufactured in the United States in 1931 the Monessen mill had manufactured 200,000. This gave rise to an inference that the nails from Hauptmann's residence and the nails from the ladder came from one or more of those 200,000 kegs.[15] Keith had narrowed the possibilities, but not nearly enough.

Pittsburgh Steel made their eight penny nails from coils of steel wire. Steel wire was made by running steel through wire drawing dies. Drawing dies wore over time until each drawing die came to make marks distinct from any other dies. Nails made from an individual coil of wire should all bear the same distinct drawing die marks. The wire then went through another set of mechanical dies which stamped the nails into the proper shape and cut them to the desired length. Stamping dies went through the same wearing process as drawing dies. Nails run through an individual stamping die should all bear the same marks. Upon closely examining the die marks on the nails, Keith found that every one of them had gone through one of eight dies. Over the course of its lifetime, the die impressions made from a single die would change. This meant that nails bearing identical die marks were not only made from the same die, they were made at the same time. If they were made at the same time, the odds were good that they came from the same coil of steel wire. After the steel had been drawn into wire and then stamped into nails, the nails would be put in a tumbler to polish them prior to putting them in kegs. The Monessen steel mill would tumble their nails in batches large enough to fill sixteen kegs. If two nails from two

---

[15] Stanley R. Keith, "Identification of the Lindbergh Ladder Nails," *The Iron Age*, 16–22, 71; (October 17, 1935), 19.

different sources came from the same coil of wire and were run through the same stamping die, then they both must have come from a single sixteen keg batch of nails.

Keith had four distinct sources of nails for examination—the ladder, the keg of nails found in Hauptmann's garage, ten nails found in the pocket of a pair of Hauptmann's overalls, and the nails used by Hauptmann to build the garage. Keith examined the die marks on the nails and identified the marks of eight separate stamping dies. For identification purposes, he labeled the dies E, S, T, V, A, U, G, and H. Keith also identified sixteen coils of wire which had gone into the making of the nails. He assigned consecutive numbers to the coils of wire. Thus, Keith could identify each of the nails by letter and number. In the batch of nails from the ladder, Keith could identify each of the eight stamping dies and eleven of the sixteen drawing dies. The only nail types missing from the ladder were E1, T6, V8, A11, and G14.[16] See Figure 3–3 for a graphic demonstration of the relationships among the nails. The conclusion was inescapable: the nails from the ladder and the nails from Hauptmann's residence all came from the same sixteen keg tumbler batch. Keith overstated his case by saying that the nails all came from the same keg. This, of course, was a reasonable inference to draw from the evidence; but scientific analysis could only get down to the same tumbler batch, not the same keg.

The decision by Wilentz to hold Keith in reserve worked out well, but if things had played out a little differently, the decision could have proven disastrous. The problem with saving witnesses for rebuttal is that the defense can deny you the opportunity of calling them by simply resting without putting on any evidence. Many

---

[16] *Ibid*, 20–22.

FIGURE 3-3
SOURCES OF NAILS

	DIE/COIL							
NAIL KEG (42)	A10	A11	E1	E2	G13	G14	H15	H16
GARAGE (275)	A10	A11	E1	E2	G13	G14	H15	H16
OVERALLS (10)	—	—	—	E2	—	—	H15	H16
LADDER (44)	A10	—	—	E2	G13	—	H15	H16

	DIE/COIL							
NAIL KEG (42)	S3	T4	T5	T6	U12	V7	V8	V9
GARAGE (275)	S3	T4	T5	T6	U12	V7	V8	V9
OVERALLS (10)	S3	—	—	—	U12	—	V8	—
LADDER (44)	S3	T4	T5	—	U12	V7	—	V9

prosecutors have lost cases by saving key witnesses to testify in rebuttal. Wilentz assuredly made the right decision when he held four handwriting examiners for rebuttal, but he is open to justifiable criticism for saving Keith until rebuttal. Keith's penchant for unnecessarily complicated explanations might have influenced Wilentz to hold him for rebuttal. Keith would never use a two syllable word when he could use one of three or four syllables, and the more roundabout the explanation, the better he liked it. We introduced our discussion of Keith's work by saying, "The conclusion that the ladder's nails came from the keg in Hauptmann's garage is simple enough, but getting to it involves a lot of explaining." It took Keith 66 words to say the same thing:

> The opinion that the 44 8d. common wire nails used in the assembly of the 11 rungs to the side members, were components of the original contents of the keg found to have been partly used by Hauptmann in constructing his garage, as an inescapable conclusion is one thing; the laborious citation of detailed circumstances, one by one, leading up to this point is quite another.[17]

---

[17] *Ibid,* 16.

Wilentz correctly believed that Arthur Koehler, who worked at the U.S. Forestry Service's Forest Products Laboratory,[18] would give the most damning evidence against Hauptmann. Koehler had initially written Lindbergh volunteering to help with analysis of the ladder, but his letter went ignored among the thousands which flooded Lindbergh's mailbox. Later, H. Norman Schwarzkopf, the director of the New Jersey State Police, requested the assistance of the U.S. Forestry Service, and the Forestry Service assigned Koehler to the case. At first Schwarzkopf would allow him to examine only slivers of wood from the ladder, but eventually he summoned Koehler to New Jersey to view the entire ladder.[19]

Based on his examination, Koehler drew a number of conclusions: (1) The builder was not a carpenter. Like Keith, Koehler overstated this conclusion by saying that the builder was not a carpenter. Apparently he was so offended by the shoddy workmanship he could not bring himself to admit that the builder had any skill as a carpenter. His overstatement, of course, could prove helpful to the defense. (2) The ladder was home-made from an assortment of types of wood—birch dowels, Douglas fir rails, North Carolina pine (NC pine) rails, and Ponderosa pine rungs. (3) The rungs, made of soft Ponderosa pine, were unworn, which meant the ladder had been purpose-built for the kidnapping. (4) The Ponderosa pine rungs had originally come from 1" x 6"[20] stock which the builder had ripped[21] to 1" x 3" size. (5)

---

[18] In Madison, Wisconsin.

[19] Shirley A. Graham, "Anatomy of the Lindbergh Kidnapping," *Journal of Forensic Science*, Vol. 42, No. 3, 368–377 (May, 1997), 369.

[20] Lumber is identified by its undressed dimensions. E.g. a 1" x 6" board measures one inch thick by six inches wide. After the board is dressed by a plane, it is slightly smaller. Thus a dressed 1" x 4" board would actually measure closer to ¾ inches by $3^5/_8$ inches.

[21] Sawed lengthwise.

The three Douglas fir rails and two NC pine rails were made from 1" x 4" lumber, but the third piece of NC pine came from a larger board which had been ripped and planed down to 1" x 4" size, suggesting that it might have come from tongue-and-groove stock. (6) The plane marks were made by a worn, unsharpened, nicked hand plane.[22] (7) The two NC pine 1" x 4" rails had originally been one board, and they were dressed on a particularly unique sort of machine plane[23] which had eight cutter heads on the wide side and six heads on the narrow side of the board. Koehler also identified the types of machine planes used to finish the other boards, but this finding proved irrelevant. (8) The third NC pine board (numbered Rail 16 for reference) had four distinct cut nail[24] holes in it. It was old but unweathered, leading Koehler to believe that it had been used in interior construction, possibly an attic or garage.[25]

Armed with these facts, Koehler suggested that if a suspect were developed, they should take care to determine (1) whether a board had been removed from interior construction in the suspect's house, and (2) whether the suspect owned a hand plane.[26] He also set about to trace the two NC pine 1" x 4" rails. He began by canvassing all east coast sawmills, asking if they used a plane like the one used to dress the rails. This canvas led him to the M.G. and J.J. Dorn Company in McCormick, South Carolina. At the Dorn Company, Koehler identified

---

[22] A plane is a device used to smooth the surface of lumber.

[23] The plane had eight heads on the wide side spinning at 0.93" rpm and six planes on the narrow side spinning at 0.86" rpm.

[24] Cut nails have a rectangular cross section due to the fact that they are cut from sheets of metal.

[25] Arthur Koehler, "Technique Used in Tracing the Lindbergh Kidnapping Ladder," *The Journal of Criminal Law and Criminology*, Vol. 27, No. 5, 356–365 (1937), 356, 357.

[26] *Ibid*, 360, 361.

the batches of 1" x 4" boards planed in the months preceding the kidnapping and determined where they had been shipped. One shipment of lumber had gone to the National Lumber and Millwork Company located in the Bronx, where the ransom had been delivered and where many of the ransom bills had been passed. On November 29, 1933 Koehler went to the lumberyard,[27] and there the trail went cold. The lumberyard operated on a cash-only basis and had no records of who had purchased the lumber. The killer probably lived close by the lumberyard, but there was no way of identifying him in such a populous borough. There was nothing else Koehler could do until the authorities developed a suspect.

Hauptmann's arrest provided a bonanza of evidence for Koehler to examine. The first item of evidence was Hauptmann's wood plane. Prior to Hauptmann's arrest, Koehler had feared that enough time had passed for the plane to have been either sharpened or worn enough to destroy its distinctive features, making it impossible to match the plane to the ladder. Koehler could not anticipate that Hauptmann would go out of the carpentry business immediately upon receiving the ransom, leaving his plane in the same condition it was in when it planed the boards of the ladder. Koehler had no difficulty matching the plane to the ladder.

The old piece of planed-down NC pine (Rail 16) proved to be the clincher, however. Koehler had concluded that Rail 16 came from inside an attic or garage and suggested that when the kidnapper was arrested, his home should be thoroughly searched to find a possible source for the pine rail. The attic of Hauptmann's home had been floored with tongue and groove NC pine, and part of one of the pine floorboards was missing. One of the outside floorboards had been sawed in two, and part

---

[27] Transcript, 2269.

had been removed. Koehler identified Rail 16 as the part which had been removed from the board in Hauptmann's attic. He did this by matching the growth rings on the two boards and showing that they were identical. Further, he found nail holes in the ceiling joists where the board had been nailed down. The nail holes in Rail 16 matched the nail holes in the joists perfectly, as to location, angle, and depth of penetration. Koehler could set the board down over the holes and drop cut nails through the boards into the joists so that the nails fit snugly. When he did so, the board aligned perfectly parallel to the other boards in the attic. At this point, one of two things should have been done. Either the joists should have been removed from the attic so that the perfect fit could be demonstrated in court for the jury, or a film should have been made of the placing of the nails into the holes. The failure to preserve this evidence caused some difficulties during Hauptmann's post-conviction litigation.

When Hauptmann asked Governor Harold G. Hoffman for clemency, Hoffman ordered a thorough re-investigation of the case. As a part of that re-investigation, Hoffman, Koehler, and others went back to Hauptmann's attic to see if the nails really fit as Koehler had described. The holes were in the correct place, they were slanted at the correct angle, but the nails would not go fully into the holes—rather than fitting flush as Koehler had said, they protruded approximately a quarter of a inch. This led to a dismantling of the attic, and the joists with the nail holes were taken to the Columbia University Physics Lab to determine why the nails wouldn't fit. Examination revealed that between the time of Koehler's examination and the subsequent examination attended by Hoffman, wood fiber had gotten into the holes, making them too shallow for the nails. After removing the wood fiber, the examiners saw that the nails fit perfectly.[28] This unfortunate incident could have been avoided had the joists been taken as evidence in the beginning.

There was a glaring weakness with the ladder evidence which the prosecution did not anticipate, and which almost scuttled the state's case—the ladder had to be put into evidence so that Koehler could testify to his conclusions, but in several material respects the ladder was very different from what it was when the police originally seized it as evidence. It had been disassembled during the investigation and reassembled for the trial. When they took the ladder apart, they gave each component a separate number, recording the component's location in the fully assembled ladder. When time came to reassemble the ladder, they could return each board to its original location and each nail to its original nail hole. Despite the care they took with disassembly and reassembly of the ladder, they had given the defense the opportunity to argue that the disassembling and reassembling process had so altered the condition of the ladder that it was inadmissible at trial. The defense challenged the ladder on the grounds that it was not substantially in the same or similar condition as when it was first found, a legal requirement demonstrated by a "chain of custody" to show that no one had altered the condition of the ladder between the time it was discovered and its introduction into evidence. Overcoming the weaknesses in the chain of custody presented Wilentz with major headaches.

The ransom notes themselves also provided a strong tie between Hauptmann and the murder. Investigators immediately recognized the importance of the notes, and they asked for help from the foremost handwriting

---

[28] George Waller, *Kidnap: The Shocking Story of the Lindbergh Case* (New York: Pocket Books, 1962), 637–641.

examiner in the nation, Albert S. Osborn. Osborn's examination of the notes revealed a number of things: First, all the anonymous notes were written in a "somewhat" disguised hand.[29] Second, the same person had written all the ransom notes. Osborn determined this from a number of things. The notes displayed a similar use of words and a similarity in the misspelling of words, most notably the word "singnature"; statements in the later notes referred to the ransom amount in the first; later notes chided Lindbergh for disobeying the first note's warning not to go to the police.[30] Additionally, the second note was written on a piece of paper torn from the paper on which the first ransom note (the nursery note) had been written; and peculiar characteristics of word and letter formation were common to all notes.[31] Then there was the peculiar symbol branded on all the notes—two interlocked blue circles with a red ball in the interlocked portion and three holes punched at regular intervals in the device. Osborn made transparencies of all the marks, and when they were placed one on top of the other, the punch holes all matched perfectly.[32] This led Osborn to conclude that they were all punched from the same pattern.[33] Later examiners believed that the signature holes were all punched simultaneously.[34]

---

[29] Transcript, 967.
[30] Transcript, 950, 951.
[31] Clark Sellers, "The Handwriting Evidence against Hauptmann," *Journal of Criminal Law and Criminology*, Vol. 27, No. 6, 874–886 (Mar.–Apr., 1937), 878, http://www.jstor.org/discover/10.2307/1137535?uid=3739600&uid=&uid=4&uid=3739256&sid=47698976249677, (accessed May 6, 2012).
[32] Transcript, 964, 965.
[33] Transcript, 952, 953.
[34] J. Vreeland Haring, *The Hand of Hauptmann: The Handwriting Expert Tells the Story of the Lindbergh Case* (Plainfield, NJ: The Hamer Publishing Company, 1937), 39.

The sentence structure of the notes suggested a German author, as did the formation of some of the individual letters in the German style. For example, the author of the ransom notes formed many (but not all) of his *h's, t's,* and *w's* in the German style.[35] Although this would not identify a specific person as the author of the notes, it did somewhat narrow the field of suspects. All they had to do was find a semi-literate German immigrant who spelled *signature* "s-i-n-g-n-a-t-u-r-e." Osborn drafted a paragraph to be used for dictation when taking handwriting samples from potential suspects. It did not follow the exact wording of the ransom notes, but it did employ many of the commonly misspelled words from the ransom notes.[36] Osborn purposely omitted the word *signature* from the paragraph, but he included other words in the document which would give the suspect ample opportunity to misplace his *n's*.

The authorities began collecting and submitting handwriting samples from multiple suspects, but Osborn's examination eliminated all of them.[37] The most notable potential suspect to be eliminated had to be Isidor Fisch. When Hauptmann offered him up as an alternate suspect, the authorities collected samples of his handwriting for examination. J. Vreeland Haring devotes an entire chapter of his book, *The Hand of Hauptmann,* to a comparison of Fisch's handwriting to the ransom notes. His finding: "There is not one scintilla of handwriting evidence to link Isidor Fisch, even in conjecture, with the kidnapper of the Lindbergh baby."[38]

The series of negative comparisons ended with Hauptmann's arrest. As Osborn had directed, investiga-

---

[35] Transcript, 967, 979, 980.
[36] Fisher, *The Lindbergh Case*, 141.
[37] Sellers, "Handwriting Evidence," 877.
[38] Haring, *Hand of Hauptmann*, 311.

tors took multiple samples of "request" writings from Hauptmann and also collected a number of "conceded" writings in Hauptmann's handwriting from among his personal effects. Wilentz had the handwriting submitted to twelve nationally renowned experts, insisting that they perform their examinations independently.[39] The experts rendered a unanimous verdict—Hauptmann wrote the ransom letters. Hauptmann not only formed his sentences in the German fashion, he also used the German *h's, t's,* and *w's,* and his poor spelling replicated the poor spelling in the ransom correspondence.

Although German diction and German lettering might be used by any German, there were multiple similarities in word and letter formation which could only be explained by concluding that Hauptmann wrote the ransom notes. Haring says, "Generally speaking, there is a duplicate in Hauptmann's penmanship for every variety found in the notes."[40] He devotes 54 pages of his book to cataloging the similarities in word and letter formation between Hauptmann's writing and the ransom notes.[41] For example, *the* was sometimes spelled h-t-e and sometimes U-e. Altogether there were six definite variations of the word *the* which were duplicated in the two sets of writings.[42] Hauptmann also had a tendency to insert *n's* in places where they didn't belong.[43] Some other common misspellings were:[44]

---

[39] Sellers, "Handwriting Evidence," 885.
[40] Haring, *Hand of Hauptmann*, 245, 246.
[41] *Ibid*, 243–298.
[42] *Ibid*, 246, 247.
[43] Sellers, "Handwriting Evidence,"880.
[44] Haring, *Hand of Hauptmann*, 247, 248, 251–253, 255, 265, 266; Sellers, "Handwriting Evidence," 880–883; Transcript, 975, 978, 979, 988, 1003, 1063, 1095.

"Anything" = a-n-y-d-i-n-g.
"Be" = b-y.
"Boat" = b-o-a-d.
"Did" = t-i-t.
"Everything" = e-v-e-r-y-d-i-n-g.
"Later" = l-a-t-t-e-r.
"Light" = l-i-g-t-h.
"Money" = m-o-n-y.
"New York" = sometimes hyphenated "New-York," sometimes not hyphenated.
"Not" = n-o-t-e.
"Our" = o-u-e-r.
"Ready" = r-e-d-y.
"Right" = r-i-g-t-h.
"Something" = s-o-m-e-d-i-n-g.
"They" = t-h-e.
"Was" = w-h-a-s.
"Where" = w-e-r-e.

As to letter formation, the size, proportions, pen pressures, and design of the numerals was common to both sets of writings. The similarities in formation were sufficient to allow examiners to duplicate Hauptmann's normal signature with individual letters cut from the ransom notes.[45] Even more remarkably, examiners were able to duplicate the initial ransom note with words and letters cut from the known writings of Hauptmann.[46] There are superficial differences between the initial ransom note and the composite, but it must be remembered that the initial ransom note was the most thoroughly disguised of the ransom notes. Hauptmann, in a move which displayed greater cunning than intellect, attempted to disguise the requested handwriting samples given to the police, but used the same disguise used in the

---

[45] Sellers, "Handwriting Evidence," 883.
[46] Haring, *Hand of Hauptmann*, 219–221.

ransom notes.[47] Some, but not all, of the common peculiarities of letter and number formation were:[48]

A: Both sets of writings had the same formation of the capital *A,* which looked like an enlargement of the German lower case *a.* American style print capital *A's* had small loops at the beginning of the initial upstroke.

C: Both sets of writings had the same distinct capital *C.*

D: Both sets of writings had the same distinct capital *D*, as well as the same three varieties of lower case *d.*

E: When capital *E's* were printed, the top line of the *E* disconnected from the perpendicular line. In the questioned and request writings, when capital *E's* were written in script, they looked like capital *C's.* In Hauptmann's conceded writings, script capital *E's* were properly formed, indicating that the malformed *E's* in the questioned and request writings were attempts at disguise.

F: Three styles of the letter *f* were found in both sets of writings.

G: When used at the beginning of words, *g's* had an open top, making them look like *y's.*

H: We have already mentioned the German *h's.* Capital *H* was formed like a reversed *N.*

I: Capital *I's* were shaped like fishhooks. Many lower case *i's* were undotted. Of 304 lower case *i's* in the ransom note, only seven were dotted. Of 106 lower case *i's* in the requested writings, only eight were dotted.

---

[47] Sellers, "Handwriting Evidence," 878.

[48] Haring, *Hand of Hauptmann*, 283–298; Sellers, "Handwriting Evidence," 883; Transcript, 976, 979, 980, 981, 984–987, 989, 990, 1000, 1009.

N: Hand-lettered capital *N's* frequently looked like *V's*. Capital *N*'s were sometimes written backwards.

O: Many *o's* were unclosed at the top. Some of them looked like *v's*.

P: There were multiple methods used for forming *p's*, and each of the methods appeared in both writings.

R: Handlettered *r's* looked like Greek *e's*. Lower case *r's* sometimes had small loops at the top right side.

S: When words began with *s*, the *s's* were disconnected from the rest of the word.

T: We have already mentioned the German *t's*. Although German *t's* can sometimes be uncrossed, both writings had non-German *t's* which were not crossed. Of 391 *t's* in the ransom note requiring crossing, only three were crossed. Of 194 *t's* in the requested writings requiring crossing, only four were crossed. In all, there were 14 distinct formations of *t* in both writings.

W: We have already mentioned the German capital *W's*.

X: Small *x's* looked like *ee's*.

Y: At the beginning of words, *y's* looked like undotted *j's*. When at the end of a word, *y's* had a short pointed base and a peculiar slant.

5: Fives had unusually long top strokes.

6: Sixes looked like script capital *O's*.

7: The top bar of the seven curved downward in the middle.

8: Some eights were unclosed at the top, resembling inverted ice tongs.

0: In numbers with multiple zeroes, the zeroes tended to diminish in size from left to right. Once in the ransom notes, and once in Hauptmann's known writing, three zeroes were linked together, and both times they looked like three script *v's* joined together.

As Haring observed, "Handwriting evidence to be of value should be cumulative. Its strength rests on the finding of several coincident diverging characteristics, rather than on the strength of any one."[49] At the trial Albert S. Osborn testified that "the presence or absence of one characteristic may be accounted to accident or coincidence, but as the number increases, the probability of accidents or coincidents disappears and conviction is irresistible."[50] Wilentz had his case organized, now all he had to do was get it before a jury in some semblance of a coherent presentation. As we shall see in the next few chapters, that was far more easily said than done.

---

[49] Haring, *Hand of Hauptmann*, 243.
[50] Transcript, 1001.

4

Preparing the Defense

Hauptmann's New Jersey defense team, led by veteran criminal defense attorney Edward J. Reilly, also included C. Lloyd Fisher, Frederick A. Pope, and Egbert Rosencrans. In preparing the defense, they engaged in an analysis and case organization very similar to the prosecution team, but they had a quite different objective. Instead of trying to prove a case theory, they would be trying to destroy the prosecution case theory.

The first line of defense in any criminal case comes during the presentation of the state's evidence when the defense seeks through cross-examination to undermine confidence in the state's witnesses. Sometimes this is all that the defense needs to do. If skillful cross-examination can raise a reasonable doubt, the jury should acquit despite the fact that they heard no affirmative defense. If counsel have an affirmative defense to present, they can use cross-examination to prepare the way for that defense. When their turn comes to present evidence, they can call witnesses to further undermine confidence in the state's evidence; to offer an innocent explanation for seemingly incriminating evidence; to suggest that someone other than the defendant committed the crime; and to prove that the defendant did not commit the crime charged. The defense they crafted can be divided into five broad categories: (1) reasonable doubt, (2) misidentification, (3) alibi, (4) other suspects, and (5) explanation. Defenses (2) through (5) could all be lumped under the heading of reasonable doubt, but for clarity of discussion, we will address them separately.

Reasonable Doubt

Reasonable doubt is always a defense in criminal cases. No matter how compelling the prosecution's case, the defense can always seize upon some real or perceived insufficiency in the evidence. Hauptmann's defense team had a number of theories of reasonable doubt that they could argue to the jury. Three of these arguments simply spoke to the sufficiency of the prosecution evidence:

(a) The totality of the evidence fails to establish guilt beyond a reasonable doubt.
(b) The prosecution cannot prove the crime occurred in Hunterdon County.
(c) The prosecution cannot prove the body was the Lindbergh baby.

Two additional reasonable doubt arguments were in the nature of affirmative defenses which the defense could try to establish by cross-examination of the state witnesses. The defense did not need to prove these arguments, just raise sufficient doubt in the minds of the jury to cause them to think the defenses might be true. These defenses are sometimes referred to as the "bad cop, no donut" defense.

(d) The police bungled the investigation.
(e) The police fabricated or changed evidence.

The defense wanted the jury to think that the investigation had been incomplete, inaccurate, and inept, and that the investigators were untrained, untalented, and unethical to the point of altering or fabricating evidence.

Reilly had great skill at attacking law enforcement, a tactic often more effective in urban trials than in rural settings such as Flemington, New Jersey, where the trial was held.

A battery of recognized experts would testify for the State on the handwriting and the wood evidence. The defense could not match the experience or credentials of these witnesses but would need to counter with some evidence of its own. One way of dealing with a host of evidence on a particular point is to pick out the weakest part of the evidence and treat it as a proxy for all the evidence. Refute the proxy and you can claim that you had refuted all the evidence. The defense adopted the tactic of focusing on the leading handwriting expert, Albert S. Osborn, and directing the jury's attention to what he had not demonstrated instead of what he had shown. They decided to deal with the wood expert, Arthur Koehler, by trying to show that he did not have adequate experience and didn't know wood as well as he testified. The available attacks on the expert testimony were:

(f) The handwriting experts are wrong and are only testifying for notoriety.
(g) The wood expert is wrong and is only testifying for notoriety.
(h) If the fingerprint examination had been done competently, it would have exonerated Hauptmann.

Misidentification

The misidentification defense could also involve both the cross-examination of prosecution witnesses and the calling of defense witnesses. Those arguments would be:

(i) Witnesses who said they saw Hauptmann in New Jersey are either mistaken or not credible, or both.

(j) Dr. Condon is mistaken or lying in his identification of Hauptmann as Cemetery John.
(k) Taxi driver Perrone is mistaken in his identification of Hauptmann as the man who gave him the ransom note to deliver to Condon.
(l) Cecile Barr is mistaken in her identification of Hauptmann as the man who used ransom money to purchase a ticket at the Sheridan Square Theater.

Alibi

Misidentification and alibi are separate defenses. The defense of misidentification is raised during the cross-examination of prosecution witnesses as to the accuracy of the identifications. The defense of alibi can be raised in addition to attacks on the identifications by showing that accused was at another place at the relevant times crime events occurred. At the time of Hauptmann's trial the courts of New Jersey did not consider the defense of alibi to be an affirmative defense. In a 1935 opinion the New Jersey Supreme Court had this to say about the defense:

> Testimony tending to break the force of the state's prima facie case, by [offering an alibi] is not the offer of an affirmative issue advanced by the defense; it is merely showing a state of facts inconsistent with an essential element of the indictment. The jury may, notwithstanding such testimony, believe that the defendant was present as charged, or they may believe that he was absent, in which event he is said to have "proved his alibi." A third result may be that the defendant's testimony may create such a degree of uncertainty as to his whereabouts that the jury are not

> satisfied, beyond reasonable doubt of his guilt of the crime for which he was indicted.[1]

At his New York habeas corpus hearing Hauptmann had failed to prove he was not in New Jersey, but he had borne the burden of proof. At the actual trial his attorneys simply had to raise a reasonable doubt as to Hauptmann's whereabouts. At the trial the defense would also have to establish alibis for times other than the day of the kidnapping. The various alibi defenses would be:

(m) Hauptmann worked the day of March 1 at Reliance Property Management.
(n) Hauptmann was at the Fredericksen bakery in New York City on the night of the crime.
(o) Hauptmann was having a music night with Hans Kloppenburg on April 2 when the ransom was paid.
(p) Hauptmann was at home for his birthday party the night Cecile Barr received the curiously folded $5 bill.

Other Suspects

Although establishing an alibi did not require proof that someone else committed the crime, such proof certainly bolstered an alibi defense. The defense, therefore, tried to turn the finger of suspicion away from Hauptmann and toward people who could plausibly be suspected of committing the crime. They could claim:

---

[1] State v. Kaplan, 115 N.J.L. 374, 180 A. 423 (Sup.Ct., 1935).

(q) People other than Hauptmann were seen with ladders before the kidnapping.
(r) People other than Hauptmann were seen with the baby after the kidnapping.
(s) The burglary was an inside job committed by various employees.
(t) Isidore Fisch was the culprit.

Hauptmann would contend that he had received the money from his business associate Isidor Fisch at the farewell party for Fisch shortly before he left to return to Germany in 1933. Hauptmann would offer witnesses to the farewell celebration who would testify that they had seen Fisch with strange bundles or large amounts of money. Other witnesses would even say they had seen Fisch with gold certificates after the ransom was paid.

The defense had an embarrassment of riches when it came to other suspects. They quite possibly had too many suspects. A shotgun style defense accusing a host of others could be self-defeating. It would be better if they had a single viable suspect to present to the jury.

Explanation

Two ugly facts tended to indicate that Hauptmann was the kidnapper. They were the facts that (1) Hauptmann had a lot of money for an unemployed man during the Depression, and (2) a lot of that money was Lindbergh ransom money. The defense had to present innocent explanations for these two facts. The defense would deal with these two embarrassing facts by offering evidence to suggest that:

(u) Fisch gave the ransom money to Hauptmann in December of 1933.

(v) Hauptmann didn't know about the ransom money until August of 1934.
(w) The Hauptmanns lived on their savings supplemented by Hauptmann's investments and money he earned doing odd jobs.

The chief problem for the defense strategy was that it had so many sub-categories. Like the prosecution case, it was complex, and complex cases often result in disjointed presentations. They require many witnesses who cannot testify in sequential order, making it difficult for the jury to compartmentalize the various contentions. It was imperative to clearly explain such a complex, multifaceted defense in opening statement so that the jury could understand how the disjointed pieces of the case fitted together.

5

The Prosecution Case

The trial began at 10:00 a.m. on the morning of January 2, 1935, at the Hunterdon County Courthouse in Flemington. The authorities had prepared the ancient courthouse as well as they could to withstand the onslaught of media and curiosity seekers. Of the 500 seats in the courtroom, they reserved 150 for the media. Color coded tickets allowed access to different areas. Red tickets allowed seating in the press section, yellow tickets admitted media telegraphers into the communications room, and white tickets went to officials who could sit inside the rail of the courtroom. No tickets were printed for the general public, who could get one of the remaining 350 seats on a first-come-first-seated basis. An additional 48 folding chairs set up inside the rail were reserved for the prospective jurors. When the courtroom filled, they would lock the door and allow no further admittance. As a precaution against souvenir hunters, the authorities wired the witness chair to the floor. Pundits predicted that the jury selection would take several days.[1]

The media intended to transmit daily transcripts of the trial testimony to the four corners of the world. They virtually took over the courthouse, cramming it with more communication equipment than had ever been used to cover any event in history. They put so much communication equipment into the attic of the courthouse

---

[1] Russell B. Porter, "Hauptmann Trial to Start Tomorrow: Clash on Jury Seen," *NYT*, January 1, 1935.

that people feared the ceiling would collapse. The County Engineer surveyed the situation and ordered that no more equipment could go in the attic.[2]

Apparently the prosecution team had shared their trial strategy with some members of the press. The *New York Times*, on January 1, published an article outlining the expected evidence and describing the approximate order in which the state intended to call their witnesses. The *Times* even described problems anticipated by the prosecution in the presentation of their case. Most notably, the *Times* disclosed that the prosecution team did not know whether John Condon would identify Hauptmann as Cemetery John. The defense, on the other hand, held their cards somewhat closer to the vest, merely saying they had several alibi witnesses in addition to Hauptmann's wife, they intended to show that Isidor Fisch gave Hauptmann the ransom money, and they intended to engage in vigorous cross-examination of the prosecution witnesses.[3]

The trial opened with a battery of lawyers in attendance. David T. Wilentz, the New Jersey Attorney General led the prosecution team, consisting of Anthony M. Hauck, the local prosecutor; George K. Large, a former judge who practiced in Flemington; and three Assistant Attorneys General—Joseph Lanigan, Robert Peacock, and Robert Stock. Edward J. Reilly led for the defense, assisted by Fred A. Pope, Egbert Rosencrans, and C. Lloyd Fisher.[4] The presiding judge was Thomas W. Trenchard, a Justice of the New Jersey Supreme Court. Although he was an appellate judge, Trenchard

---

[2] "Huge Wire Service Set up for Trial," *NYT*, January 2, 1935.

[3] Russell B. Porter, "Hauptmann Trial to Start Tomorrow: Clash on Jury Seen," *NYT*.

[4] "Digest of the Opening Session of the Hauptmann Trial," *NYT*, January 3, 1935.

often sat as judge on trials in lower courts.[5] He had a reputation as an excellent trial judge. In his three decades on the bench he never had a murder conviction reversed.[6]

Hauck and Fisher, being local attorneys, did the bulk of the voir dire examination. Although the pundits had predicted a lengthy jury selection process, it only took two days. This difference between expectation and reality has a simple explanation. High profile cases tend to be tried in larger jurisdictions with enormous jury pools. Rarely do the lawyers actually know anyone on the panel of prospective jurors. Hunterdon County was a small community where almost everyone knew almost everyone else. In such jurisdictions, local lawyers know the prospective jurors far better than lawyers in large jurisdictions. In Hunterdon County, Hauck and Fisher would likely know whether they wanted a particular juror before asking a single question. Given that dynamic, it was no wonder that the local attorneys handled the voir dire and no wonder that the voir dire concluded so quickly.

Instead of asking a battery of searching questions, the lawyers asked rather perfunctory questions. The examination of Charles F. Walton is typical of the sort of questions asked:

BY MR. FISHER:

Q: Mr. Walton, are you married?

A. Yes, sir.

Q: And do you have a family?

A. Yes, sir.

Q: What?

A. Four children: three boys and a girl.

Q: How old is the youngest child?

---

[5] He would, of course, recuse himself from hearing appeals involving cases that he had sat on as a trial judge.

[6] "T.W. Trenchard, Hauptmann Judge Dies at Home," *NYT*, July 24, 1974.

A. Nine.

Q: Have you formed any opinion as to the guilt or innocence of the defendant in this case?

A. Not exactly, no.

Q: Have you read the Winchell column in *The Daily Mirror*?

A. No, I haven't.

Q: Or heard his broadcast?

A. Well, occasionally.

Q: Do you feel, Mr. Walton, if you were permitted to sit on this jury that you would be guided by the evidence and render a fair verdict in accordance with the evidence as presented to you?

A. I would, sir.

Q: And do you understand that rule of law is that the defendant is innocent until he is proved guilty beyond a reasonable doubt?

A. Yes, sir.

Q: And would you be willing to give him the benefit of that reasonable doubt?

A. Yes, sir.

Q: Did you receive this so-called pamphlet, Criminal File No. 2310?

A. I did.

[This pamphlet was a parody of the Lindbergh case which had been mailed to every member of the prospective jury panel].

Q: And did the receipt of that alter your opinion one way or the other about this case?

A. No.

Q: Have any threats of any kind been made to you in connection with the probability of your serving on this jury?

A. No, they haven't.

Q: You are in such position that you can dismiss from your mind entirely anything that has gone along heretofore; is that correct?

A. Yes, sir. Yes, sir.

BY MR. FISHER: You may examine.

BY MR. HAUCK:

Q: Mr. Walton, have you any conscientious or religious scruples against capital punishment?

A. No.

Q: I understood you to answer Mr. Fisher in the beginning of his examination as to whether or not you had formed an opinion that you said not exactly.

A. Well, not to any extent, not any more than anyone else would that read the paper.

Q: In other words, even though you might have been affected in some small manner, you could be guided by the evidence and by the law as charged to you by the court solely?

A. Yes.

Walton was then sworn as a juror.[7] He later became the foreman.[8] Apparently at that time in New Jersey, the first juror sworn became the foreman. By the end of the first day, ten jurors had taken the oath.[9] This sort of questioning would never pass muster in a modern capital case voir dire. Each answer Walton gave would produce a litany of follow-up questions. Defense counsel would have inquired into everything that Walton had ever heard about the case, everything he had ever read about the case, and every thought he had ever thought about the case. Walton

---

[7] "Digest of the Opening Session of the Hauptmann Trial," *NYT*, January 3, 1935.

[8] "Bookkeeper, 55, Carpenter, 60, Fill Jury, With Average Age Increased to 44½ Years," *NYT*, January 4, 1935.

[9] "10 Hauptmann Case Jurors, 4 Women, Quickly Chosen; Col. Lindbergh a Spectator," *NYT*, January 3, 1935.

would have been required to state any opinion he ever formed or expressed concerning Hauptmann's possible guilt or innocence, and the defense would have inquired thoroughly into the exact nature of Walton's feelings about the death penalty. The defense would also make a searching inquiry into every aspect of Walton's background which might have any influence whatsoever on his ability to sit as a fair and impartial juror. These inquiries would include, but not be limited to, Walton's feelings about law enforcement officers, his prior experiences with the justice system, and whether anyone he knew had been the victim of a homicide.

The prosecution would also have been obliged to ask far more detailed questions in an effort to defend against the possibility that the defense would lead the potential juror into saying something that might give rise to grounds for a challenge for cause. Both sides had unlimited challenges for cause, meaning that they could strike any number of jurors off the panel if they could state a good cause for believing that the juror could not be fair and impartial. In addition, each side had a limited number of peremptory challenges which they could use to remove jurors without having to state any reason. The defense had twenty peremptory challenges, and the prosecution had twelve. The sooner the defense ran out of peremptory challenges, the sooner the jury would be seated. By the end of the first day, the defense had exercised fifteen of its twenty challenges, and the prosecution had exercised seven.[10]

On the second day of the trial the crowd ignored the sheriff's order that there would be no standees in the courtroom, and 275 additional unticketed observers crowded into the courtroom and stood in the aisles nearest the

---

[10] *Ibid.*

walls.[11] Samuel J. Foley, the Bronx District Attorney, attended the trial at the request of Wilentz. Foley pledged his full support for the New Jersey prosecution and announced his intention to attend every day of the trial.[12] The demand for instant access to news of the trial had necessitated the addition of another teletype line directly from Flemington to London, England.[13] The last two jurors were seated quickly, and Wilentz made his opening statement. The defense reserved making their opening until after the state rested.

Mark Twain once said, "We have a criminal jury system which is superior to any in the world; and its efficiency is only marred by the difficulty of finding twelve men every day who don't know anything and can't read." Although he meant his aphorism as a joke, it speaks to a real problem with jury selection. Jurors who know too much about a case can be disqualified from service, and many lawyers think that the more ignorant the juror, the better. Consequently, jurors seldom know anything about the facts of the case which they must decide, and the lawyers must fully educate the jurors on the facts of the case as they try to persuade the jury to return a favorable verdict. The opening statement is the first opportunity to begin educating the jury. Advocates may not argue their case during opening statement; they must limit themselves to giving a clear and concise account of what they expect the evidence to prove, not what they think the evidence means. Although argument is prohibited in opening statement, there is no prohibition against stating the facts persuasively.

The opening statement is important because of the near impossibility of telling a story in strict chronological

---

[11] "Court Room Walls Lined by Standees," *NYT*, January 4, 1935.

[12] "Foley Attends Trial," *NYT*, January 4, 1935.

[13] "Direct Wire to London Set up for Trial News," *NYT*, January 4, 1935.

order through the presentation of witnesses. One witness may have information about the beginning and end of the case, but not the middle. Another witness knows very little about the case, but you must call her to establish an evidentiary foundation for important evidence. Witnesses' schedules have to be accommodated. All these factors can lead to an evidentiary presentation which is jumbled at best and incoherent at worst. In the opening statement the advocate gets to give a coherent account of the case, familiarize the jury with the evidence to be presented, and introduce them to the various themes which will play out during the presentation of evidence. Given a good opening statement, the jurors can hear the disjointed items of evidence and testimony and place them in order on the framework of the opening statement.

In evaluating Wilentz's opening statement, it should be remembered that he was prosecuting his first criminal case. He made a good opening statement for a rookie prosecutor, but this case demanded more talent than a rookie possesses. Let us look at what he needed to do in his opening and evaluate how well he did it. Wilentz had three objectives to accomplish in the opening statement: (1) establish his case theory, (2) give the jury a narrative statement of the case, and (3) map out for the jury how he intended to persuade them to accept his narrative statement and case theory. He had two triads to establish: a triad of people and a triad of tangible evidence. Hauptmann, Cemetery John, and the Lindbergh baby, the first triad, had to be connected. Wilentz had to put both Hauptmann and Cemetery John in the Lindbergh baby's bedroom on the night of the kidnapping, and he had to prove that Hauptmann was Cemetery John. In order to do this, he had to demonstrate to the jury how the evidentiary triad of the ladder, the ransom letters, and the ransom money, tied Hauptmann, Cemetery John, and Charles Lindbergh, Jr. all together. As we said in Chapter

3, this evidentiary triad could be referred to thematically as Ladder, Letters, and Loot.

Wilentz began his opening statement by introducing the legal theory: "[W]here the death of anyone ensues in the commission of a burglary, that killing is murder—murder in the first degree."[14] He told the jury that Hauptmann "broke into and entered at night the Lindbergh home with intent to commit a battery upon the child and with the intent to steal the child and his clothing."[15] And then Wilentz made a grave tactical error which came back to haunt the case when it went up on appeal after Hauptmann's conviction. In order to explain his error, we must discuss the mechanics of proving up a murder case.

To prove Hauptmann guilty of first degree murder, the prosecution had to establish three things: (1) That the Lindbergh baby was dead; (2) that the death was caused by the criminal act of Richard Hauptmann; and (3) that the killing (a) was premeditated, or (b) occurred during the commission of common law burglary. The medical examiner had determined that the child died from a blow to the head but could not say how the blow was inflicted. This left Wilentz with no proof of exactly how Hauptmann had killed the baby. The circumstances were open to two reasonable interpretations: (1) Hauptmann planned from the outset to kill the baby and either killed it in the nursery or shortly after leaving the home; or (2) the homemade ladder, barely strong enough to support Hauptmann as he climbed into the window, broke under the added weight of the baby; and when the ladder broke, Hauptmann dropped the baby, accidentally killing it. Either interpretation made Hauptmann guilty of first

---

[14] Transcript, 1.

[15] Transcript, 2.

degree murder, and it would have been perfectly proper for the prosecution to argue both theories to the jury.

The fact narration in the opening statement should have been stated broadly enough to cover either accidental death or premeditation. By leaving his options open in this way, Wilentz would have been free to argue both theories to the jury. "Ladies and gentlemen, Bruno Richard Hauptmann killed the child while he was committing a burglary. Whether he intended to kill or accidentally killed, he is still guilty of first degree murder." If he restricted himself to one theory in opening, he would be hard pressed to reverse his course and argue the other in closing. First, juries have been known to acquit because the prosecution couldn't make up their minds about how a defendant inflicted the fatal blow. Second, changing theories so radically allows the defense to argue that the case should be reversed because of a variance between allegation and proof.[16]

Wilentz told the jury that as Hauptmann went "down that ladder of his, the ladder broke. He had more weight going down than he had when he was coming up. And down he went with this child. In the commission of that burglary, that child was instantaneously killed...."[17] He had restricted his proof, and he came to regret it. In closing the defense asked why the child had not cried out when Hauptmann took it from the crib. Wilentz answered the question by changing his theory from accidental death to premeditated murder: "Why? There was no cry left in the child. Did he use the chisel to crush the skull at the time or to knock it into insensibility? Is that a fair inference? What

---

[16] State v. Jones, 115 N.J.L. 257, 179 A. 320 (Ct.Err. & App., 1935) (Reversing murder conviction because the state opened with a theory of felony murder during a burglary and closed with a theory of felony murder during a robbery).

[17] Transcript, 2.

else was the chisel there for? To knock that child into insensibility right there in that room."[18] This gave the defense an opportunity, but they frittered it away. They raised the issue on appeal, but the appeals court turned a deaf ear to their plea because "there was apparently no objection made, no exception taken, no request for an opportunity to reply to the argument freshly presented, no request for a jury charge based thereon."[19]

After establishing his legal theory, Wilentz began to give his factual narrative to the jury. Inexperienced trial lawyers often assume the jury knows more about the case than they actually do. This causes them to confuse the jury by omitting essential facts and explanations. Wilentz did just this. He mentioned a number of witnesses whom he failed to introduce to the jury—Henry Breckinridge,[20] John Condon,[21] Jafsie,[22] "The Boss,"[23] Mrs. Schoenfeld.[24] Although he knew the broad outline of the story, he did not know the details. Consequently, he often qualified his description of events—"I think,"[25] "I suppose,"[26] "or whatever it was,"[27] "or something like that,"[28] "I think it was,"[29] "or whatever it was,"[30] "or

---

[18] Transcript, 4407.
[19] State v. Hauptmann, 115 N.J.L. 412, 421, 180 A. 809, 816 (Ct. Err. & App., 1935). Given the tenor of the court's additional comments on the issue, it is doubtful that they would have reversed even if the defense had properly preserved their objection.
[20] Transcript, 3.
[21] Transcript, 4.
[22] Transcript, 5.
[23] Transcript, 7.
[24] Transcript, 12.
[25] Transcript, 4.
[26] Transcript, 5.
[27] Transcript, 6.
[28] Transcript, 6.
[29] Transcript, 8.
[30] Transcript, 8.

whatever her name is."[31] His assumption that the jury knew details of the transactions which they may well not have known led him to give a disjointed, choppy narrative which sometimes was inaccurate and misleading. He gave the false impression that Charles Lindbergh was present at Dr. Condon's house when the child's sleeping suit arrived.[32] He described the discovery of the child's body as though both Charles Lindbergh and Bessie Gow were present when it was lifted from the shallow grave.[33] He could have avoided all this uncertainty and confusion by simply painting with a broader brush.

Wilentz also did a poor job of establishing his two essential triads. As to the triad of characters—Hauptmann, Cemetery John, and the kidnapped child—he neither mentioned Cemetery John nor did he give the jury any inkling as to how Cemetery John and Hauptmann were connected. He did no better with his triad of tangible evidence—the ladder, the ransom letters, and the ransom money. As to the ransom money, he never once mentioned the tracking of the serial numbers, nor did he describe the tracking of the license tag number which the gas station attendant wrote on the ten dollar bill Hauptmann gave him. Twelve handwriting examiners identified the ransom letters as coming from the hand of Hauptmann, but Wilentz never mentioned any of them.

The ladder was arguably the most important piece of evidence against Hauptmann, and it would have been nice to set up its importance in opening statement—to tell how it was examined and to explain how the examination tied it back to Hauptmann—but when Wilentz discussed the significance of the ladder, he said nothing about how the identification was made. He simply said:

---

[31] Transcript, 12.
[32] Transcript, 5.
[33] Transcript, 8.

> [H]auptmann took part of that attic of his and built the ladder with it,—and we will prove that to you *beyond any doubt*. One rung of that ladder, one side of that ladder, comes right from his attic, put on there with his tools, and we will prove it to you, *no matter how difficult it may sound*,—we will prove it to you so that there will be *no doubt about it*.[34]

[Emphasis supplied]. Nothing can ever be proved beyond all doubt. That is why the burden of proof in a criminal case is "beyond a reasonable doubt," and not "beyond all doubt" or "beyond a shadow of a doubt." Wilentz in one breath said it sounded difficult to connect the ladder to Hauptmann, and in the next breath he promised to connect it to Hauptman "beyond any doubt." Wilentz took a great risk by assuming a higher burden of proof than the law requires—the jury just might have held him to it.

Wilentz ended his opening statement with another high-risk strategy. Good advocates try to close out any forensic speech with a strong motivational statement urging the jury to find in their favor. Instead of adopting such a course, Wilentz said:

> Now men and women of the jury, *if we do not prove these facts* to you, why, you *acquit him*, you *acquit him; if we do not prove them* to you, *you acquit him*. But *if we do*, as we are confident we will be able to, and as we expect to, let me just tell you, representing the State of New Jersey, that this State will not compromise with murder or murderers. We demand the penalty of murder in the first degree.

[Emphasis supplied]. Oftentimes when a prosecutor invites a jury to acquit, they follow his instructions.

---

[34] Transcript, 11.

Wilentz extended that invitation to the jury three times, and then he said, "if we do [prove these facts]." He seemed to be doubtful himself about whether he could carry his burden. Good trial lawyers often doubt their ability to carry a particular burden of proof, but they never share those doubts with the jury.

There is an old saying that lawyers often win cases in spite of their efforts rather than because of them. A good case is often strong enough to survive a bad opening statement, but a bad opening statement will often kill a good case. A good opening statement coupled with a good case is almost always a winner. Now that we have thoroughly critiqued the opening statement that Wilentz made, let us offer an opening statement which he could have made.

> Ladies and gentlemen of the jury, Bruno Richard Hauptmann kidnapped and killed 20 month old Charles A. Lindbergh, Jr. and then he conned the boy's parents by pretending their child was still alive and promising to return the child if they paid him a ransom. But before he could become a kidnapper and a killer, he had to become a burglar. On the night of March 1, 1932, he placed a handmade ladder against the side of the Lindberghs' home here in Hunterdon County and used it to climb into the second story window of little Charles's bedroom, where he took the child out of his bed. During the course of that burglary, he killed little Charles by causing the boy to suffer a terrific blow to his head. Hauptmann left the house with the dead child, but he left the ladder and a wood chisel behind as he fled. A few miles away from the home he walked a short distance off the highway and buried little Charles face down in a shallow grave.
>
> It was about 10:00 that evening when little Charles's nurse went into the bedroom to check on him. When she couldn't find him, she went to Colonel Lindbergh and raised the alarm. Lindbergh armed himself with a Springfield rifle and went outside to

search for his son while his wife, the nurse, and the rest of the servants searched the house. When Colonel Lindbergh returned, he asked his butler to telephone the police and went back upstairs to look at the bedroom. He saw what looked like the marks of footprints leading from the window to the crib, and he saw an envelope on the window sill.

When the police arrived, Colonel Lindbergh showed them the envelope, and they opened it. The envelope contained a crudely written letter which told Lindbergh not to call the police and demanded $50,000 in ransom. Hauptmann had drawn a symbol on the letter which he said would identify any further messages—two interlocked blue circles with a red circle in the middle and three holes punched through the paper. This was the first of a series of letters demanding ransom and promising the safe return of the child, and each one of them had the same symbol—two blue circles, a red circle, and three holes. The second letter came in the mail addressed to "Mr. Col. Lindbergh, Hopewell, NJ," and the third came to Lindbergh's lawyer. Then another man entered into the ransom correspondence.

Dr. John Condon, a retired professor who lived in the Bronx, wanted to do something to try to help the Lindberghs, and he decided to put an ad in the *Bronx News* offering to add $1,000 of his own money to the ransom payment and volunteering to act as a go-between in the ransom negotiations. Hauptmann, who also lived in the Bronx, saw the ad and sent Condon a letter accepting him as a go-between. Condon took the letter to Colonel Lindbergh, Lindbergh saw that the letter had the symbol on it, and he agreed to use Condon as the go-between. This began an awkward correspondence between Condon and Hauptmann. Hauptmann would send Condon letters and Condon would put his replies in the paper using the code name Jafsie, which he devised from his initials—J.F.C.

They finally arranged a face-to-face meeting. The two met at Woodlawn Cemetery in the Bronx. Condon tested Hauptmann's bona fides by showing him some things that Colonel Lindbergh had given him and asking Hauptmann if he knew what they were. Hauptmann replied that they were the safety pins that had been used to secure the baby's blanket on the night he was kidnapped. Hauptmann identified himself as "John," and Condon nicknamed him "Cemetery John." Condon pleaded with Hauptmann to let him see little Charles, but Hauptmann refused, saying he was just the messenger and "Number One would smack me out." They worked out a compromise. Hauptmann agreed to send Condon an article of the baby's clothing. Then they parted company and went their separate ways, but before they did, Hauptmann asked an ominous question, "Will I burn if the child dies?"

Shortly after the meeting between Dr. Condon and Hauptmann, a package came to Condon's home, and it contained a sleeping suit. Colonel Lindbergh identified it as his son's suit, and they made preparations to deliver the ransom. At Lindbergh's request, the authorities had stayed out of the ransom negotiations, but they insisted that they be allowed to record the serial numbers of the ransom money. Colonel Lindbergh agreed, and the authorities decided to do something else to make the money more easily identifiable. President Roosevelt was about to call in all the gold certificates in circulation. People could take their gold certificates to the bank and exchange them, but after the deadline for turning in gold certificates it would be unlawful to possess them. The authorities took Colonel Lindbergh's money and swapped it for bills which they provided. There were fives, tens, twenties, and fifties in the ransom. None of the fives were gold certificates, but most of the rest were. The authorities recorded the serial numbers of all the bills and put the numbers on a flyer which they intended to send to all banks after the recovery of the child.

On the evening set for the ransom payment, Dr. Condon and Colonel Lindbergh waited at Condon's home for instructions, which a messenger delivered to the front door. The two men followed Hauptmann's written instructions and arrived near St. Raymond's Cemetery in the Bronx. Lindbergh drove. When they stopped to wait, Hauptmann yelled, "Hey Doctor, over here," and Condon went alone to meet with Hauptmann. Hauptmann asked where the money was, and Condon told him it was in the car. Condon tried to bargain Hauptmann down from the $70,000 he had demanded, and when Hauptmann said he would accept $50,000, Condon went back to the car to get it. He and Lindbergh removed $20,000 in fifties from the ransom, and Condon took it back to Hauptmann. Hauptmann looked over the money, thanked Condon, and gave Condon a note bearing false directions to a "Boad Nelly" which was supposedly in the Massachusetts Bay. The directions said that they would find the child on the "Boad Nelly" with two nurses who were innocent. Lindbergh flew to the Massachusetts Bay, but try as he might, he could never find the "Boad Nelly." To this day, no one has ever found the "Boad Nelly."

While Lindbergh searched for his son, two workmen discovered little Charles' body where Hauptmann had left it. Despite its state of decomposition both Lindbergh and the baby's nurse identified the body. They identified little Charles from his facial features and from a twisted toe on his foot. Also, little Charles was still wearing a hand sewn shirt which his nurse had made for him on the very evening of his abduction. The nurse still had the cloth that she cut the shirt from, and they were able to match the cloth to the shirt.

The very day that he got the ransom money, Hauptmann quit his job and never had a steady job ever again. Up to that point, he kept meticulous financial records. He stopped after the ransom was paid. After the serial numbers went out to banks across the U.S. and after the deadline passed for turning in gold certificates, it would have been dangerous to deposit a huge number of gold certificates in a bank. Hauptmann began passing single gold certificates around New York City, making small purchases and getting change in return. On one occasion, he bought a thirty five cent movie ticket with a five dollar bill from the ransom payment. The bills started turning up at various locations around New York City, and Hauptmann began making lots of bank deposits consisting of the coins he got in change for his gold certificates. He also began making extravagant purchases, buying an expensive set of binoculars, a $400 Victrola record player, and a hunting rifle. He took a vacation to Florida, went hunting in Maine, and sent his wife to Germany. And all during this time he was losing money hand over fist in the stock market. Hauptmann finally got caught when he used a $10 gold certificate to buy gas at the Warner-Quinlan gas station in the Bronx. The gold certificate made the attendant suspicious, and he asked Hauptmann about it. Not satisfied with the explanation he got, the attendant wrote Hauptmann's license tag number on the bill. Eventually the bill got deposited in a bank. The bank identified the serial number and turned the bill over to the authorities, and the authorities traced it in two directions. Using bank records they found the gas station where Hauptmann passed the bill, and using the tag number, they found Hauptmann's home address.

But the authorities hadn't been idle in the two years between the baby's disappearance and Hauptmann's arrest. They had worked very hard following the few leads that they had. Their first lead was the ladder that Hauptmann had left behind. It was handmade from an assortment of 1" x 4" boards and was divided into three sections so it could be taken apart and carried in an automobile. In fact, it fit quite neatly into Hauptmann's car. They tried to lift latent fingerprints off of the ladder but failed. Despite their best efforts, they could not raise useful prints off of the ladder. They next looked at the materials the ladder was made from. It looked to be made from an assortment of scrap lumber pieces such as what a carpenter might have left over from doing several jobs. Some of the boards were North Carolina pine, some were

Ponderosa pine, and some were Douglas fir. The authorities numbered each piece of wood from the ladder, and they took the ladder apart for examination. They labeled each nail to show where it was pulled from, and when they got through with the ladder, they put it back together. They called on Arthur Koehler, a wood expert from the U.S. Department of Forestry, to come in and examine the wood from the ladder. Koehler was particularly interested in three North Carolina pine boards—Rails 12, 13, and 16.

Koehler determined that Rail 16 came from a different source than Rails 12 and 13. He said it was old and might have been nailed inside a garage or attic. He said when they found a suspect, to look for places where the board might fit. Koehler also tried to locate the source of Rails 12 and 13. Through some excellent scientific work that you will hear about in the testimony, he determined that the rails came from a sawmill in South Carolina. He then traced the shipment of those rails to the National Lumber and Millwork Company in the Bronx. Now this company used to have an employee by the name of Bruno Richard Hauptmann. They made no connection between Hauptmann and the lumber at that time, because it was still a year before the authorities learned that Hauptmann even existed. After Hauptmann's arrest, the authorities thoroughly examined Hauptmann's home and found where Rail 16 came from. It had been sawed off of a board that was still in Hauptmann's attic.

The wood wasn't all they examined from the ladder. They examined the nails also, and they were able to determine that the Pittsburgh Steel Company in Monessen, Pennsylvania had made the nails. This discovery was also made long before Hauptmann's arrest. After Hauptmann's arrest, they found a keg of nails in his garage. The nails from that keg, and the nails used to build Hauptmann's garage, matched the nails in the ladder. And they came from the same factory that made the nails in the ladder—the Pittsburgh Steel Company in Monessen, Pennsylvania. More than that, scientific examination traced all the nails back to a single batch of nails made at the factory.

Several handwriting examiners looked at the ransom letters and all came to the same conclusion—the person who wrote the ransom letter found in the Lindbergh baby's bedroom wrote all the other letters. After Hauptmann's arrest, they identified Hauptmann as the writer of all the letters. They discovered one more item of handwriting evidence after Hauptmann's arrest. They found Dr. Condon's address and telephone number written on a board in Hauptmann's closet. Hauptmann admitted that he wrote the information on the board and explained that he was in his closet reading in the paper about the Lindbergh case and decided to write Condon's address on the board.

The final item of evidence that they ran down was the ransom money. All the banks were on the lookout for those bills, and as gold certificates got scarcer and scarcer, it got easier and easier to determine whether the ones that came in were from the ransom money. Whenever tellers found a ransom bill, they called the authorities, and the authorities traced each bill back to the place where it was passed. Far and away the vast majority of those bills were passed in New York City. When Hauptmann got arrested, he had a ransom bill in his pocket. He assured the authorities that the bill in his pocket and the bill passed at the gas station were the only ransom money that he ever had, but a thorough search of Hauptmann's home and garage told a different story. They found $14,590 more dollars hidden in the garage, all of it ransom money.

So the ladder, the letters, and the loot, along with other evidence you will hear and see during the trial, all point to Bruno Richard Hauptmann as the kidnapper of the Lindbergh baby, the killer of the Lindbergh baby, and the con man who swindled Charles Lindbergh, Sr. out of $50,000. But before he could become a kidnapper, before he could become a killer, before he could become a con man, he had to become a burglar and sneak into the Lindbergh home in the dead

> of the night and steal away Charles and Anne Lindbergh's most precious possession—their only child. At the end of the trial, you will be satisfied beyond a reasonable doubt that Bruno Richard Hauptmann is guilty of murder in the first degree.

This opening statement immediately introduces the case theory and describes the three essential items of circumstantial evidence. It then gives a factual narrative that describes how the circumstantial evidence formed a web around Hauptmann from which he could not escape. The conclusion summarizes the case strengths and assures the jury that they will be satisfied of Hauptmann's guilt. Other and better opening statements could be written for the case, but this one does a serviceable job of covering all essential points.

After making his opening statement, Wilentz immediately began the presentation of the evidence with the Disappearance module. He first called Walter E. Roberts, a surveyor, to introduce maps of the area which established venue by showing that the Lindbergh home was in Hunterdon County. Wilentz also used Roberts to introduce a floor plan of the Lindbergh home.[35] He next called Anne Lindbergh to testify about the circumstances of her son's disappearance. Reilly declined to cross-examine her. Charles Lindbergh testified next, and the day ended with his direct examination incomplete. After the trial recessed for the day, attorneys for both sides held press conferences, with the prosecutors praising Mrs. Lindbergh's testimony and the defense discounting it. Reilly made the first of many flamboyant statements to the press, claiming that he intended to prove that the kidnapping was perpetrated by a gang of five criminals which included some of the servants in the Lindbergh household. He said

---

[35] Transcript, 77.

that he would begin his attack on the state's case the following day, and would show that the ladder was never used in the kidnapping. Reilly then said he intended to spend the bulk of the next day cross-examining Lindbergh. "I have an awful lot of questions to ask Colonel Lindbergh, an awful lot of things I want answers to."[36] The prosecution also shared its plans for case presentation with the press, giving the names and testimony synopses for the next several witnesses. They were not willing to share their plans for calling John Condon, however.[37] Their reluctance probably stemmed from the fact that they assessed Condon as a loose cannon and were not really sure when they should call him.

Pandemonium continued to reign on the third day of the trial, as people began to line up at 6:00 a.m. to get seats at the trial.[38] Attendees realized that their passes, which were good for only one day, were not being screened properly and began showing expired passes to the officers on duty. When the sheriff realized that many spectators were gaining an unauthorized second entrance into the courtroom, he closed the doors to everyone and decreed that henceforth, he would have passes collected at the door to prevent their reuse.[39] The circuslike atmosphere was not confined to the spectators. Trenchard, upset over the publication of photographs depicting the Lindberghs testifying, lectured the media representatives and warned that publication of further photographs of the trial would result in the exclusion of cameras from the

---

[36] "Inside Job, Reilly Says," *NYT*, January 4, 1935.
[37] *Ibid.*
[38] "Youthful Throng Waits at Court as Cold Weather Keeps Elders Away," *NYT*.
[39] "Court Room Doors Closed in Confusion over Passes," *NYT*, January 5, 1935.

courtroom.[40] On cross-examination Reilly asked Lindbergh if he were armed. This provoked an objection from Wilentz which the judge sustained, but Lindbergh answered the question, "No, I am not."[41] Reilly asked this question because the previous day some spectators had noticed Lindbergh carrying a revolver in a shoulder holster. Because of threats on his life, Lindbergh had been carrying the revolver for years.[42] He had somehow learned that Reilly intended to make an issue of the firearm and left his gun outside the courtroom.

Problems began to crop up almost immediately. Wilentz allowed the court reporter to number the evidentiary exhibits, and the reporter made a pig's breakfast of the numbering system. Exhibits are first marked for identification so that the lawyer can establish the relevancy, authenticity, and integrity of the evidentiary exhibit. After the laying of a sufficient evidentiary predicate to establish the relevance of the exhibit, the judge allows the exhibit to be marked into evidence. Ideally, the exhibit receives the same evidence number as the identification number. Many courts use a system where the exhibit receives an identification letter and an exhibit number when it goes into evidence. This makes for difficulty in reading transcripts, with an exhibit being referred to as "Exhibit A" for a portion of the trial and "Exhibit 1" later in the transcript. Things get messy when the prosecution has more than 26 exhibits. Usually the 27th and 28th exhibits receive the designation "AA" and "BB," and so on. The State had approximately 308 evidentiary exhibits.[43] If they had used the letter/number procedure,

---

[40] "Photographing of Lindberghs Stirs Court; Ban on Pictures at Trial to Be Enforced," *NYT*, January 5, 1935.
[41] Transcript, 117, 118.
[42] "Lindbergh Stops Carrying Revolver in Court Room," *NYT*, January 5, 1935.
[43] Transcript, 4324.

that means that the last state's exhibit for identification would have been "Exhibit VVVVVVVVVVVV." What the reporter did was even worse. Exhibits received a number for identification and a number in evidence. This would have been fine if the numbers had been the same. They weren't. For example, State's Exhibit 6 for identification was a photograph of the Lindbergh child. It was also a photograph taken on the grounds of the Lindbergh home.[44] Identification Exhibit 6 (the photo of the child) became Evidentiary Exhibit 6, while Identification Exhibit 6 (the photo of the grounds) became Evidentiary Exhibit 37,[45] which pre-empted Identification Exhibit 37, a note.[46] State's Exhibit for Identification 34 was both a chisel and an envelope, with the chisel eventually becoming Evidentiary Exhibit 210[47] and the envelope becoming Evidentiary Exhibit 60.[48] Mistakes like this abound throughout the official index of exhibits.[49] It could not help but to promote confusion, something which never helps the prosecution. The prosecutor should control the numbering of exhibits, not the clerk or the court reporter; and the prosecutor should take care that the numbering system makes sense.

The witnesses for the Disappearance module consisted of those who lived in the Lindbergh home, the first responding officers, and some questionable eyewitnesses putting Hauptmann in the vicinity of the crime. Of the witnesses for this module, Charles and Anne Lindbergh made by far the strongest two witnesses. Anne Lindbergh made such a sympathetic witness that any sort of rigorous cross-examination would be suicidal. Charles Lindbergh

---

[44] Transcript, 399, 400, 402, 403, 408.
[45] *Ibid.*
[46] Transcript, 105.
[47] Transcript, 371, 372, 374, 401, 1492, 1493.
[48] Transcript, 104, 639, 640.
[49] Transcript, 4674–4685.

was vulnerable to cross-examination concerning a number of questionable actions on his part, but his intellect, his powerful personality, and his universal esteem enabled him to weather Reilly's rigorous cross and emerge relatively unscathed. The other Disappearance witnesses would be vulnerable. Neither Bessie Gow (the child's nurse) nor Elsie Whateley (the Lindbergh's maid) had the force of character to fully combat the expected cross-examination. The police officers who first arrived on the scene proved easy targets for cross-examination because they did not have the training and experience necessary to deal with the intricacies of crime scene investigation. A case like the Lindbergh kidnapping comes along once in a career, and even today first-responder officers from small town police agencies find themselves at sea trying to cope with the monumental problems presented by a high profile case. The New Jersey State Police proved not much better than the local constabulary. The agency was little more than ten years old at the time of the kidnapping, and it had not been many years since it had transitioned from the horse to the motor car as its principal mode of transportation.[50] In the 1930's the agency's primary duty consisted of traffic enforcement, and training was minimal because they took it as an article of faith that "a real detective is born rather than made."[51]

In Chapter 3 we discussed dividing the case presentation into modules and identified nine prosecution modules for the Lindbergh case—Arrest, Autopsy, Correspondence, Delivery, Disappearance, Finances,

---

[50] "New Jersey State Police History: 1920's The History Begins," http://www.njsp.org/about/20s.html (accessed October 30, 2013).

[51] "New Jersey State Police History: 1930s Blue and Cavalry Yellow," http://www.njsp.org/about/30s.html (accessed October 30, 2013).

Handwriting, Ladder, and Ransom. When presenting a module, the advocate should strive to deal with that module in its entirety before moving on to another. This allows the jury to hear the evidence in a less disjointed fashion than if the witnesses are scattered randomly throughout the presentation. Sometimes the logistics of bringing witnesses from distant cities and the necessity of laying evidentiary foundations make it impossible to deal with the modules so cleanly, but the advocate should strive to keep the presentation of the module as compact as possible. Another problem that crops up with the modular presentation comes when witnesses have essential knowledge of more than one module. Wilentz immediately confronted this problem with Charles Lindbergh, who played a central role in three modules—the Disappearance, the Correspondence, and the Delivery. Wilentz had the option of either calling Lindbergh once and dealing with all the modules at one time or calling Lindbergh to the stand three separate times for the three separate modules. He decided to call Lindbergh once, deal with everything, and then return to the Disappearance module. This method of dealing with the problem disrupted the Disappearance module, and it may have been better to save Lindbergh until the conclusion of the Disappearance module and use him as a transition from that module to the next modules, which would be the Correspondence and Delivery modules.

The first week of trial ended with the testimony of Elsie Whateley. The international news media had transmitted over 2,500,000 words of transcript to London and were planning to open a telegraph line to Sydney, Australia.[52] Over the weekend, tens of thousands of people came to Hopewell and Flemington to gawk at the

---

[52] "2,500,000 Words on Wires. Peak-Load of Trial Carried Day Lindbergh Was Cross-Examined," *NYT*, January 7, 1935.

Lindbergh home and the hole in the ground which marked the spot where the baby's body had been recovered. The sheriff admitted the curious into the courthouse in groups of 200, and by the end of Saturday 5,000 had viewed the courtroom.[53]

The second week of the trial began with the testimony of Bessie Gow and several more officers to wrap up the Disappearance module. This last part of the Disappearance module involved mighty efforts by Wilentz to get the ladder introduced into evidence. The numbering of exhibits proved a nuisance, but the evidentiary problem presented by the ladder could have sounded the death knell for the prosecution's hopes for a conviction. Try as he might, Wilentz couldn't get the ladder into evidence. Before an exhibit can come into evidence, the proponent must authenticate it, a procedure which can be summarized with the acronym MIRA—Mark, Identify, Relevance, Authenticate. In order to identify the exhibit, the proponent must show that it is not only the item involved in the case, it is in substantially the same condition as it was when it was seized. Sometimes the identification process includes establishing a chain of custody for the item—proving where the item has been and who has had it from the time that it was seized as evidence until the time it is offered at trial. The ladder had been fingerprinted, disassembled, reassembled, shipped back and forth across the country, and studied by multiple experts. The broken rail on the ladder had even been repaired. All of this handling made the ladder difficult to authenticate. Wilentz tried to get the ladder into evidence on Monday during the second week of the trial and failed.[54] He used New Jersey State Trooper Lewis Bornmann as the sponsor of the exhibit, and things went badly. Wilentz had the ladder marked, he had Lewis

---

[53] "60,000 see scenes of Lindbergh case," *NYT*, January 6, 1935.
[54] Transcript, 368–370.

Bornmann identify it, he established its relevance by showing that it was on the grounds of the Lindbergh home the night of the crime, but he made no attempt to authenticate it. Then he merely offered it into evidence. Reilly objected on the grounds that the ladder had not been shown to be in substantially the same condition as it was when it was seized. Wilentz then embarked on a series of questions which established that the ladder definitely was not in the same condition as it was when seized:

Q: Officer, is this ladder substantially in the same condition as it was that night when you found it?

A: Yes, sir; it is.

Q: This white board, however, wasn't on it, was it?

A: No, that has been put on it since.

Q: Will you tell us in what other manner it is different now than it was then? For instance, I see a number here, No. 2 with F. K. on there; do you know what that is?

A: Yes, that is Trooper Kelly's initials placed on there that night immediately after—

Q: The writing is his writing?

A: Yes, sir.

Q: And these numbers alongside of the nails, they have been—

A: The nails were removed for the purpose of analysis.

Q: For the purpose of analysis. And they are put back now with those—at any rate these little clips were not on at the time?

A: No, sir; they were not, nor were those white—

Q: Those white numbers, these identifying marks that you are speaking of now were not on at the time?

A: No, sir.

Q: On this piece of board I notice a cut. That cut was not there at the time?

A: No, sir; it was not.

Q: Except for that, those changes that I have indicated to you which I take it were made for the purpose of making tests—

A: They were.

Q: (Continuing.) Is it the same ladder?

A: Yes.[55]

Except for the facts that the ladder now had a new board added to it, it had been written on, the nails had all been pulled out and put back in, clips had been added to it, white numbers had been placed on it, and a piece had been cut out of one of the boards, it was unchanged. Trenchard ruled:

> It may well be that it is desirable before this ladder be actually offered in evidence that it be made to appear, so far as counsel are able to make it appear, in whose custody this ladder has been, and what has been done with it.[56]

Trenchard meant that he wanted the prosecution to establish a full chain of custody and account for every change that had been made to the ladder—a daunting task. Wilentz didn't give up. He tried again the very next day, calling Arthur Koehler, the wood expert. Koehler explained that he had cut the piece out of the ladder, and that he had supervised the affixing of the new board to the ladder. A rail had been sawn in two, and the new board was nailed on to hold the two pieces together. On cross-examination, Koehler testified that the first time he saw the ladder, the rail was in one piece, but the next time he saw it, the rail had been cut in two. Koehler had no idea who cut the rail in two. Koehler further testified on

---

[55] Transcript, 365–366.
[56] Transcript, 370.

cross that he had also pulled all the nails out of the ladder. Koehler said he turned the nails over to someone else, and had no personal knowledge of what happened to them before they were returned to him. He could not positively say that he got the same nails back that he had sent off, but he assured defense counsel that he had been told they were the same nails. Trenchard refused to allow the ladder into evidence.[57] Finally, on January 22, during the fourth week of the trial, after an epic struggle, Wilentz got the ladder into evidence.[58]

In the midst of his efforts to get the ladder admitted, Wilentz called Amandus Hochmuth, an octogenarian who lived at "[t]he corner of what they call the Mercer County Highway and the road that goes up to Mr. Lindbergh's place."[59] Hochmuth testified that on the day of the kidnapping he saw "a car coming around the corner [at a] pretty good speed."[60] The car nearly went into the ditch, and Hochmuth saw the driver's face from a distance of approximately 25 feet. He identified the driver as Hauptmann. Wilentz established that Hauptmann was driving from the direction of Hopewell, and then he asked:

> **Q:** Hopewell. And did it make the turn, as you said, into the lane?
>
> **A:** Yes.[61]

A careful listener might infer from the question and answer that the lane Hauptmann turned into was the lane leading to Lindbergh's home and that Hauptmann drove down the lane in the direction of Lindbergh's home, but Wilentz never made those facts clear. State's Exhibit 1

---

[57] Transcript, 471–479.
[58] Transcript, 1946–1956.
[59] Transcript, 445.
[60] *Ibid.*
[61] Transcript, 448.

was a map of the area surrounding Lindbergh's home. Now would have been a good time to bring that map out to have Hochmuth show where he lived in relation to the Lindbergh home and trace the route taken by Hauptmann's car. It would have been even better if he had used an aerial photograph of the intersection to illustrate Hochmuth's testimony. He certainly knew where to find a pilot.

Hochmuth stood ready to testify that he saw a ladder folded up in the passenger compartment of the car, but Wilentz never made that fact clear. The sum total of the testimony he got out of Hochmuth about the ladder was:

> **Q:** Did it get into the ditch?
>
> **A:** Not yet, but it stopped there, and he pulled the ladder over to him.
>
> ...
>
> **Q:** Yes, sir. Alright, sir. Now you said just now something about a ladder: Was there a ladder in the car?
>
> **A:** I saw something, some of the ladder in it.[62]

Wilentz followed this up with some inconsequential questions about how long Hochmuth had lived in Hopewell and who lived with him, and then concluded the questioning:

> **Q:** Thank you, sir. That is all. Oh. You remember the color of the car? Yes, I omitted that.
>
> **A:** Yes. A dirty green.[63]

Because the ladder was a moderately important piece of evidence, Wilentz should have placed more emphasis

---

[62] *Ibid.*
[63] Transcript, 450.

on questioning about it. He then turned Hochmuth over for cross-examination, and Reilly did a workmanlike job of discrediting the man's testimony. Wilentz attempted to repair the damage with a redirect examination which merely reemphasized the damage Reilly had done on cross, and Hochmuth's testimony concluded.

Although it was important to put Hauptmann in the vicinity of the Lindbergh home, Wilentz declined to call another witness who would do just that. A young man who claimed to have been hitchhiking in the vicinity of the Lindbergh home on the night of the kidnapping said that Hauptmann gave him a ride. According to the witness, Hauptmann had three other men in the car with him. No mention was made of a ladder being in the car.[64] The witness, whose name was Charles Garrick, demonstrates the often two-edged nature of testimony. Garrick gave some support to the theory that Hauptmann committed the kidnapping, but his testimony was in such conflict with the other evidence that Wilentz would have weakened his case by calling the man.

Wilentz also declined to call another witness who could possibly have corroborated Hochmuth's testimony. No matter how well investigated a case may be, if a high profile trial stretches to more than a few days, additional evidence turns up. This sometimes comes about as the result of someone reading or hearing about the trial, remembering things they previously thought unimportant, and coming forward with the information. The day before Hochmuth testified, a Bronx mechanic named Harry Snofsky was going through some old bills and found a bill for repairs on a green Dodge. The bill was made out to a customer named R. Hauptmann and dated three days after Condon delivered the ransom to Cemetery John. Snofsky reported the matter to the New York police, and

---

[64] "Coast Man Identifies Hauptmann," *NYT*, January 9, 1935.

by the end of Condon's testimony, the report had been given to Wilentz. Wilentz did two things: He checked out the story, and he released the story to the news media.[65] Wilentz jumped the gun in releasing the story to the media, because he never called Snofsky as a witness. It goes without saying that the media should have learned of Snofsky's identity, if at all, when he took the stand to testify at the trial.

Upon concluding the Disappearance module, Wilentz turned to the Correspondence and Delivery modules. He had already broached the subjects of both Correspondence and Delivery with the testimony of Charles Lindbergh, who played an integral role in both modules. Except for the testimony of the nearsighted Amandus Hochmuth, nothing about the Disappearance module had directly incriminated Hauptmann, but that would change with the Correspondence and Delivery modules. Wilentz depended on two important witnesses to identify Hauptmann—Lindbergh and John Condon. Lindbergh's identification should logically carry little weight, but the force of his personality would give the identification power far beyond its mere logical significance. When Lindbergh went with Condon to deliver the ransom, he heard a voice calling to Condon, "Hey, Doctor." On the witness stand Lindbergh identified Bruno Richard Hauptmann as the man who spoke those words. It strains credulity to think that Lindbergh, hearing two words spoken in 1932, could identify the speaker in 1935. Lindbergh, however, made an excellent witness. The *New York Times* had this to say about his testimony:

> When the Colonel stepped down from the witness stand, it was obvious that he had made the strongest kind of a witness for the State. There was no mistaking

---

[65] "Story of Auto Link to Suspect Sifted," NYT, January 11, 1935.

> the profound effect his frank, open countenance, his straightforward answers to all questions, his evident intention to be scrupulously fair, and his general air of sincerity created upon the spectators in the courtroom.[66]

Lindbergh had given his testimony about the correspondence and the ransom delivery on the first week of trial. After he testified, Wilentz presented several more days of testimony about the disappearance before he returned to the Correspondence module. The eccentric John F. Condon would serve as the heart and soul of both the Correspondence module and the Delivery module, and Wilentz wanted to surround him with as many corroborative witnesses as possible. He therefore called a number of witnesses before Condon testified who did little more than flesh out the details of the negotiations. One witness, however, served a much more important purpose. Joseph Anthony Perrone helped to identify Hauptmann.

Three ransom notes had been sent to Lindbergh by the time John F. Condon interjected himself into the case. Condon placed an ad in the *Bronx Home News* offering to act as a go-between, and the kidnapper answered him. On March 12, 1932, as Perrone drove his taxi on Gun Hill Road in the Bronx, a man approached him and asked him if he knew where 2974 Decatur Avenue was. Perrone said yes, and the man handed him a dollar bill and an envelope addressed to John Condon, 2974 Decatur Avenue. Perrone delivered the envelope, which contained a ransom letter. Despite the fact that during the investigation he had tentatively identified several other men as the culprit,[67] Perrone positively identified Haupt-

---

[66] Russell B. Porter, "Ransom Deals Retraced: Colonel Swears Voice at the Bronx Cemetery Was Hauptmann's," *NYT*, January 5, 1935.

[67] "Hoffman Attacks another Witness; Points to Bronx Taxi Man's Many Partial Identifications before Hauptmann Trial," *NYT*, February 28, 1936.

mann at the trial. Although Reilly's cross-examination consisted of a vociferous attack on Perrone, the best avenue of attack was denied him because he knew nothing of Perrone's many tentative identifications of other men. It was not until after Governor Harold G. Hoffman undertook his own post-conviction investigation of the Hauptmann case that this information came to light. Today the prosecution has a duty to turn such information over to the defense, and the post-conviction discovery of these identifications could call the propriety of the conviction into question. If the reviewing court decides that the nondisclosure gives rise to a "reasonable probability of a different result," then the defendant is entitled to a new trial. "Reasonable probability of a different result" does not mean that the defendant would certainly have been acquitted had the information been disclosed. It simply means that there is sufficient likelihood (even less than 50%) of a different result (not necessarily an acquittal) sufficient to "undermine confidence" in the verdict.[68] Before 1963, however, the prosecution had no such duty.[69] The revelation resulted in something of a mini-scandal, but Hauptmann's conviction stood.

On the question of whether the disclosure would probably have changed the result, we have the testimony of seven of the jurors. During the height of the furor over Hoffman's revelation, a reporter canvassed as many of the jury as he could find to see if their verdict would have been different. Every juror who was questioned maintained that they would still have found Hauptmann guilty. Jury foreman Charles Walton summed up the jurors' sentiments in this way: "Even if they threw out the testimony of every one of the identification witnesses—

---

[68] Banks v. Dretke, 540 U.S. 668, 124 S.Ct. 1256 (2004).
[69] Brady v. Maryland, 373 U.S. 83 (1963).

Millard Whited, Dr. Condon, Joseph Perrone, and Amandus Hochmuth—there is still the ransom money, the handwriting, and the ladder."[70] Wilentz might not have appreciated the power of the triad Ladder, Letters, and Loot, but the jury did.

Wilentz ended the Disappearance module with Amandus Hochmuth, who identified Hauptmann, and led off the Correspondence module with Perrone, who also identified Hauptmann. Neither man made a sterling witness, but prosecutors cannot procure witnesses from central casting. They must take the witnesses as they come. Trouble came from another direction on this, the fourth day of testimony. The lights in the courthouse went out. Officials of the New Jersey Power and Light Company said extra lights installed for the newsreel cameras had overloaded the system and blown a fuse. Although the outage disrupted news coverage, testimony continued in the darkened courtroom as repairmen replaced the blown fuse.[71] Wilentz called a number of auxiliary witnesses to flesh out and corroborate John Condon's testimony but deferred calling Condon himself until the next day. Reactions to the day's events were varied. The press quoted Hauptmann as saying that Hochmuth was mistaken and Perrone was lying.[72] Reilly called Hochmuth a "poor, misguided old man," and promised "some surprises in the forthcoming cross-examination of Dr. John F. Condon."[73]

The trial was fast coming to the point where Wilentz had to call Condon. Wilentz did what he could to shore up Condon by leading up to him with corroborative

---

[70] Kenneth T. Downs, "Bruno Jurors Standing Pat," *Reading Eagle*, February 29, 1936, https://news.google.com (accessed March 20, 2015).

[71] Russell B. Porter, "Court Room Lights Fail," *NYT*, January 9, 1935.

[72] "Hauptmann Assails Two State Witnesses," *NYT*, January 9, 1935.

[73] "Pope Not to Quit Defense," *NYT*, January 9, 1935.

testimony and following him with additional corroboration. The corroborative testimony presented few problems, but Condon's erratic behavior could very well scuttle the case. We have already discussed Joseph Perrone, who preceded Condon on the witness stand and identified Hauptmann as the man who gave him the ransom letter to deliver to Condon. Several other men who became involved in Condon's initial meeting with Lindbergh also testified and added weight to the corroboration. It was now time to call Condon and hope that he would do something which he had so far refused to do—identify Hauptmann as Cemetery John. After asking the preliminary accrediting questions, Wilentz had Condon briefly describe the delivery of the ransom to Cemetery John and then asked:

> **Q:** And who did you give that money to?
> **A:** John.
> **Q:** Who is John?
> **A:** John is Bruno Richard Hauptmann.[74]

Wilentz must have breathed a sigh of relief at this point. He had cleared the first hurdle of Condon's testimony—the identification. It remained to be seen how Condon dealt with the second hurdle—cross-examination by an experienced criminal defense attorney. Wilentz then backtracked to the beginning of Condon's involvement in the case and took him through his testimony in chronological order. Twice more during the direct he asked the identity of John, and twice more he received the reply "John is Bruno Richard Hauptmann."[75] Wilentz concluded his direct examination by having Condon recite the description of Cemetery John which he had

---

[74] Transcript, 593.
[75] Transcript, 622, 661.

given the police over two years before the trial. According to the papers, it "fitted Hauptmann rather closely."[76] The jury never saw something else that fitted Hauptmann rather closely—the police sketch of Cemetery John made with Condon's assistance.[77] Wilentz missed an opportunity to corroborate Condon's identification of Hauptmann when he failed to offer the sketch into evidence. When Wilentz finished his direct examination, he said, "You may inquire, sir," and the duel between the veteran defense attorney and the septuagenarian educator began. All that Wilentz could do at this point was cross his fingers and occasionally try to help Condon with a well-timed objection.

Reilly began by inquiring into Condon's knowledge of boxing. He established that both he and Condon would be classified as heavyweights and then said, "So we start out even?" Condon, who had gotten a laugh out of the jury when he had proclaimed Reilly a heavyweight, got another laugh with the reply "Right—that is physically." Trenchard called the courtroom back to order and directed Reilly to go on with his examination.[78] Condon had won the first corps-a-corps of their verbal duel. He would win several more on this, his first day of testimony. The press loved Condon. The *New York Times* reported:

> He testified for nearly five hours, of which two were occupied by a severe cross-examination by Edward F. Reilly, chief defense counsel. The cross-examination failed to shake Dr. Condon's story or his identification on any vital point, although the lawyer made Dr.

---

[76] Russell B. Porter, "Condon Names Hauptmann as 'John' Who Got Ransom; Parries Defense Attack," *NYT*, January 10, 1935.

[77] Richard T. Cahill Jr., *Hauptmann's Ladder: A Step-by-Step Analysis of the Lindbergh Kidnapping* (Kent, Ohio: Kent State University Press, 2014), 87.

[78] Transcript, 674.

> Condon admit that he did not say that Hauptmann was "John" at the time he viewed him in jail in New York, right after his arrest.
>
> . . .
>
> When Mr. Reilly attacked him, Dr. Condon counter-attacked. When Mr. Reilly thundered, Dr. Condon thundered back. When Mr. Reilly adopted an air of exaggerated courtesy, Dr. Condon adopted the same air. When Mr. Reilly became crafty, Dr. Condon became crafty.[79]

Reilly adopted the wrong strategy for the examination of Condon. Instead of attacking the implausibility of Condon's testimony, he attacked Condon personally. What Reilly succeeded in doing by aggressive verbal sparring with Condon was to highlight Condon's wit in repartee, which in turn masked the implausibility of his testimony. A representative exchange between the two came on the issue of Condon's failure to identify Hauptmann at the lineup.

> **Q:** Yes. You never once told any newspaper man that this defendant was John, did you?
>
> **A:** Which defendant?
>
> **Q:** This defendant here.
>
> **A:** Oh. I never did. I never told or mentioned his name to them or in public, never—note the words Colonel—of affirmation or denial. I make a distinction between "identification" and "declaration of identification." [In the early Twentieth Century it was customary to address lawyers as "colonel."]
>
> **Q:** In other words, I am to understand that you split hairs in words?

---

[79] Russell B. Porter, "Condon Names Hauptmann as 'John' Who Got Ransom; Parries Defense Attack," *NYT*, January 10, 1935.

A: No hairs at all. A man's life is at stake and I want to be honest about it.

Q: There was nothing preventing you from telling the press, was there, that this was the right man?

A: Yes, there was; yes, there was.

Q: If you wanted to be honest about it, why did you not blazon forth that fact to the world when they asked you?

A: Because I didn't wish to do it and perhaps interfere with this case itself. [There is an old saying among trial lawyers that the cross-examiner should never ask "Why." Condon's response to Reilly's "Why" question demonstrates the wisdom of this maxim].

Q: If you were honest and telling the truth, do you not know that nothing could interfere with the truth, no matter how many times you said it was the man?

A: It didn't. It didn't. It didn't interfere because I didn't say.

Q: In Greenwich Street, New York police station, you said it was not the man, did you not?

A: No, sir. Get all the people that were there, I did not.

Q: You never said it was the man?

A: I never said it was or was not.

Q: Because you know you are not sure?

A: Because I made the distinction between declaration and identification. The identification meant what I knew mentally, the declaration meant what I said to others. There isn't a man who breathes has ever heard me say that that was the man but one.

Q: You were brought there for the purpose of identifying Hauptmann, were you not?

A: I was, yes, sir.

Q: And you didn't identify him, did you?

A: No, sir. Beg pardon, there is the word "identification" again. I take exception to your language. It would make a mistake and when you begin to divide the identification and declaration and denial, you would make it appear as though I were dishonest and I am not. I won't—is that too severe, Judge?

THE COURT: No.

Q: Come on, I can take it.

A: That is good. I want you to know, Counselor, that the identification is purely a mental process after the senses have known, after the senses have distinguished, and unless that is taken that way to answer quickly, fast, I don't know but what it might be a kind of trap that you were getting me. The declaration is where I tell it to others. Identification is what I know myself.[80]

Reilly should have attacked the plausibility of the testimony, not the personality of the testifier. Snide remarks and personal assaults proved counterproductive and resulted in this portion of the cross-examination being diverted down a rabbit trail of arguing over the meaning of words. He would have done better by asking a line of tight and controlling single-fact questions. Such a line of questioning might have gone thus:

Q: You attended a lineup at the Greenwich Street police station in New York?

A: Yes.

Reilly should expect Condon to append a verbal barrage to his affirmation, but he should not take the bait. Rather he must relentlessly pursue the non-identification.

Q: The police asked you if anyone appearing in the lineup was the John whom you met in the cemetery?

A: Yes.

---

[80] Transcript, 688–690.

Q: Bruno Richard Hauptmann was in the lineup?

A: Yes.

Q: At that time you did not identify Mr. Hauptmann as John?

A: I identified Mr. Hauptmann at that time but I made no declaration of identification.

At this point in the actual cross-examination Reilly sought to belittle Condon as a hair-splitter. Two types of witnesses engage in this type of splitting of hairs—evasive witnesses and pedants. Condon may have been evasive, but he was also a pedant. It would have been far better to give Condon enough rope to unwittingly betray his evasiveness than to attack him with a charge of lack of candor.

Q: So you identified Mr. Hauptmann as John?

A: Yes.

Q: But you did not make a declaration of identification?

A: No.

Instead of battling with a witness over the definition of words, Reilly should have adopted Condon's definition and work the definition against Condon. A better line of questioning could have gone like this:

Q: *So when you left the police station that day, you had told nobody that Mr. Hauptmann was John?*

A: *No.*

A myriad of short, single-fact questions could be spun out to hammer home the fact that, despite the earnest desire of the police to learn the identity of John, Condon withheld vital evidence from the police.

> ***Q:*** *And you never told Mr. Wilentz that Mr. Hauptmann was John?*
>
> ***A:*** *No.*
>
> ***Q:*** *The first time you have ever told anyone that Mr. Hauptmann was John is today in this courtroom?*
>
> ***A:*** *Yes.*

Another barrage of short, single-fact questions could have been asked to accentuate the preposterous nature of Condon's assertion, leading the jury to the conclusion that Condon was a lunatic or a liar. With such a series of questions, Reilly could have highlighted the implausibility and made Condon's verbosity look like evasion rather than self-defense against a relentless attack. Russell B. Porter, writing for The *New York Times*, had this assessment of Condon's first day on the stand: "Dr. Condon at the end of the day, despite his advanced age, was more vigorous and effective than at the beginning of his testimony."[81]

Although the defense team tried to put on the faces of victors, the first engagement on cross-examination went to Condon. But there was always tomorrow. Reilly still had questions to ask on cross-examination. The next day Reilly tried manfully to suggest that Condon was the mastermind behind the kidnapping, but the ploy failed. Reilly's failure with Condon exemplifies another maxim, "When you cross-examine, you can hurt your case by examining crossly." Given Condon's performance the previous day, Reilly would have had much better luck trying to portray Condon as a crackpot rather than a criminal mastermind.

Wilentz immediately followed Condon with Henry Breckinridge, Lindbergh's attorney, who figured prom-

---

[81] Russell B. Porter, "Condon Names Hauptmann as 'John' Who Got Ransom; Parries Defense Attack," *NYT*, January 10, 1935.

inently in the ransom negotiations. Breckinridge strongly supported Condon's testimony, and on the issue of whether Condon might be the mastermind who engineered the kidnapping, he had this to say:

> **Q:** Tell me whether Dr. Condon ever suggested or urged that this money should be paid.
>
> **A:** He did not.
>
> **Q:** Isn't it a fact that he urged that the money shouldn't be paid?
>
> **A:** Except upon a c. o. d. delivery.
>
> **Q:** Except when the child was delivered, you mean?
>
> **A:** Yes, sir.[82]

Having finished the Correspondence and Delivery modules, it was now time to move on the Handwriting module. The preliminary Handwriting testimony began on Thursday, January 10, and the module continued for four more days until its conclusion on January 16. Wilentz had to prove that Hauptmann was responsible for the ransom letters by (1) placing the letters into evidence, (2) placing handwriting samples identified to Hauptmann into evidence, and (3) producing testimony which showed that the same person authored both groups of documents. Wilentz had accomplished the first task during the Correspondence module; he now turned to the second. He called three officers in rapid succession, and had each of them testify to collecting known handwriting samples from Hauptmann. That chore completed, Wilentz was now almost ready to begin calling handwriting examiners.

On Friday, January 11, Wilentz called Colonel Schwarzkopf to testify about collection of handwriting samples and Special Agent Frank J. Wilson of the Internal Revenue Service to testify about the preparation

---

[82] Transcript, 833.

and tracing of the ransom money. Wilson described how the serial numbers of the bills were recorded and how they sought to recover those bills by publishing the list of serial numbers. Wilson also testified that he matched the money recovered from Hauptmann to the list of serial numbers, and Wilentz concluded his direct examination with the fact that since Hauptmann's arrest not a single ransom bill had been recovered. Defense attorney C. Lloyd Fisher opened his cross-examination by repeating Wilentz's last question:

> **Q.** Do you mean to say, Mr. Wilson, as a positive fact it is within your knowledge that not a single ransom note has been passed since the apprehension of Hauptmann?
>
> **A.** Not that I know of.[83]

He asked the question twice more with the same result and ended the line of questioning by getting the witness to agree that he didn't know whether a note might have appeared anywhere in the whole world. The cross didn't get any better. Before he concluded, Fisher had wrung the following harmful admissions from Wilson: The first ransom bill that was recovered came from a bank near the Majestic Hotel, just a few days after Hauptmann had quit his job at the Majestic;[84] the second and third bills were located on Broadway; and with the exception of two bills located just outside New York, all the recovered bills were found in New York.[85] Wilentz missed a good opportunity to use Wilson as a summary witness. He could have had Wilson indicate on an enlarged map of New York where each of the bills had

---

[83] Transcript, 897.
[84] Transcript, 907.
[85] Transcript, 908–918.

been recovered, giving powerful visual proof that the kidnapper was most likely a New Yorker who passed a lot of bills in the Bronx.

Wilentz called Albert S. Osborn as his first expert in the Handwriting module. Osborn first testified to his credentials as a handwriting examiner, mentioning his 30 years of experience and his authorship of two books, *Questioned Documents* and *The Problem of Proof.* Reilly did not contest Osborn's experience, and Trenchard ruled "It seems to be in effect conceded that the gentleman qualifies as an expert on handwriting."[86] Under the questioning of Assistant Attorney General Joseph Lanigan, Osborn described how he had come into the case in May of 1932 and how he had eliminated 100 possible suspects by finding that they did not write the ransom notes. Osborn testified that Bruno Richard Hauptmann had written all of the ransom notes. He then cataloged the similarities he found between the hand of Hauptmann and the ransom notes, and demonstrated the similarities with five huge posters containing enlarged photographs of the peculiar letters from both the known and questioned documents. Lanigan's direct of Osborn followed a classic pattern for presentation of expert testimony—expertise, examination, expert opinion, explanation. Russell B. Porter, writing for the *New York Times*, summed up his testimony by saying, "Mr. Osborn's whole testimony supported the state's theory that Hauptmann was the kidnapper, murderer, and collector of the ransom,"[87] a succinct statement of the kidnapper, killer, con man case theory we suggested for Wilentz in Chapter 3.

---

[86] Transcript, 944.

[87] Russell B. Porter, "Expert says Hauptmann Wrote All Ransom Notes; $14,600 in Bills Identified," *NYT*, January 12, 1935.

Initially, Wilentz intended to call only two of his handwriting experts, holding the others for rebuttal, and to give abbreviated examinations of those whom he called. Osborn's testimony changed Wilentz's mind. Osborn captivated the jury. He had them hanging on his every word and intently studying the exhibits he used. His testimony was so well received that Wilentz decided to call more experts and to have them testify at length about their findings.[88]

Before calling any more experts, however, Wilentz slipped in another witness to corroborate John Condon's testimony. Hildegarde Olga Alexander testified that she saw a man watching Condon at a subway station. Condon seemed unaware of the man, but the man seemed very interested in Condon. Wilentz had her describe what she saw in detail and asked if she had ever seen the man at any other time. She saw him a few weeks later in the Bronx. Wilentz then asked, "Who was the man you saw in that station watching Dr. Condon on this night in March and whom you saw a few nights afterwards walking down Fordham Road?" Alexander replied, "I say the man was Bruno Richard Hauptmann."[89] Alexander withstood a vigorous cross-examination by Reilly. His cross may very well have increased her credibility before the jury. Russell B. Porter wrote that Alexander "spoke in a voice that could hardly be heard until Mr. Reilly, cross-examining her with questions intended to discredit her veracity, made her angry, and she raised her voice and answered him in a loud, determined tone."[90] A vociferous cross-examination, if it does not destroy the witness,

---

[88] Russell B. Porter, "Week's Fight Due over Handwriting in Hauptmann Case," *NYT*, January 13, 1935.

[89] Transcript, 1056–1057.

[90] Russell B. Porter, "Woman Swears She Saw Hauptmann Watch Condon Before Ransom Was Paid," *NYT*, January 15, 1935.

sometimes has the effect of motivating the witness to go from timorous and unsure to bold and certain.

Wilentz returned to the handwriting testimony and called seven more experts ending with Clark Sellers, the expert whom he considered his second strongest. Sellers first examined the ransom notes and stated his belief that they were all written by the same person. Then he was shown two groups of writings: (1) writings Hauptmann made at the "request" of law enforcement officers, and (2) writings "conceded" to be his because they came from documents he admittedly authored. After being shown these three groups of writings, Sellers testified clearly and emphatically that "if Mr. Bruno Richard Hauptmann wrote these conceded and request writings, then he wrote these ransom notes." Sellers went on to say, "I am not only saying that Mr. Hauptmann wrote them [the ransom notes], but I am saying that no one else did...." Sellers went on to describe in detail the similarities which led him to that conclusion, but possibly the most persuasive part of his explanation came with Exhibit S–164. "At the right hand lower portion of this Exhibit S–164 is the name 'Hauptmann,' as written by Mr. Hauptmann in [a conceded document]," he explained, "and below it characters cut out and pasted below the name 'Hauptmann,' cut from the ransom notes, so that those cutouts spell the name Hauptmann."[91] The similarities between the two signatures were remarkable. After the trial Sellers wrote:

> In many cases it is possible to take from the writings of a person the letters that spell his name, and reconstruct a replica of that writer's signature. In the Hauptmann case it was possible to reconstruct from the body of the ransom letters a replica of his own

---

[91] Transcript, 1389–1404.

> signature. In fact, as can be seen from [S–164], there were so many habitual characteristics of Hauptmann's handwriting in those ransom letters, that he might just as well have signed his name to every one of them....[92]

Wilentz moved on to the Autopsy module. He first called the two men who discovered the body, Orville Wilson and William J. Allen. The two were driving down the Mount Rose Road when Allen had to answer the call of nature. He stopped their truck by the side of the road and walked into the bushes to relieve himself. There, in a shallow trench, Allen found the body. Cross-examination of Allen emphasized that the body had been dumped within eyesight of the Lindbergh mansion.[93] The cross of Wilson established that the body lay not in Hunterdon County but in Mercer County.[94] The coroner and a few officers testified next, mainly to establish an investigation of the crime scene and the delivery of the body to Dr. Charles H. Mitchell, the County Physician, for autopsy. During the recovery of the body one of the officers displayed his expertise as a crime scene investigator by poking a hole in the child's skull with a stick. Dr. Mitchell established that the hole was not a gunshot wound, but that the baby had died "instantaneously" from a massive skull fracture. Mitchell testified:

> To the effect that I think it [death] occurred immediately is proven by the extent of this fracture. It was so great, covered such an area, in my estimation, from my experience, that proved conclusively it was instantaneous or almost so.[95]

---

[92] Sellers, "Handwriting Evidence," 883–885.
[93] Transcript, 1439.
[94] Transcript, 1447.
[95] Transcript, 1487.

On cross Reilly tried to show that Mitchell was under-qualified, performed a shoddy examination of the body, and should have sent for assistance from a more experienced pathologist. There may have been room to argue over the precise cause of death, but given the circumstances of the child's disappearance and the discovery of his decomposed body concealed in bushes in a shallow trench or grave, the odds overwhelmingly favored death by homicide. When an abduction victim's body is finally found, it is often so decomposed that the precise cause of death is problematical; but when the body is found concealed and only partially clothed, the manner of death will usually be found to be homicide.[96] Although you might quibble with Dr. Mitchell's qualifications or his opinion as to the cause and speed of the child's death, no competent medical examiner would disagree with his bottom line conclusion that the death resulted from a homicide.

Another point not made at trial has become something of a bone of contention in its aftermath. Dr. Mitchell's hands were so crippled that he could not personally dissect the body. He had an assistant dissect the body as he stood by directing the procedure and taking notes. Some have contended that this fact disqualified him from voicing an opinion and actually made him vulnerable to a prosecution for perjury. Dr. Mitchell did nothing wrong. Medical examiners sometimes employ assistants to actually do the dissection of the body while they oversee the process. These employees are called dieners, which is the German word for servant.[97]

---

[96] George R. Dekle Sr., *The Last Murder: The Investigation, Prosecution, and Execution of Ted Bundy* (Santa Barbara: Praeger, 2011), 75, 194–195, 206–207.

[97] Thomas D. Kinney and Kenneth R. Broda, "The Pathologist's Assistant." *Human Pathology* 5, no. 5 (1974): 503–505.

After calling Dr. Mitchell, Wilentz spent the rest of the day describing the preparation of the ransom money and the recording of the serial numbers. He ended the day with a description of how Hauptmann was finally identified as a suspect. On September 15, 1934, Bruno Richard Hauptmann drove into the Warner-Quinlan gas station at the corner of 127th Street and Lexington Avenue in Manhattan. Walter Lyle, the station manager, asked Hauptmann if he wanted to fill the tank, but Hauptmann said he just wanted $5 worth. Lyle pumped the gas and Hauptmann took an envelope out of his pocket and removed a $10 gold certificate. Lyle examined the bill and said, "You don't see many more of these." Hauptmann replied, "No, I only have about a hundred left." His suspicions aroused, Lyle noted the tag number of Hauptmann's car and wrote it down on the margin of the bill. When the bill made its way to the Corn Exchange Bank, they compared it against the list of ransom serial numbers and determined that it was a part of the ransom money. They notified the authorities, who took the bill in custody and began trying to determine where and by whom the bill had been passed. Tracing the tag number written on the bill, officers identified Bruno Richard Hauptmann as the owner of the car bearing that tag. Tracing the bill back to the Warner-Quinlan station, they found Walter Lyle and John Joseph Lyons, another attendant at the station, both of whom identified Bruno Richard Hauptmann as the man who passed the $10 gold certificate.

When he finished with this, Wilentz was ready to begin the Arrest module. He called Agent Thomas H. Sisk of the FBI, who assisted in the arrest of Hauptmann. According to Sisk, when arrested, Hauptmann had another twenty dollar gold certificate in his pocket. The serial number matched one of the ransom bills. When asked about the bill, Hauptmann said it was one of about 300 gold certificates he had accumulated over the last few months. He said he had gotten the bills from several banks, but could name only one—the Central Savings Bank of New York. When the officers said they could go to the bank to check out his story, Hauptmann retracted it and said that he accumulated the bills from various places. When the officers asked to see the other bills, Hauptmann accompanied them back to his home, where he showed them $120 in gold coins. The officers told him that they were after gold certificates, and he said the one from his pocket was the last of the gold certificates. They began a thorough search of his house which turned up no additional gold certificates. During the search, they noticed that Hauptmann kept looking out the window in the direction of his garage. Upon being asked what he had in the garage, he said, "Nothing." The officers searched the garage and found two loose planks in the floor. Pulling up the planks, they found some freshly disturbed earth, and buried under that earth they found a crockery container with nothing but a little water at the bottom. Hauptmann denied any knowledge of the container at first, but after the discovery of the other ransom money hidden in the garage, he admitted that he had used the container to store the gold certificates. During Sisk's testimony, Hauptmann became agitated and blurted out, "Mister, mister, you stop lying. You are telling a story."[98]

Wilentz ended the day by calling an engineer to authenticate a map of the Bronx. After introducing the map, Wilentz had the engineer point out places of interest around the Bronx including the two cemeteries, Hauptmann's home, and Condon's home.[99] This was an ineffective use of the map. The engineer should have been called before Condon took the stand. Then during

---

[98] Transcript, 1582–1590.
[99] Transcript, 1599–1615.

Condon's direct examination, Wilentz could have had Condon point out his home and the various places he met with Hauptmann, including the two cemeteries. When Sisk took the stand, he could have pointed to the place where Hauptmann lived.

Wilentz's first witness on the following day directly contradicted Agent Sisk about Hauptmann's statements. Sergeant John Wallace of the New Jersey State Police, who assisted with Hauptmann's arrest, had a very different recollection of Hauptmann's statements concerning the twenty dollar gold certificate. As Wallace remembered, before they went back to Hauptmann's house, Hauptmann had told them the twenty dollar bill was the last gold certificate he had, and had told them that he had $120 in gold coins at his home.[100] Wilentz blundered here. He should have known before they took the stand that Sisk and Wallace had differing recollections of Hauptmann's statements concerning the gold certificates. He should have ascertained which of the two versions was the correct one, and placed only the correct one before the jury. As it was, Wilentz provided the defense with a witness to impeach Agent Sisk. The first questions asked of Wallace on cross-examination were aimed at emphasizing the differences between his testimony and Sisk's.

Despite his difference of opinion with Agent Sisk, Wallace was an important witness. He testified to the seizure of the plane that Koehler later proved to have been used to build the ladder, and he identified and authenticated several bundles of ransom money discovered in Hauptmann's garage the day after the arrest. He also testified that when confronted with the money, Hauptmann acknowledged possession of it.[101]

---

[100] Transcript, 1637–1638.
[101] Transcript, 1646–1665.

Hauptmann denied that there was any more ransom money in the garage, but Wilentz would later offer testimony that a week after Hauptmann's arrest, detectives found $850 more ransom money in the garage. Wilentz also offered testimony that a board was found inside a closet in Hauptmann's house, and that John F. Condon's address and telephone number were written on the board. The last witness Wilentz called in the Arrest module was a court stenographer. The stenographer had taken down a transcript of an interrogation of Hauptmann by the District Attorney. During that interview, Hauptmann admitted to writing Condon's address and phone number on the board. He explained how he came to write on the board:

> **Q:** Why did you write it on the board?
>
> **A:** I must have read it in the paper about the story. I was a little bit interest, and keep a little bit record of it and maybe I was just in the closet and was reading the paper and put down the address.
>
> **Q:** How did you come to put the telephone number on there?
>
> **A:** I can't give you any explanation about the telephone number.
>
> **Q:** Your only explanation for writing Dr. Condon's address on this board and telephone number is that you were probably reading the paper in the closet and you marked it down, is that correct?
>
> **A:** It is possible that a shelf or two shelfs in the closet and after a while I put newspapers always on the closet and we just got the paper where this case was in and I followed the story of course and I put the address on there.
>
> **Q:** That is why you marked it on the door?
>
> **A:** That is the only explanation I can give.[102]

---

[102] Transcript, 1763.

In the midst of the witnesses testifying about Hauptmann's arrest and subsequent interrogation, Wilentz called three witnesses who were relevant to other aspects of the case. Ella Achenbach testified that she saw Hauptmann limping a day or two after the kidnapping; Walter Lyle testified about writing Hauptmann's tag number on the gold certificate passed at the Warner-Quinlan gas station, and Stanley Keith testified in support of the ladder, which Wilentz still had not gotten into evidence. As he neared the finish line with his case, the presentation became more and more disjointed. With only the Finances and Ladder modules remaining, Wilentz still had to present several witnesses from other modules. He chose to disperse these witnesses among the witnesses to his last two modules.

On Monday, January 21, the thirteenth day of the trial, Wilentz called William E. Frank, from the Intelligence Unit of the U.S. Treasury Department, who had done a study of Hauptmann's finances. Testifying from bank and brokerage records which Wilentz had previously introduced into evidence, Frank testified that between April 2, 1932, and September 19, 1934, "The amount deposited in the brokerage accounts [belonging to Hauptmann] were $16,942.75, the total in the bank accounts [belonging to Hauptmann] was $9,073.25. Adding to that the three figures $14,600 [found in Hauptmann's garage], $3,750 [from a mortgage], and $120 [in gold coins] brings a total of $44,486."[103] Wilentz followed Frank with the testimony of Edward F. Morton, the construction timekeeper for the Majestic Apartments, who testified from the time records he kept that Hauptmann worked at the Majestic on Friday, April 1, 1932, but did not work on Saturday, April 2, the day the ransom was delivered. Morton further testified that

---

[103] Transcript, 1819.

Hauptmann returned to work on Monday, April 4, and quit his job at the end of the day.

Cecile Barr, a ticket taker at Loew's Sheridan Square Theater in Greenwich Village, identified Hauptmann as the person who gave her an oddly folded $5 bill on November 26, 1933. The bill found its way to the Corn Exchange Bank with the other receipts for the night. The next morning William M. Cody processed the deposit and recognized that the oddly folded bill was within the range of serial numbers for the Lindbergh ransom money. He notified his supervisor who called the police. James J. Finn of the New York Police Department responded to the bank and took the bill into his custody. He traced the bill back to the theater and identified Cecile Barr as the person who took the bill. This testimony placed Lindbergh ransom money into the hands of Hauptmann before Isidor Fisch supposedly gave him the ransom money.

The prosecution case began to draw to a close. Two more witnesses, Millard Whited and Charles Rossiter, testified they saw Hauptmann in the area of the Lindbergh home in February of 1932. Rossiter made an excellent witness, but Whited had credibility problems. The defense caught him in several prior inconsistent statements, and they established that he held his peace about seeing Hauptmann at times when one would expect him to have mentioned it.[104] Wilentz finally got the ladder into evidence, and then began the tedious business of preparing the way for Arthur Koehler, who would be the last witness. Koehler's account of tracing Rails 12 and 13 from the sawmill which sawed them to the Bronx lumberyard required testimony from the sawmill operator and the lumberyard employees, and his tracing of Rail 16 to Hauptmann's attic also required a number of witnesses

---

[104] Russell B. Porter, "Ladder into Evidence after a 15-Day Struggle; Two More Identify Hauptmann" *NYT*, January 23, 1935.

to testify in support of his conclusions. The *New York Times* characterized Koehler's testimony by saying:

> A United States Government expert on wood, backed by a detective of the New Jersey State Police and two police carpenters from New York City, gave testimony, which the state of New Jersey believes to have been more damaging to Hauptmann than any of the eighty-seven witnesses … in the sixteen days that the state of New Jersey has been presenting its case….[105]

And with this final salvo, Wilentz rested his case.

---

[105] Russell B. Porter, "Expert Traces Tool Marks on Ladder to Hauptmann; Part of Wood to His Attic," *NYT*, January 24, 1935.

6

The Defense Case Part 1
Hauptmann Testifies

When C. Lloyd Fisher rose to deliver the defense opening statement on the afternoon of January 24, he needed to get the jury's attention early and keep it. It was already the afternoon of the seventeenth day of trial, and the jurors were not fresh. Fisher gave his statement after the jurors had heard the testimony of more than 80 prosecution witnesses and seen more than 250 items of prosecution evidence. This begs the question whether it would have been better for the defense to present its opening statement directly after the prosecution opening so that the jurors would hear the prosecution witnesses against the backdrop of the defense theory. The conventional argument in favor of delaying opening statement goes something like this. You don't know how the prosecution evidence is going to play out. If you make an opening statement, you run the risk of locking yourself into a specific defense and won't have the flexibility to respond to unexpected prosecution evidence. On the other hand, there are compelling arguments in favor of immediately making an opening statement. Something has to be done to neutralize the prosecution's case, and the sooner it is neutralized the better. The earliest chance to answer the prosecution's case comes immediately after the prosecution ends its opening statement. When the defense held their opening statement in reserve, they gave up that opportunity.

Opening statements are not arguments—they are the occasion to tell the jurors what the evidence will be; not what the evidence means. Lawyers must wait until summation or closing argument to explain to jurors what the evidence means. Fisher had given a cogent outline of his legal theory in an interview published by the *New York Times* on January 14.[1] Fisher had defended John Hughes Curtis, the Norfolk shipbuilder convicted of interfering with the kidnapping investigation by telling authorities he was in contact with the kidnappers. Fisher felt that when the state convicted Curtis they had taken the position that a gang had kidnapped the child. In light of the position they had taken in the Curtis case, he felt the prosecutors could not properly present a theory that Hauptmann was a "lone wolf" and that there was no conspiracy to kidnap the Lindbergh child. Fisher told Russell B. Porter of the *New York Times* that the prosecutions of Curtis and Hauptmann were inconsistent.

> If the defendant today, Hauptmann, is guilty of having committed this crime or committing it alone—"a lone wolf" as the State says—then [John Hughes Curtis] was not guilty. On the other hand, if Curtis was guilty as charged—of dealing with a gang and then refusing to reveal the identity of gang members—Hauptmann cannot be guilty as charged.[2]

Reilly had broached the subject of Curtis when he cross-examined Lindbergh,[3] and Fisher had extensively cross-examined Frank Kelly of the NJSP about Curtis,[4] but Fisher never mentioned the Curtis incident in his

---

[1] Russell B. Porter, "Week's Fight Due over Handwriting in Hauptmann Case," *NYT*, January 14, 1935.
[2] *Ibid.*
[3] Transcript, 196–203.
[4] Transcript, 898–906.

opening statement. Nor did Reilly mention it in final argument. They raised the issue in the assignments of error on appeal,[5] but it seems that the defense squandered an opportunity to argue the matter to the jury.

A good speech of any kind can be divided into three simple parts: beginning, middle, and end. For Fisher, he would need a beginning that would capture the attention of already tired jurors and lead them into the middle, the core of the defense evidence. He would need to end on a high note—something that would motivate the jury to be receptive to the defense case even against all the prosecution evidence they had already heard. Fisher began rather formally.

> If it please your Honor and ladies and gentlemen of the jury: I am fully cognizant of the grave importance of the trial of this indictment. I appreciate truly how keen a responsibility is mine. I shall humbly and in language as simple as I can command give you briefly the facts and the circumstances upon which we rely to gain for the defendant, Bruno Richard Hauptmann, an acquittal at your hands.[6]

Did Fisher's statement that he would use "language as simple" as he could make the jurors think he was talking down to them? Rather than presenting an idea of the defense proof, Fisher then explained his duty to the jury:

> That is now our responsibility: The fair presentation of all the facts and circumstances attendant to the trial of this indictment which we shall contend will preserve the life and the liberty of this defendant.[7]

---

[5] Transcript, 4572–4573.
[6] Transcript, 2376.
[7] Transcript, 2376.

> Until these facts and circumstances are fully proven, that responsibility continues to be his and ours. When we have fully and completely presented all those facts and circumstances which we feel are material to the proper presentation of this defense, then that responsibility shifts, it is no longer mine, or that of my associates. That responsibility for the life and liberty of Hauptmann then becomes yours.[8]

When Fisher told the jury that the defense had the "responsibility [for t]he fair presentation of all the facts and circumstances," he was shifting the burden of proof from the state to the defense. If the jurors perceived that the defense had the responsibility to clear Hauptmann, they would be looking to the defense for proof of innocence rather than to the prosecution for proof of guilt. Telling the jurors that they were responsible for Hauptmann's life and liberty may have also been a mistake. He apparently hoped that this statement would cause the jurors to balk at thinking it was their responsibility to send Hauptmann to his death, but they could just as well have balked at the prospect of setting a notorious killer free. Fisher could have taken the safer course of reminding the jurors that it was their duty to follow the law and the evidence, and it would become the law's responsibility for handling any outcome from the trial.

Fisher next re-read the indictment in the case. Many defense attorneys quickly remind jurors that an indictment is simply an accusation, not evidence, because indictments necessarily contain strong accusations against the accused. After seventeen days of testimony and exhibits, the jurors were well aware of the accusations against Hauptmann; but Fisher was trying to make another narrow legal point that the indictment was not

[8] Transcript, 2376–2377.

specific in its charges. Staying on technicalities, Fisher next told the jury that the defense had demanded a bill of particulars and that the state had filed an answer. Fisher did not explain what a bill of particulars was, and his statement on this point could only confuse the jury. Fisher's mentioning the bill of particulars gave Wilentz a chance to object and break the momentum of the defense opening as the attorneys and the judge resolved the objection. Justice Trenchard ruled the bill of particulars was not a proper subject for opening statement.[9] This ruling threw Fisher off balance, and he had to work to regain the momentum lost during the objection. What he said next did nothing to regain that momentum:

> We submit that in our defense we will attempt and we believe successfully to prove to you a complete alibi for the defendant Hauptmann on each and every occasion that he has been named as being present at a given point in the evidence thus far produced, and I refer now particularly to March 1st, 1932, to April 2nd, 1932, and to November 26th, 1932.[10]

Fisher was referring to the day and evening of the kidnapping (March 1), the evening the ransom was paid (April 2), and the evening the theater ticket was sold (November 26), but giving the dates of these incidents rather than describing them could only confuse the jury. The dates confused Fisher himself, causing him to mistakenly place the theater incident in the wrong year. He said the incident happened in 1932 when it actually happened in 1933. Fisher would have been more effective by referring to the events themselves rather than their dates.

---

[9] Transcript, 2379.
[10] Transcript, 2380.

Having missed an opportunity for a strong beginning, Fisher was much more effective in relating what the defense proof would show. Using such phrases as "We will follow him downtown for you"[11] and "His wife, a frugal, hardworking housewife,"[12] Fisher laid out the alibi for the day and evening of March 1. He said that the night of April 2, the ransom payment, was "a very easy night for Mr. Hauptmann to recall"[13] because the first Tuesday of each month was a music night. When he returned to the evening that Cecile Barr said Hauptmann used a ransom bill to buy a movie ticket, he again got the date wrong, saying it was 1934 instead of 1933.

Fisher went on to explain that the defense could not match the State's witnesses on the handwriting evidence for financial reasons. He described Hauptmann's funds as "completely and totally exhausted" and told the jury that Hauptmann's defense had been "almost entirely financed through the members of his counsel."[14] Wilentz objected to what appeared to be a plea for sympathy for the condition of Hauptmann and the defense, and Justice Trenchard sustained the objection, reminding Fisher that "The very purpose of an opening is to state the facts which counsel expects to prove."[15] Jurors are regularly told that sympathy and prejudice have no place in their deliberations and decisions, but the defense would bring up the lack of defense resources whenever it could during the trial. Fisher then led the jurors through the Hauptmanns' finances, offering explanations for the money they had and explaining away the business transactions with Fisch.

---

[11] Transcript, 2380.
[12] Transcript, 2381.
[13] Transcript, 2381.
[14] Transcript, 2383.
[15] Transcript, 2384.

Fisher moved to what would become a major focus of argument—the investigation. "We believe we will be able to show you that no case in all history was as badly handled or as badly mangled as this case, and we refer specifically to the witness Kelly and his testimony about the ladder."[16] He told the jury that Dr. Erastus Meade Hudson, whom the authorities had called in to assist the investigation, found 800 fingerprints on the ladder where the police had found none. He then set up the testimony of Sebastian Benjamin Lupica, who had seen a man with a ladder near the Lindbergh estate the evening of the abduction by saying "We will produce before you, we believe, the man who has always been considered by the State Police of New Jersey to have been the last man and the only man to actually see the man who did the kidnapping."[17] Fisher noted that Lupica had been in the courtroom all through the State's case but had not been called as a State's witness.

Fisher then turned to the handwriting evidence. He said that Hauptmann's funds were so exhausted that the defense could not bring them a host of outstanding experts. Wilentz objected to these statements as improper statement, and Justice Trenchard was inclined to think Fisher was going too far away from proper opening statement. But what had Fisher just said? Had he told the jurors that the defense really could not overcome the testimony of the State handwriting experts that the jurors had already heard testify? After claiming to be unable to afford experts, Fisher told the jurors that the defense would produce competent handwriting experts who would show them beyond any doubts in their minds that it was not the handwriting of Bruno Richard Hauptmann. With these words Fisher assumed the dual burdens of producing many

---

[16] Transcript, 2392.
[17] Transcript, 2394.

experts to testify that the handwriting was not Hauptmann's and having those experts testify persuasively that Hauptmann didn't write the letters. The defense would only produce one handwriting expert, failing on both counts to carry the burden of proof Fisher assumed.

Fisher also promised defense proof that the state had miscalculated Hauptmann's finances by counting sums of money twice. Fisher said Hauptmann would draw money out of his accounts, then change his mind and redeposit the same money—not new money—and the state would add both the withdrawal and the redeposit. "The great State of New Jersey has attempted to prove to you by evidence that is all fresh money coming out of his pocket. We will prove to you, ladies and gentlemen, that such is not the case."[18] This strategy would have been more effective if Reilly had used the terms "old money" and "fresh money" in his direct examinations so the jury could follow the defense contention.

After stumbling out of the gate, Fisher had recovered and delivered a good presentation of the defense case. He needed a strong ending to urge the jury to act.

> We are here battling along with our back to the wall, so far as financing goes, and we will prove that on this witness stand, and we will do the very best we can. We will give you everything we have got, everything we can get in this courtroom, by way of testimony. We will hide nothing and produce everything and, when you have heard all the testimony, we trust that if you are not already satisfied that the State of New Jersey has utterly failed to make out a case against Bruno Richard Hauptmann, we are quite sure you will be convinced, after you have heard such testimony related as we will present.[19]

---

[18] Transcript, 2386.
[19] Transcript, 2394–2395.

Edward J. Reilly began the presentation of the defense at 3:07 p.m. on January 24, 1935, almost immediately after Lloyd Fisher completed the opening statement. Bruno Richard Hauptmann took the stand as the first defense witness, just as Lindbergh took the witness stand early in the prosecution's case. It made logical sense to begin the defense presentation with Hauptmann because his testimony was essential to almost every aspect of the defense, but he had to make a good impression on the jury. If the jury found his testimony incredible, it would poison everything that came afterward in the defense. Hauptmann weathered a blistering cross-examination by Wilentz and did not conclude his testimony until January 30. Unlike Lindbergh, Hauptmann did not make a good witness. Anna Hauptmann followed her husband onto the stand. Just as Charles and Anne Lindbergh formed the opening tandem of witnesses for the prosecution, Anna and Richard Hauptmann formed the opening tandem for the defense. Although Reilly had spared Anne Lindbergh the ordeal of withstanding a cross-examination, Wilentz showed no such consideration for Anna Hauptmann.

The defense called no fewer than 50 witnesses in addition to Hauptmann and his wife to testify to various matters, but they called the defense witnesses in a haphazard, unordered fashion, which suggests that the defense team did not subdivide their presentation into modules. Had they done so, they could have made a more cogent presentation. For the purpose of discussion and analysis, we will subdivide the defense case into discrete modules:

1. HAUPTMANN'S DIRECT EXAMINATION
   Since Bruno Richard Hauptmann would provide evidence concerning multiple modules, it is sensible to consider his testimony a separate module.

2. HAUPTMANN'S FINANCES
   Since Hauptmann's testimony was so important to this module, we could include it under Hauptmann's Direct Examination. There were a number of supporting witnesses, however, and for the purpose of analysis it is better to consider it separately.

3. HAUPTMANN'S CROSS-EXAMINATION.
   Hauptmann had to be prepared to undergo the Attorney General's cross-examination, and the defense had to anticipate the structure of that cross and devise a strategy for dealing with it.

4. THE ALIBIS
   a. March 1 (when the crime occurred)
   b. April 2 (when the ransom was delivered)
   c. November 26 (when Cecile Barr received the five dollar ransom bill)

5. SCIENTIFIC EVIDENCE
   a. The Ladder
   b. The Handwriting

6. THE SHODDY POLICE INVESTIGATION

7. REASONABLE DOUBTS about Hauptmann's guilt, including, but not limited to:
   a. Hauptmann's ignorance of the Lindbergh's schedule and the floor plan of the house.
   b. Venue of the murder. Did it occur in Hunterdon County?
   c. Identity of the body as Charles A. Lindbergh, Jr.

8. OTHER SUSPECTS, including:
   a. Oliver Whateley
   b. Bessie Gow
   c. Elizabeth (Elsie) Whateley
   d. Isidore Fisch
   e. Violet Sharpe
   f. Red Johnson

g. The Purple Gang
h. Person or persons unknown

We will discuss each of these modules in the order set out above, but we must remember that there is considerable overlap among the modules.

1. HAUPTMANN'S DIRECT EXAMINATION

Hauptmann began by contending that he was in New York City when the crime occurred. He found his testimony constrained, however, by what had happened at the hearing in which he contested extradition from New York. James M. Fawcett, Hauptmann's attorney at the New York hearing, had presented testimony that on the day of the crime Hauptmann worked for Reliance Property Management, Inc., at the Majestic Hotel and on the evening of the crime had gone to the Fredericksen bakery to pick up his wife, but he had not offered a solid alibi for either event. Fawcett placed into evidence two Reliance payroll checks endorsed by Hauptmann, but they tended to show that he worked eleven days in March, beginning on the 21st, and two days in April before resigning.[20]

On direct examination Reilly asked Hauptmann about working at the Majestic for Reliance. Hauptmann testified he went to the Majestic on March 1 at eight o'clock

---

[20] It would have been very easy for the defense team to subpoena the Reliance payroll checks for the period March 1 to March 15 to see if Richard Hauptmann had been paid during that period. Had they done so they would have learned that the Reliance time book for the pay period covering the date of the kidnapping does not include Hauptmann's name. The book is now in the custody of the New Jersey State Police Museum in Ewing Township, NJ.

in the morning, and that he talked to the supervisor. The supervisor told Hauptmann to come back on the fifteenth of March because he only hired men on the first and the fifteenth. Hauptmann thus abandoned the Majestic alibi for March 1 by saying that he began work on March 15. He added, "I quitted on 2nd of April."[21] Coincidentally, on the evening of April 2, John Condon delivered the ransom payment to Cemetery John.[22] There would be no daytime alibi for Hauptmann for March 1.

Reilly turned Hauptmann's attention to the evening of March 1. Hauptmann said that he went to the bakery around seven o'clock to call for Anna. Reilly asked whether the Fredericksens had a dog, and Hauptmann said they did, adding that he usually let the dog out for a walk. Hauptmann said that he took the dog down to the corner of Boston Post Road, then came back to the gasoline station. He recounted meeting a man at the gasoline station who talked to him about the dog.[23] Hauptmann said that he and Anna had left the bakery after nine o'clock. They got home and went right to bed.

2. HAUPTMANN'S FINANCES

The prosecution had proved that Hauptmann possessed and passed Lindbergh ransom money. Hauptmann stuck with the story he had told the police and the extradition court—that Fisch had given him a package in December of 1933, and he had not discovered that it contained money until August of 1934 when leaking

---

[21] Transcript, 2435–2436.
[22] Transcript, 2437.
[23] This would set up the later corroboration testimony by August Van Henke about meeting Hauptmann at the gasoline station with the dog.

water revealed its contents. Hauptmann testified that Fisch arrived at his farewell party with a "little bundle under his arm." He came in and he and Hauptmann went into the kitchen. Hauptmann said Fisch had told him, "I leave it. I leave it something, if you don't mind, keep care of it and put it in a tight place."[24] Hauptmann said Fisch told him there was paper in the bundle. Hauptmann put the bundle in the kitchen closet on the top shelf. The box wasn't disturbed until the middle of August 1934 when there had been a nasty storm outside. Hauptmann was looking for a broom in the kitchen closet and must have hit the box with the broom handle. "I looked up, and that way I saw that it is money. I damaged the box."[25] Hauptmann told Reilly he took the money to the garage. He said he only saw gold certificates in the box and didn't count it in the beginning. Reilly asked if that was the money found in his garage, and Hauptmann replied that it was. Other than Hauptmann, the defense had no one who could testify that Fisch gave Hauptmann any money; so they would pursue a several-part strategy to prove Fisch had a large amount of money, some of which were gold certificates. Witnesses would testify that there had been a farewell party for Fisch in December, 1933; and a witness would corroborate Hauptmann's testimony about the leak in the kitchen closet which led to Hauptmann's discovery of the money.

Anna Hauptmann said that Fisch had left suitcases and some boxes at the Hauptmann house before he left for Germany, but that had been before the farewell party. Reilly asked her, "So that if he had anything at the party you didn't see him bring it, did you?" Anna answered, "No."[26] Anna said she had never seen the box on the top

---

[24] Transcript, 2448.
[25] Transcript, 2448.
[26] Transcript, 2925.

shelf, and Reilly had to offer some explanation for that. Anna told Reilly that she had to stand on her toes to reach that shelf. "Did you know anything about any box, shoe box, card board box on the top shelf of the broom closet?" Anna said she never used that shelf.[27] Wilentz asked Anna, "Every day you went to that closet and you never saw any shoe box on the top shelf, did you?" Anna said she didn't know what was on the top shelf.[28] Anna later admitted that she kept soap coupons on the top shelf in a tobacco box. She would take the tobacco box down every three months or so, but she never saw a shoe box on the shelf. There is an interesting issue that Wilentz did not appear to see. The kitchen closet was very narrow, and the broom would not fit in the closet horizontally. If the shoe box had been on the top shelf near the front of the shelf, it should have been visible to anyone entering the closet or looking in from the kitchen. Anna testified she never saw the box, suggesting that, if it had been there, it was not near the front edge of the top shelf. If the box were pushed back from the front edge of the shelf, it would have been difficult if not impossible for Hauptman to have accidentally hit the wet box with the broom handle as he claimed he did. Wilentz had questioned Hauptmann about whether things on the top shelf of the closet could be seen from the kitchen.

> **Q:** Now of course if I stood here and that was the closet, I could easily see that shelf, couldn't I? Just like you can see it on this picture as you look away from it?
>
> **A:** Yes. This door was usually closed.

---

[27] Transcript, 2925.
[28] Transcript, 2933.

Q: Oh, sure, but I mean if the door was open and I was standing five feet away from it, I could see the whole top shelf, couldn't I?

A: Yes, you could see it partly, not quite.

Hauptmann was trying to deflect the question. Wilentz had created an apparent inconsistency between Hauptmann and his wife. Hauptmann had said the third shelf could be seen from the kitchen, but Anna had never seen a box on that shelf. How could Hauptmann have hit the box if it were recessed and out of sight? Wilentz wanted this point clearly established for the jury. "And you hit the box somehow?" Hauptmann answered "Yes."[29] Wilentz could have considered a courtroom demonstration of how Hauptmann had been able to get the broom handle parallel enough with the third shelf in the narrow closet to have hit the box that wasn't at the leading edge of the shelf. However, Wilentz had no idea what Hauptmann would do on the demonstration and realized that whatever happened would be fixed in the jurors' minds. He moved on.

The defense called a number of witnesses to testify about attending the party for Isidor Fisch before he departed for Germany to bolster Hauptmann's claim that he had received the money from Fisch at the farewell party. Hans Kloppenburg, who had tried to establish an alibi for Hauptmann for April 2, 1932, the night the ransom was paid, also testified about the farewell party for Isidor Fisch. He got to the party at the Hauptmanns' between six and seven o'clock p.m. He saw Fisch arrive. Fisch immediately began talking with Hauptmann, and Kloppenburg saw that Fisch had a package with him. Kloppenburg described the package as five to six inches high, seven to eight inches wide, and about fourteen

---

[29] Transcript, 2699.

inches long. He last saw Fisch with the package in Hauptmann's kitchen. When Fisch came back from the kitchen, he didn't have the package. On cross-examination Kloppenburg said that he was pretty sure Fisch left after one o'clock in the morning. He admitted to Wilentz that he had not seen Fisch leave, so he couldn't testify that Fisch had left the package with Hauptmann. Wilentz had secured the admission that weakened Kloppenburg's testimony, but he was not content and pressed on. "You don't know whether the package you saw Fisch come in with, you don't know whether or not he took it back with him, do you?" Wilentz, having scored his point, saw it evaporate with Kloppenburg's answer. "I am sure that he left it in the kitchen and he didn't take it; I don't think so."[30]

The defense called other witnesses who had attended the farewell party. Louise and Otto Wollenberg, Bertha Hoff, Victor Schussler, and Hilda and Otto Heyne. None of these witnesses saw Fisch with a package; they could only corroborate that there had been a party for Fisch. Reilly carefully did not ask these witnesses about seeing a package, hoping that the sheer number of witnesses would corroborate Hauptmann's assertion about Fisch giving him the money. Gustave Miller testified that he had been called to fix the leak in the Hauptmann's kitchen closet. As with the Fisch farewell party, Miller could only corroborate that there had been a leak. He had not seen any box with money. He was asked about whether any boards were missing from the attic, but he couldn't say. There had been some lumber in the cellar, but he could not recognize the attic board, S–226, as being among them.

Reilly called Bertha Hoff of Brooklyn to testify about a visit from a man named Budreau and a man she didn't

---

[30] Transcript, 3367–3368.

know around Thanksgiving, 1933. The men came about two o'clock and stayed about half an hour. She identified Exhibit D–39, the photograph of Fisch, as the man with Budreau.[31] She told Reilly that Fisch had some bundles with him. When asked to describe the bundles, Wilentz objected to the materiality of the bundles. Reilly argued that the purpose of the witness was to show that Fisch had tried to leave bundles with Hoff in November, 1933, just prior to leaving a bundle with Hauptmann at the Fisch farewell party. Wilentz complained that the defense couldn't prove the bundle Fisch left with Hauptmann was one of the bundles Hoff saw. Reilly in response argued his theory to Justice Trenchard.

> Now, if the Court please we might just as well face the issue, after the Attorney General has summed up to the jury. During the day I am prepared to prove, if my witnesses come from New York, that the man who jumped over the cemetery wall was Idisor Fisch, that the money was handed to Isidor Fisch, that Isidor Fisch from that date on not only approached one, but many persons in New York, trying to dispose of this money. I am going to trace every connection of Isidor Fisch with this money until he left on the steamer. I hope to be able to prove by witnesses when he arrived in Hamburg, his actions before the immigration authorities in Germany. I am going to trace everything I can to show that Isidor Fisch and not this defendant received the money from Dr. Condon, tried to dispose of it, tried to leave it, not only with this woman but other people, finally left it with Hauptmann, and the development of the innocence of this defendant.[32]

---

[31] D–39 is not listed in the official index of exhibits, but it is a photograph of Isidor Fisch.
[32] Transcript, 3533.

Trenchard said he was inclined to exclude the question, suggesting Reilly might be able to establish the proper predicate later. Reilly then withdrew Mrs. Hoff from the witness stand.

George Steinweg, who was in the steamship and tourist business, testified that he had sold Fisch and Henry Uhlig tickets on the steamer *Manhattan* to Germany, departing on December 6, 1933. Fisch had made the two reservations on August 18 and made final payment of $410 for both tickets on November 14. Fisch also purchased American Express checks in German marks, $1500 for Fisch and $500 for Uhlig. Steinweg further testified, "He had quite considerable more money in his wallet, because I asked him to buy more checks; but Mr. Fisch said that his friends would send some more money afterward if he needed it."[33] Steinweg testified that Fisch had a very bad coughing spell when he reserved and later bought the tickets and checks. Reilly showed Steinweg Exhibit D–39, the photograph of Fisch, but Steinweg said he could not recognize it as Fisch. Reilly then showed Steinweg D–5, another photograph of Fisch, but Steinweg would only say it was "about that." Reilly pressed for an identification, but Steinweg said he had a doubt about it.

Steinweg had not identified the man he had seen as Fisch, but Wilentz felt he needed to challenge Fisch having so much money. Wilentz asked argumentatively, "And on November the 14th, 1933, don't you know that Hauptmann gave him $2000 for that very purpose?" Steinweg replied that he didn't know. [34] He asked Steinweg if he had been in court when Hauptmann testified that he had given Fisch $2000 for the trip. Steinweg said no. Steinweg was allowed to leave the

---

[33] Transcript, 3626.
[34] Transcript, 3269.

witness stand. Wilentz had no need to attack Steinweg, who had simply sold Fisch a ticket.

Reilly called Sam Streppone, a radio repairman, to the stand. Streppone said that Fisch came to his store on May 10, 1933, to get his radio repaired. He presented Reilly with a record of the repair order which became D–49. Fisch had left a package about the size of a shoebox in the store for six hours before returning to retrieve it. There was no indication that the package left with Streppone was the package Hauptmann claimed contained the money. Wilentz immediately attacked the credibility of Streppone by asking if he had been adjudged insane some years ago. Streppone replied that he had been discharged in 1928 with no psychosis. On redirect Reilly had Streppone say he had spent three months at Central Islip. On recross-examination Streppone said that he had been in an institution for mental disorders about five times. Streppone said that he had been hospitalized because he had threatened bodily harm to a woman. He said that doctors called his condition manic-depressive psychosis. Streppone admitted that he had been treated as recently as July 5, 1934, at Bellevue Hospital. Streppone then left the witness stand.

Oscar John Bruchmann, a taxi driver, provided additional proof that Fisch had money. He identified D–39 as being a photograph of Fisch and said he had worked with Fisch in his Knickerbocker Pie Baking Company for about a year in 1930–1931. He next saw Fisch in May, 1933, when Fisch used his taxi. He said that Fisch pulled a roll of bills out of his pocket and gave him a five-dollar bill to take him down to Sixth Avenue. Bruchmann volunteered that he didn't know if the money Fisch had was gold certificates. Wilentz objected to that statement, and Trenchard ordered it stricken from the record. Wilentz did not offer any cross-examination.

Theron J. Main testified that on August 2 or 3 he had gone to the bank to get a draft cashed. A man he identified as Fisch from Exhibit D–39 was in a restaurant about 2:30 a.m. playing a prize game and drinking beer. He saw Fisch give the bartender a $20 gold note. Fisch followed him out of the restaurant and exhibited gold notes to him. He later saw Fisch's photograph in the *Buffalo Evening News* in January, 1935. He had been with Fisch about half an hour. On cross-examination Wilentz asked about the gold notes and what Main meant by that. "Well, it is yellow on one side and green on the other," Main answered.[35] Wilentz produced a $20 bill for comparison. "Take a look at it. One side of it would be green, the front of it would be like that, is that it substantially?" Main replied, "Why, I would say similar to that." Wilentz continued, "And the back of it would be yellow?" Main answered, "Yes."[36] Main said there was no doubt in his mind that he had seen a gold back. Wilentz locked him in on the gold back; and, in an argumentative question asked, "Haven't you read in every paper in this country that gold bills didn't have any yellow backs or gold backs to them?"[37] Prior to the 1928 series, gold certificates were green on one side and yellow on the other. The 1928 Series eliminated the yellow back side and bore a gold seal and gold serial numbers on the front and a green back. If Main had seen Fisch with "gold backs," it could not have been any of the Series 1928 gold certificates in the Lindbergh ransom money.[38]

William E. Frank had testified for the State as a summary witness about Hauptmann's finances and transactions. His opinion was that Hauptmann's finances depended on the ransom money for his transactions.

---

[35] Transcript, 3759.
[36] Transcript, 3759.
[37] Transcript, 3760.
[38] FBI New York File 62–3057, page 208.

Reilly would have to question Hauptmann about his finances to explain where his money had come from. Reilly's examination of Hauptmann on his finances covered 34 pages of transcript, a dizzying recitation of deposits and withdrawals, but he asked no questions about Hauptmann's household budget—nothing about rent, food, clothing, car, medical bills, or anything like that. The jurors were left with a confusing series of unexplained deposits and withdrawals to consider. After the verdict was rendered, Author P. J. O'Brien examined the jury room and found written computations in which the jurors had tried to analyze Hauptmann's investments, but O'Brien could not decipher the jury's figures,[39] possibly because the jury could not decipher Hauptmann's account of his finances.

3. HAUPTMANN'S CROSS-EXAMINATION

Experienced trial lawyers have long known that when preparing witnesses to testify, it is essential to prepare them to withstand cross-examination by the opposing attorney. Almost 2,000 years ago the Roman rhetorician Quintilian wrote:

> One who produces a voluntary witness may well know what he is going to say; he therefore appears to have an easier task in questioning him. But even this part requires acumen and watchfulness; care must be taken that the witness is not frightened, inconsistent, or unwise. Witnesses are confused, and are drawn into traps by the advocates on the other side; they do more damage by being caught like this than they would have done good by a firm and fearless performance. They must therefore

---

[39] O'Brien, *The Lindberghs*, 301.

> be carefully rehearsed at home and tested by various questions of the kind that the other side may raise.[40]

Judging from the way that Wilentz demolished Hauptmann on cross-examination, it does not appear that the defense team heeded Quintilian's advice. Before Hauptmann took the stand, someone from the defense team should have vigorously cross-examined Hauptmann to give him practice in responding to the difficult questions that he would certainly be asked. Having once been raked over the coals, Hauptmann would have been better able to cope with cross-examination and might have cut a somewhat better figure than he did.

Cross-examination serves as the first line of attack on any evidence which the defense presents during its case. A skillful prosecutor seeks to accomplish one or more of the following objectives: (1) to gain admissions which either (a) support the prosecution theory or (b) undermine the defense theory; (2) to demonstrate the unreliability of the testimony; or (3) to demonstrate the unreliability of the witness. Wilentz understood the objects he needed to achieve on cross, but he lacked skill in the techniques for achieving them. As we have already seen in the previous chapter, he sometimes shot himself in the foot with his questioning. As we shall soon see, he tended to conduct rambling, poorly organized, and overly lengthy cross-examinations. Despite these shortcomings, he still inflicted serious damage to the defense case.

Reilly had good reasons to call Hauptmann as his first witness, but he also had excellent reasons to save him for later. Hauptmann was a vulnerable witness who had already given conflicting statements and testimony. Although he steadfastly maintained his innocence, some of his statements included damning admissions. Wilentz could use

---

[40] Quintilian, *The Orator's Education*, 5.7.10–11

Hauptmann's admissions to bolster his case theory, and if Hauptmann denied or evaded, he could use the admissions to undermine the defense theory by portraying Hauptmann as a liar. Cross-examining Hauptmann presented no simple task, but the material was there to both build the state's case and destroy Hauptmann's credibility. If the jury decided Hauptmann was a liar, then the defense would suffer a devastating blow which would undermine all the rest of the defense evidence.

Reilly, as a seasoned defense attorney, had confronted such problems with his clients before, and he knew that he had options for softening the blows that could be inflicted on cross-examination. The two most popular methods are (1) keep your client off the witness stand, or (2) call your client last. It may have gone better for Hauptmann if Reilly had been able to convince him not to testify, but the final decision on that issue belonged to Hauptmann, not Reilly.

Wilentz began his cross of Hauptmann by getting him to make a roundabout admission that he had lied at his habeas corpus hearing in the Bronx.

Q: All right. So that you stand now on the story that you have given today?

A: I do.

Q: You stand on the story that you gave in the Bronx, in the court house.

A: To a certain extent.

Q: Well, I am talking about the story that you swore to before a court in The Bronx. Do you stand on that?

A: To a certain extent, yes.

Q: And to a certain extent, no?

A: To a certain extent, no.[41]

---

[41] Transcript, 2538.

Then Wilentz got him to make a similar admission about lying in a statement before the Bronx District Attorney.

> **Q:** Did you lie to District Attorney Foley or did you tell him the truth?
>
> . . .
>
> **A:** I told the truth to District Attorney Foley about my treatment in The Bronx; that is correct.
>
> **Q:** About this case, not about the treatment, about the Lindbergh case, the murder, did you tell him the truth about that?
>
> **A:** To a certain extent.
>
> **Q:** And to a certain extent you didn't tell him the truth, is that it?
>
> **A:** I was —
>
> **Q:** Did you tell him the truth only to a certain extent and lie to another extent?[42]

Wilentz should not have cut Hauptmann off. Cutting the witness off as he did was both legally and tactically wrong. It would have been interesting to hear Hauptmann's explanation of how he was not lying when he made untrue statements. Pope objected to the manner in which Wilentz was questioning Hauptmann and Justice Trenchard agreed. Wilentz dropped the line of questioning and moved on to Hauptmann's criminal record. He would later return to the subject and continue to press Hauptmann for a flat admission that he had lied. Hauptmann would refuse to cooperate.

Wilentz walked Hauptmann through an admission that he had gone to prison in Germany for selling stolen property and after four years had been released on parole.

---

[42] Transcript, 2539.

Hauptmann admitted that he had been out approximately two weeks and then gotten arrested and put in jail again. Then Wilentz got Hauptmann to describe how he had broken out of jail.[43] Wilentz got Hauptmann to swear that he had only been convicted of one crime.

> **Q:** So you mean you were only convicted of one crime, is that it?
>
> **A:** Yes, sir.
>
> **Q:** Only convicted once?
>
> **A:** Convicted once.[44]

Wilentz immediately impeached Hauptmann by reminding him of a second conviction.

> **Q:** Isn't it a fact that you were also convicted of breaking and entering into the Mayor's home on March the 15th and 16th, 1919?
>
> **A:** It is about right. I can't remember,
>
> **Q:** Breaking in through a window—you went through a window, didn't you?
>
> **A:** Yes.[45]
>
> **MR. POPE:** I object to that question. He may ask him if he was charged with the crime and convicted. He may not go into the detail.
>
> **THE COURT:** There is a limitation there.[46]

New Jersey law held that a witness could be impeached by showing a prior conviction of crime, and even the nature of the charge, but not the details of the commission of the crime.[47] If Pope had interposed a

---

[43] Transcript, 2540–2542.
[44] Transcript, 2542.
[45] Transcript, 2543
[46] *Ibid.*
[47] State v. Sands, 76 N.J. 127, 386 A.2d 378 (1978).

timely objection when Wilentz first asked about the circumstances of Hauptmann's selling stolen property conviction and escape, the jury would probably never have heard that Hauptmann had committed a burglary by going through a window. Wilentz then impeached Hauptmann with another conviction.

> **Q:** Isn't it a fact that you were convicted, you and another man were convicted of holding up two women with a gun?
>
> **A:** It is.

Wilentz tried to get Hauptmann to admit the two women were pushing baby carriages when he robbed them, but Pope again objected and Trenchard again sustained.[48] Although neither the fact that Hauptmann had previously been convicted of crimes nor the circumstances of those crimes are direct legal proof that he was guilty of murder, his prior convictions did give the jurors a legal basis for disbelieving his testimony. It might be difficult, however, for the jury to make this distinction. Wilentz also tried to get Hauptmann to admit to two more convictions, but he was through cooperating. Having no real proof to refute Hauptmann's denials, Wilentz moved on to questioning Hauptmann about his illegal entry into the United States.

> **Q:** And you sneaked on a boat and tried to sneak into this country, didn't you?
>
> **A:** That is true.
>
> **Q:** And they sent you back?
>
> **A:** Yes, sir.

---

[48] *Id.*

Q: Then you sneaked on another boat and tried to sneak into the country and they sent you back again, didn't they?

A: Yes, sir.

Q: And finally, you sneaked in the last time?

A: Yes, sir.

Q: And you have been here ever since?

A: Yes, sir.[49]

By this time Wilentz had ripped Hauptmann's credibility to shreds. He was now ready to move on to attempting to get Hauptmann to make admissions supportive of the prosecution theory. The conventional wisdom teaches that the cross-examiner should first get helpful admissions and then attack the credibility of the witness. Wilentz correctly departed from the conventional wisdom here, because Hauptmann was going to stubbornly refuse to admit the obvious. When a witness denies a fact asserted in a question, the jury almost reflexively makes a decision about who is telling the truth—the lawyer or the witness. If Wilentz had begun by trying to get helpful admission, some of the jurors might have felt sympathetic to Hauptmann and credited his denials. Reversing the conventional order of questioning assured that the jury would be predisposed to credit Wilentz's assertions over Hauptmann's denials.

Wilentz then prominently displayed a photographic enlargement of a portion of the final ransom note delivered to Lindbergh after the ransom was paid. This final ransom note told Lindbergh he could find his son alive and well on the "boad Nelly." After setting up the photographic enlargement, Wilentz was ready to begin his cross-examination. What follows is an abridged and edited version of the long and sometimes disjointed examination.

---

[49] Transcript, 2544–2545.

Q: Yes. Now I want to show you a little book and ask you if it is yours. Is that your handwriting? Take your time about it. Look at it.

A: Yes, that's my handwriting.

Q: That is your handwriting?

A: Yes.

Q: Take a look at this word particularly [Wilentz points to the word "boad"]. Tell me if that is your handwriting, that one word there.

A: It looks like my handwriting, but I can't remember I ever put it in.

Q: You can't remember what?

A: No, no.

Q: Don't mix it up now. Just stay with that word there for a minute; two dollars and fifty cents. You see that word?

A: Yes.

Q: Alongside of it?

A: Yes.

Q: Are they your figures?

A: They must be my figures.

Q: They must be your figures. Now let's get to this word that you use.

A: Yes.

Q: Yes. That [the word "boad"] is your word then, isn't it?

A: I can't remember if I ever put it in.

Q: Why did you spell "boat" b-o-a-d?

A: This book is probably eight years old.

Q: All right. Why did you spell b-o-a-d?

A: Well, after you make improvement in your writing.

Q: All right. So that at one time you used to spell "boat" b-o-a-d?

A: Probably eight or ten years ago, and I am not quite sure if I put it in.

Q: But the word "boad" in there you won't say that is not in your handwriting, will you?

A: I wouldn't say yes either.

Q: You don't say yes or no?

A: I don't say yes or no because I can't remember ever putting it in.

Q: The reason you don't say yes or no is because you know you wrote "boad" when you got the fifty thousand from Condon, isn't that right?

A: No, sir.

Q: Boad Nelly. Look at it.

A: No.

Q: Do you see the word "boad Nelly"?

A: I see it, certainly.

Q: Look at it again right underneath there, again "boad", do you see that?

A: I see it.

Q: B-o-a-d?

A: I see it.

Q: Let me see this exhibit for identification [S–252]. Do you see that?

A: I see that.

Q: Same spelling?

A: Same spelling.[50]

Russell B. Porter, covering the trial for the *New York Times*, noted that Hauptmann's "look of terror was easy to read" during this portion of the cross-examination.[51] Kathleen Norris, also writing for the *Times*, found

---

[50] Transcript, 2548–2550.

[51] Russell B. Porter, "Admissions by Hauptmann Open Cross-Examination: Shaken by Bitter Attack," *NYT*, January 26, 1935.

Hauptmann to be a pitiful figure as he shrank back in his chair under the Attorney General's attack.[52]

Wilentz then showed Hauptmann another page of the notebook, had Hauptmann identify the word "New York" as his handwriting, and had him underline where he wrote "New York" in six different places on the page. Wilentz marked the page S–257, and then had Hauptmann look at a photographic enlargement of the word "New York" from a ransom note. When Wilentz questioned Hauptmann about similarities between his admitted writing "New York" and the writing "New York" on the ransom note, Hauptmann claimed there was a great difference between the two.[53] Wilentz published S–257 to the jury so that they could compare Hauptmann's admitted "New York" writing to the photographic enlargement of "New York" from the ransom note. Wilentz then walked Hauptmann through a number of comparisons between examples of his known handwriting and the handwriting on the ransom notes. At times Hauptmann would agree to the similarities, and at others he would claim to see no similarity. When Hauptmann did this, Wilentz displayed the handwriting to the jury. Hauptmann evaded and temporized as he attempted to thwart the relentless demonstrations of similarities between his handwriting and the handwriting on the ransom notes.

Wilentz quite possibly did the greatest damage to Hauptmann's credibility when confronting him with Exhibit S–204. This was the board from Hauptmann's closet on which someone had written John Condon's address and telephone number–2984 Decatur, Sedgewick 3–7154. During his interrogation by the Bronx District

---

[52] Kathleen Norris, "Mrs. Norris Finds Prisoner 'Pitiful,'" *NYT*, January 26, 1935.
[53] Transcript, 2578–2580.

Attorney, Hauptmann had identified the board as coming from his home and also agreed that the handwriting was his. He begrudgingly repeated these admissions before the Bronx Supreme Court at his extradition hearing. Wilentz had transcripts of both admissions. When Hauptmann tried to deny that the board had come from his house and refused to identify the handwriting as his, Wilentz used the transcripts to impeach Hauptmann with his prior inconsistent statements. Wilentz's lack of experience as a prosecutor was evident as he stumbled through the impeachment from the transcripts. He eventually made his points, however, and Hauptmann's credibility took a beating in the eyes of the jury. What follows is an edited rendition of the questioning omitting the repetitions, redundancies, and arguments among counsel.[54]

Q: Do you know what this is, Mr. Defendant? (Exhibiting the plank S–204 to the witness.) You do, don't you?

A: A piece of board, yes.

Q: That is from your closet, isn't it?

A: I am not quite sure.

Q: That is your handwriting on there, isn't it?

A: No. … The numbers look familiar upwards. I can't remember for putting it on.

Q: Did you remember better when you were talking to District Attorney Foley?

A: At that time I was quite excited.

Q: Were you excited when you got before a Supreme Court Justice in the State of New York in your extradition proceedings?

A: I say yes.

Q: You didn't tell the truth there, you mean?

A: Well, I was quite excited then.

---

[54] Transcript, 2659–2665.

Q: Do you remember that you had a hearing before a Supreme Court Justice by the name of Mr. Justice Hammer in the Bronx court house in New York?

A: I remember that, yes.

Q: And you were asked this question with reference to Exhibit 204 —

MR. REILLY: Page, please.

MR. WILENTZ: 83.

Q: You were asked the question: "Finally one day thereafter you were brought in and questioned by District Attorney Foley, were you not?" and your answer was "Yes." "And District Attorney Foley asked you if you recognized a certain piece of wood or lumber, do you remember that?" And your answer was "Yes." Is that correct?

A: I will—let's explain before you read further —

Q: No. Wait a minute. I am going to let you explain when I find out what your answer is. Did District Attorney Foley ask you—No. Withdraw that. Isn't this the question that was asked of you in the Bronx County Court before a Supreme Court Justice while you were under oath?

A: I can't remember the, what the question was.

Q: "And District Attorney Foley asked you if you recognized a certain piece of wood or lumber, do you remember that?" And your answer is "Yes." Is that correct?

A: Well, I really can't remember what—all the questions.

Q: Isn't that the question "And you said, 'Yes,' that was your handwriting, is that so, yes." Was that question put to you?

A: I really can't remember this question.

Q: Then the Court says—he can't remember the question—then the Court says: "You better mark this Exhibit A:" You see this Exhibit A—referring to the board.

A: I see it.

Q: You see it?

A: All right.

Q: And then the next question that I asked you in The Bronx, so that when you looked at Exhibit A, which was presented to you by the District Attorney of Bronx County, and you looked at the handwriting thereon, you said that was your handwriting, isn't that so, and your answer there was, "I said that is my lumber; I could not make out the handwriting." Do you remember that?

A: I can't remember them questions.

Q: Did you say that was your lumber, but that you couldn't remember the handwriting in the Bronx court?

A: I guess I did.

Q: Now, the next question, "You said the number on there is your handwriting," do you remember that question?

A: No, I don't.

Q: And didn't you answer "Yes" to that question? You said the number on there is your handwriting, yes, in the Bronx Court, before Supreme Court Justice Hammer—didn't you say yes?

A: I can't remember this.

Q: Will you say that you didn't say "Yes"?

A: No, I said nothing about it.

Q: Well, you remember, do you—you were there, weren't you?

A: I suppose I was there.

Q: Sitting on the stand?

A: Yes.

Q: And then you were asked this question: "What about the Decatur"— and you were shown the word on the board—"What about the Decatur?" And your answer was, was it not? "A: I could not make out whether that was my handwriting and numbers." Do you remember that?

A: I can't remember my answer.

Q: Now let me give you the next one: "The numbers are in your handwriting, are they not?" You remember being asked that again; and you said "They are." Do you remember that?

A: That's what I said, I can't remember what I said of it.

Q: Didn't you swear in the Bronx County Court House before Supreme Court Justice Hammer, swear unto God, that it was?

A: I did.

Q: And the numbers you talked about were 2974, isn't that so? It is a little blurred now, isn't it?

A: Looks like it.

Wilentz turned his attention to the $20 bill Hauptmann had in his pocket when he was arrested:

Q: Now, let's get back to the time you were arrested and they found this twenty dollar bill on you, the ransom money bill, and the police asked you where you got it. Right?

A: Yes.

Q: And you said to the police, "This twenty dollar bill, yes, I had three hundred dollars worth. I saved it, got it from friends and got it from the banks and this is the last of the gold bills.

A: Yes, I told them that.

Q: You knew at the very time that you told them that you were not telling the truth, isn't that right?

A: That is right.[55]

Wilentz confronted Hauptmann with lie after lie, some of which he admitted and others he tried to evade.

---

[55] Transcript, 2692–2693.

Hauptmann had spent money lavishly after he quit work on April 2, 1932. Wilentz wanted to know where the money came from.

Q: In May, 1932 you bought a radio for $400, didn't you?
A: Yes.
Q: In cash?
A: Yes.
Q: What date in May, do you know?
A: No, I can't remember which day.
Q: After April the 2nd, 1932, you bought some field glasses too, didn't you?
A: I guess was in July.
Q: 1932?
A: Yes, July, I guess.
Q: How much did you pay for the field glasses?
A: Well, $126.
Q: $126?
A: Yes.
Q: Before March the 1st, 1932, did you own field glasses?
A: Yes; yes.
Q: You did own field glasses?
A: Yes.
Q: But after March the 1st, 1932, and particularly in July, I think you said, you spent $125 for a new pair of field glasses?
A: Yes.
Q: Now, before you bought that radio you already had a Victrola in your home, hadn't you?
A: Yes.
Q: Did you buy a canoe and take a hunting trip?
A: Yes.[56]

---

[56] Transcript, 2728–2729.

. . .

Q: After April 2, 1933, you told us you bought—you told us about the radio and you told us about the field glasses. Did you buy a canoe?

A: Yes.

Q: Did you take a hunting trip, several hunting trips?

A: Well, I really can say only one.

Q: Did you take a trip to Florida?

A: Yes.

Q: And your wife went to Germany?

A: Yes.

Q: And during all that time neither you nor your wife worked?

A: I was working—Well, I made enough money on the market and on the fur.

Q: Now please answer the question. During that time you didn't work, did you?

A: I did work.

Q: In the market?

A: Yes. In the market and as carpenter.

Q: Well, about how much would you say you earned as a carpenter, from 1932, April 1932, until September, 1934?

A: Couple hundred dollars.

Q: A couple of hundred dollars?

A: Yes.

Q: Your wife quit work too, when she went to Germany, didn't she?

A: Yes.

Q: So that from June, or from April, 1932, April the 2nd, 1932, to September, 1934, when you were arrested, you made $200 as a carpenter and your wife did no work at all either, she quit work?

A: Yes, she quit work.[57]

---

[57] Transcript, 2752.

Wilentz suspended his cross examination to call a translator to translate a letter Hauptmann had written to Isidore Fisch's family in Germany. After Fisch died, they had written him asking whether Hauptmann had any money or other property belonging to Fisch, and Hauptmann's reply letter said nothing about Fisch having any money. He did, however, tell the family:

> I still have two trunks belonging to Isidor in my apartment. There are no important things in them, but if you should be interested I will send the same to Germany. There are photographs, linen, and other small things in them.[58]

This was problematical for two reasons. First, Hauptmann had explained some of his newfound wealth by saying it came from business deals with Fisch. Second, Hauptmann said nothing to Fisch's family about the box containing over $14,000 in cash. Hauptmann tried to justify his concealment of some of Fisch's financial dealings with him by saying that Fisch lost money and it would have done no good to worry them by telling them that "he losed so much money." [59] His explanation for not telling them about the box full of ransom money was less than convincing.

> **Q:** You sent him [Fisch's brother] stories about two trunks but nothing about the money box.
>
> **A:** In this time I didn't know it.
>
> **Q:** Well, you finally found out about it and didn't tell him anyway.
>
> **A:** I was going to tell him.
>
> **Q:** But you didn't tell him.

---

[58] Transcript, 2825–2826.
[59] Transcript, 2853.

A: Not yet.

Q: Two trunks with nothing in it, linens—you looked through the trunks.

A: Yes.

Q: You forgot all about the money box.

A: Give me a chance to answer.

Q: Yes, sir. I will. You forgot about the money box, didn't you?

A: I found it out in all this 1934.

Q: You forgot about it?

A: And I didn't write. I didn't have any chance to write then.

Q: That's because you forgot it?

A: Yes.

Q: Isn't that it? You had it in the closet but you forgot about it?

A: I forgot about it.

Q: That's what I am asking you.

A: Yes.

Q: You forgot about it. So you didn't write to him?

A: I couldn't write; I couldn't write.

Q: Because you forgot about it?

A: I forgot about it.[60]

In response to a request from Fisch's family, Hauptmann had told them about boxes full of photographs and linens but had neglected to tell them about the box full of money. He had thoroughly inspected the boxes full of clothing, but he claimed never to have looked into the box full of money. When he did discover the money in the box, he didn't notify Fisch's family. His claim to have inspected the linen boxes but not the money box can be rejected out of hand as ridiculous. This leads

---

[60] Transcript, 2853–2854.

to one of two conclusions, neither of which helped Hauptmann's credibility. Either Hauptmann said nothing about the money box because he was trying to steal the money from Fisch's relatives or he didn't tell them about the money box because Fisch gave him no money box.

Hauptmann, at first composed, became more and more agitated by the Attorney General's questioning. Russell B. Porter described Hauptmann's demeanor during the second day of cross examination in this way:

> Now for the first time, in today's cross-examination, Hauptmann got really angry. He set his jaw, thrust forward his chin and his whole body, and grasped the witness chair with taut arms.
>
> His voice, which he had kept down to a low-pitched monotone most of the day, rose in an almost hysterical shout. His deep-sunken eyes, which had shown bland indifference, suddenly blazed into a cold, hard look of hatred turned point-blank upon his questioner.[61]

The bombardment of cross-questioning continued, scoring more points, until Wilentz finally finished questioning, Hauptmann's believability was finished as well. Reilly tried to repair some of the damage with a redirect examination, but as often happens the redirect examination merely gave Wilentz the opportunity to damage Hauptmann further with a recross-examination. Wilentz got Hauptmann to admit to passing Lindbergh ransom money at a grocery store and then went outside the scope of the redirect to ask a few more questions on the issue of the board bearing Condon's address and phone number. Wilentz established that when Hauptmann

---

[61] Russell B. Porter, "Hauptmann Admits Lying and Says Wilentz Lies Too; Still Protests His Innocence," *NYT*, January 26, 1935.

was confronted with the board in the Bronx, he had examined it with a magnifying glass.

> **Q:** And when you saw this piece of wood with that writing on it you said, "That's my lumber." Isn't that so—in the Bronx.
>
> **A:** I did.[62]

The debacle of Hauptmann's cross-examination infected everything else the defense did. Even if he were being truthful about his innocence of the murder, his patent falsehood as to such important points destroyed him in the eyes of the jury. At the time of Hauptmann's trial, New Jersey recognized the legal doctrine of *falsus in uno falsus in omnibus* (false in one thing false in everything). This doctrine held that if a jury determined that a witness had willfully perjured himself as to a material fact, they were permitted, if they saw fit, to completely disbelieve everything he said.[63] Had the state asked, the judge could have lawfully instructed the jury:

> If you find that a witness has willfully, knowingly, or intentionally testified falsely concerning a material fact in the case, you may reject all or any portion of the testimony given by such witness.[64]

Even without such an instruction, the jury might be inclined to reject all of Hauptmann's evidence. Having rejected all of Hauptmann's testimony, the jury would then be inclined to disbelieve all other testimony offered by the defense. Anyone skilled in the art of persuasion knows that poor arguments tend to weaken good ones,

---

62 Transcript, 2907.

63 Addis v. Rushmore, 74 N.J.L. 649, 65 A. 1036 (Ct.Err. & App., 1907).

64 Coleman v. Public Service Coordinated Transport, 120 N.J.L. 384, 199 A. 772, 773 (Sup.Ct., 1938).

and false evidence casts doubt on truthful testimony. When asked what he thought about Hauptmann's testimony, the comedian Jack Benny, who attended the trial and watched the cross-examination, deadpanned, "What Bruno needs is a second act."[65]

[65] Fisher, *The Lindbergh Case*, 327.

7

The Defense Case Part 2
Reasonable Doubts

Edward J. Reilly knew his way around a courtroom. He had practiced law for over twenty years and had, by his count, defended over 1,000 people charged with murder. He reveled in the notoriety of sensational cases, and his flamboyant style had earned him the reputation of being New York's most entertaining lawyer.[1] Reilly had won his share of high profile cases, and he was supremely confident of his abilities—one might even say overconfident. Reilly was so confident of his abilities that he had developed a habit of flying by the seat of his pants, trying cases without notes and without taking notes, waiting for "the one unforeseen break which will turn defeat into victory,"[2] and then pouncing. This may well have contributed to Hauptmann's undoing.

In the criminal courtrooms of the early Twentieth Century such a technique could lead to great success. They had no discovery, and cases were often an exercise in trial-by-ambush. In such situations, with little chance to prepare, advocates had to have resilience, resourcefulness, and readiness to improvise. The inability to learn much about the other side's case sometimes led to

---

[1] Milton MacKay, "Profiles: For the Defence," *The New Yorker Magazine*, January 12, 1935, 22–25, http://www.newyorker.com/magazine/1935/01/12/for-the-defence (accessed March 25, 2015).
[2] Ibid, 24.

inadequate investigation of one's own case. A defense lawyer could feel safe calling a witness about whom he knew very little because the witness would be a surprise to the prosecution, and the quick pace of trials made it impossible to adequately investigate the witness. Sometimes lawyers would even take the chance of calling witnesses whom they knew to be dangerous to their side of the case, relying on the probability that the other side would not know the weakness and not be able to capitalize on it.

Reilly was used to springing witnesses on the prosecution at the last minute and then watching them flounder as they tried to cross-examine without adequate investigation. It was not going to be like that in the Lindbergh case. Wilentz had a veritable army of investigators at his disposal to conduct lightning investigations of all the defense witnesses as soon as they became known. Wilentz would string out the cross-examination until the time for the evening recess and say he had more questions for the next day. Over the evening he would be debriefed on what the investigation revealed, and the next morning he would be equipped to impeach the witnesses.[3] Reilly never adjusted to this. He would repeatedly call easily impeached witnesses, and Wilentz would destroy them.

It appears that Reilly's only countermeasure to this tactic was to complain bitterly that the New York and New Jersey police were threatening his witnesses. When presented with the complaint, Justice Trenchard said they should bring him some affidavits from the threatened

---

[3] Ludovic Kennedy, *The Airman and the Carpenter: The Lindbergh Kidnapping and the Framing of Richard Hauptmann* (New York: Viking Penguin, Inc., 1985), 314.

witnesses, and he would take remedial measures.[4] No affidavits were forthcoming. Reilly should have done a little preliminary investigation of his witnesses himself. If he had done so, he might never have called many of them. This defect in Reilly's trial performance began to show itself in the Alibi modules.

4a. ALIBI: March 1

Fawcett had called four witnesses for the bakery alibi—Hauptmann, his wife, and the Fredericksens. Kate Fredericksen testified that she took Tuesdays and Fridays off, and Anna must have worked the evening of March 1 since it was a Tuesday. Kate was not a true alibi witness—she only bolstered Anna's testimony. Neither Christian Fredericksen nor Anna Hauptmann could say for certain that Hauptmann was at the bakery on March 1. They could only testify that it was routine practice for Hauptmann to pick up Anna when she worked evenings, and that she routinely worked on Tuesdays.

Reilly opened the bakery alibi with Christian Fredericksen. "Now who was in the habit in February and March, 1932, of bringing Anna Hauptmann to work?" he asked. Fredericksen replied, "Her husband would usually bring her to work."[5] Establishing that Anna worked later on Tuesdays and Fridays when Kate Fredericksen was off, Reilly asked about how Anna would get home on those evenings. Fredericksen answered, "Well, her husband usually always come; as a rule he always come." Fredericksen continued with "usually" by stating that

---

[4] "His Witnesses Threatened, Reilly Charges; Court Hears Complaint against Police," *NYT*, January 31, 1935.
[5] Transcript, 2407.

Hauptmann "usually came in and have supper there." Reilly understood that "usually" was not good enough for a solid alibi and asked Fredericksen about his "best recollection" of Tuesday evening, March 1. "My best recollection is that Bruno usually called for her, he must have been there that night too, but I can't swear to it."[6] When an alibi witness testifies that he "can't swear to" the alibi, the defense has problems.

Wilentz wanted to solidify the conditional answers. He got Fredericksen to repeat that he couldn't swear to seeing Hauptmann there that Tuesday night;[7] and ended his questioning with:

> **Q:** So you don't know whether he was there at all?
>
> **A:** No, not positive sure; I can't swear to it.[8]

Anna Hauptmann testified about her work routine and habit at the Fredericksen Bakery—that she worked late on Tuesday and Friday evenings when Kate Fredericksen was off. She said that she had worked on Tuesday night, March 1, 1932, and Hauptmann came to the bakery that night to pick her up sometime between quarter to seven and quarter after seven and stayed there until Anna could leave.

There was a marked contrast between the tone of the Attorney General's cross-examination of Hauptmann and the examination of his wife. The *New York Times* noted that "Mr. Wilentz was very gentle in his tone and manner of questioning her."[9] Nevertheless, the cross-examination by Wilentz took full advantage of Anna's testimony at the New York hearing. At the habeas corpus hearing

---

[6] Transcript, 2409.

[7] Transcript, 2413.

[8] Transcript, 2414.

[9] Russell B. Porter, "Three Hauptmann Alibis Backed by Wife on Stand; Another Witness Waivers," *NYT*, January 31, 1935.

Wilentz had highlighted inconsistencies between Anna's testimony and what she told the police. He now could use both her testimony at the New York hearing and her statements to the police to show inconsistencies with her trial testimony. To impeach a witness with a prior inconsistent statement, the attorney typically reads the prior questions and answers to the witness and asks if the witness remembers those answers and statements. The defense attorneys surely talked to Anna about this and prepared her as best they could. Wilentz read the testimony from the hearing to Anna.

> **Q:** And did you not tell Inspector Bruckman and others who where there present at the time that you had no recollection at all of what happened March the 1st, and that it was too far back, that you don't know whether your husband was with you or not?
>
> **A:** I did tell him that.[10]

Fawcett had only presented four witnesses for the alibi of the evening of March 1, 1932. The defense added four more: Elvert Carlstrom, Louis Kiss, August Van Henke, and Walter Manley. Author Ovid Demaris characterized the new witnesses as "the weirdest collection of alibi witnesses ever assembled in one courtroom,"[11] and the seeming popularity of Fredericksen's Bakery on the night of the kidnapping became a source of amusement for the audience, with one wit saying that it was busier than Grand Central Station.[12]

---

[10] Transcript, 2946.

[11] Ovid Demaris, *The Lindbergh Kidnapping Case: The True Story of the Crime that Shocked the World* (Derby, Conn.: Monarch Books, 1961), 132.

[12] A. Scott Berg, *Lindbergh* (New York: Berkley Publishing Group, 1999), 328.

Elvert Carlstrom testified that he had left Dunellen, New Jersey, and come to New York on the evening of March 1. While in New York he had gone to the Fredericksens' bakery. He could remember the evening of March 1, 1932, because it was his birthday. Carlstrom's direct examination was curiously devoid of detail as to why he had gone to New York and what he had done after leaving the bakery. The birthday would provide a reason to remember the date, but the paucity of additional detail proved problematical. Carlstrom had frequented the bakery in the past and knew both the Fredericksens and Anna Hauptmann. Carlstrom testified that he'd never met Hauptmann before, but he vividly remembered Hauptmann because Hauptmann had laughed at him and made him angry. He testified that he had come forward after seeing photographs of Hauptmann in the newspaper.

Wilentz conducted a rambling cross-examination of Carlstrom which took up the remainder of the day. In addition to admitting that he knew Anna Hauptmann, Carlstrom became confused and evasive about what he did for the rest of the evening after he saw Hauptmann. He refused to give more than the first name of the lady he had gone to see in the Bronx that night, and he claimed not to know the first name of another person mentioned during his testimony—his good friend Mr. Larsen. Much of what Wilentz did on cross of Carlstrom was ineffective, but Wilentz wanted to string the cross-examination out as long as possible.

The investigation of Carlstrom reaped dividends. By the next morning Wilentz had an affidavit from Arthur Larsen, a co-worker of Carlstrom, who swore that on the night of March 1, he was in Dunellen, New Jersey, with Elvert Carlstrom working on a job for Oscar Christiansen.[13] Wilentz had Larsen in the courtroom as he continued his cross-examination.

Q: Now the Mr. Larsen you talked about yesterday, will you take a look over there? Where is Mr. Larsen? Stand up, please, Mr. Larsen. (A man stood up in the courtroom.)

Q: Is this the Mr. Larsen you talked about?

A: Yes, Arthur Larsen.

Q: You know his name today. ...[14]

The cross-examination from that point on destroyed Carlstrom's credibility. Both Larsen and Christiansen testified in rebuttal. Wilentz had also learned the name of the young lady Carlstrom refused to identify. Her name was Esther Ellerson and she was a good friend of Anna Hauptmann.[15]

Louis Kiss saw an article about a dog having been at the bakery the evening of March 1, 1932, and had called Reilly's home phone number to say that he had been at the bakery and remembered the dog. Carlstrom had not said anything about a dog being at the bakery. Kiss recalled a man telling a woman that someone wanted to take the dog away, but he didn't get much of a glimpse of the man. Kiss told Reilly that he remembered the bakery because that night he was supposed to take two pints of whiskey to the home of a friend named Leo Singer in the Bronx, but he had taken the wrong train. He passed the bakery around 8:15 p.m. and went inside for coffee. He was almost finished with his coffee when a police dog ran in. He said that the woman serving him coffee talked to a

---

[13] "His Witnesses Threatened, Reilly Charges; Court Hears Complaint about Police," *NYT*, January 31, 1935.
[14] Transcript, 3054.
[15] "Police Rush Check of Carlstrom's Story," *NYT*, January 30, 1935.

man about the dog in German, "Somebody want to take away the dog." Kiss remembered the whole thing because of the German. He identified Hauptmann as the man speaking German. He said he heard about the Lindbergh kidnapping later that night on the radio.[16]

Wilentz was again forced to confront a story he didn't believe, but Kiss had two memory markers for that evening: seeing the man speaking German about the dog and later hearing about the kidnapping. Wilentz had to impeach the testimony somehow. He spent a lot of time on Kiss' background, perhaps only accomplishing personalizing the witness in front of the jury. Some of his questions appeared to be nitpicking, focusing on small details and technicalities. He questioned Kiss' recollection that his wife had taken their son to the hospital on Washington's birthday, February 22, instead of his original testimony that it had been him who took the child. Kiss had said that it was one week later exactly that he had gone to the bakery. Wilentz challenged "exactly," pointing out that one week later exactly from Washington's birthday would have been Monday, February 29, not March 1.[17] Other than a few inconsistencies and the fact that Kiss had sold illegal whiskey and rum during Prohibition, Wilentz did little to impeach Kiss.

The real damage to Kiss's testimony came on rebuttal when Wilentz called Leo Singer to the stand. Singer testified that Kiss had visited in his home only once, and that visit came toward the end of March or beginning of April, well after the kidnapping. Singer could be certain of this because on March 10, he had purchased a new radio, and when Kiss came to his home they discussed the new radio.[18]

---

[16] Transcript, 3067–3077.
[17] Transcript, 3078–3114.
[18] Transcript, 4267–4269.

August Van Henke testified that he had lost his police dog Rex in February, 1932. On the evening of March 1, he stopped at a gas station on Ryder Avenue near Boston Post Road. He saw a man with a dog that looked like his missing dog. He talked with the man who identified himself as Hauptmann; and, after examining the dog, he determined it was not his. He went home and heard people talking about radio accounts of the kidnapping. He contacted Fawcett after Hauptmann was arrested. Van Henke could not put Hauptmann at the bakery, but he corroborated the alibi accounts of Hauptmann being at the bakery that same evening with a police dog.

Wilentz didn't want to spend a lot of time on Van Henke's story. He asked Van Henke if he knew August Wunstorf, and Van Henke replied "That is me."[19] Van Henke said that he had used the name August Wunstorf on account of a little family trouble because he had operated a saloon during Prohibition. He admitted that he had run book for horse races. He conceded that his establishment had been raided a couple of times, but he contended that it was Walter Goodwin who ran the illegal operations in Van Henke's restaurant/saloon. Wilentz asked Van Henke about his restaurant on Lenox Avenue, insinuating that the restaurant had rented out rooms on the second floor to men and women. Van Henke denied any knowledge of anything on the second floor, saying he had never been up there. Wilentz then asked who August Marhenke was, and Van Henke replied it was he who used that name in addition to August Wunstorf. Wilentz now had some arguments against Van Henke's credibility, but he had not done any direct damage to Van Henke's story about the dog and seeing Hauptmann.

Walter Manley testified that he had been to Fredericksen's bakery twice, and that on March 1, 1932 he had

---

[19] Transcript, 3122.

bought some Danish pastry and bread at the bakery. Anna waited on him, and he saw Hauptmann sitting in the front of the bakery sipping coffee. Two months before the trial, Manley told a coworker about being at the bakery and seeing Hauptmann, and the coworker contacted Reilly. Wilentz asked Manley about his knowledge of Anna and Hauptmann. Manley said that he had known Anna since '28 or '29, but he didn't know Hauptmann before the night at the bakery. Wilentz used the popular tactic of pointing out that the witness had important information about the case but didn't tell anyone who could do anything about it. Manley admitted that after he had seen the photographs and news articles, he had not gone to tell the Bronx judge, the Bronx District Attorney, or any authorities. He had not contacted Fawcett. Other than showing that Manley had important information and did not act upon it, Wilentz' cross-examination accomplished very little.

4b. ALIBI: April 2

Reilly wanted to provide evidence that Hauptmann could not have been the Cemetery John who received the ransom from Condon because Hauptmann was at home with Anna and Hans Kloppenburg the evening it was delivered. Hauptmann testified that April 2 was a Saturday and that he had worked that day at the Majestic Apartment. When he was working, he usually left the house at seven o'clock and worked until five o'clock in the afternoon. The Majestic was about eight miles from the Hauptmann home. Despite earlier testimony from the Reliance timekeeper that he had not worked April 2, Hauptmann said that he had worked that day and was paid for it. Hauptmann added, "I originally resigned on Saturday; on Monday I went down to try to get my pay check, but I get answer I got to wait till the 15th."[20] Reilly asked when Hauptmann had gotten home on Saturday, and Hauptmann replied that it was around six o'clock. He said that around seven o'clock Hans Kloppenburg came to the house because the first Saturday of each month was their music evening. Reilly asked if a Jimmie had been there with them, and Hauptmann could not recall. When asked to explain the music evening, Hauptmann said that Kloppenburg played the guitar and he played the mandolin. They would play for about an hour or an hour and a half until between 11 P.M. and midnight.

Anna Hauptmann testified that she remembered April 2, 1932. Reilly asked, "Do you remember who was in your home that night?" She replied, "Yes, I do, Hans Kloppenburg was with us."[21] Anna explained that Kloppenburg and Hauptmann got together the first Saturday night of each month for a music night. Hans Kloppenburg corroborated Anna's alibi for Hauptmann. He said that they had played music, had some coffee and cake, and that he had left between eleven and twelve o'clock when Hauptmann drove him to White Plains Avenue. Kloppenburg explained that he could remember the date because he and Hauptmann routinely met to play music. "On April 2nd, 1932, I was in Hauptmann's home. The first thing I remember we had a whole lot of joke about the first of April and the second reason is that we had the first Saturday of each month our week ends with music."[22] Kloppenburg gave Hauptmann a "habit alibi." Witnesses may not recall a specific date, but they do recall a routine or habit such as the first Saturday of a month.

---

[20] Transcript, 2437.
[21] Transcript, 2929.
[22] Transcript, 3373.

On cross-examination Wilentz established that Kloppenburg was very friendly with Mr. and Mrs. Hauptmann. After testing Kloppenburg's recollection of dates, Wilentz turned to Kloppenburg's statement to the Bronx District Attorney after Hauptmann's arrest in September, 1934. Wilentz asked if he remembered being asked about seeing Hauptmann in March, 1932. Kloppenburg had told the Bronx officials that he could not recall exactly when he had seen Hauptmann in March, but he had seen Hauptmann that month. Wilentz then reminded Kloppenburg of the statement he had made to the Bronx District Attorney.

Q. Nobody was forcing you to say anything except the truth, were they?

A. That's right.

Q. And you made your statement of your own free will?

A. Yes.

Q. And you were asked about the month of March and the month of April, 1932, weren't you?

A. Uh-huh.

Q. And do you remember this question being asked you, referring to Hauptmann: "Do you remember whether you saw him in the month of March, 1932?" And you answered: "I can't remember exactly days, but I saw him that month?"

A. That's right.

Q. Do you remember him?

A. That's right.

Q. Then you were asked: "Can you tell me one day in the month of April, 1932, when you saw him, any one day in particular?" "A. I don't know. That is too long ago." Is that correct?

A. I don't remember I said.

Q. Yes. You said "That's too long ago?"

A. That's right.

Q. April, 1932?

A. That's right.

Q. So in October, 1934, when you were making your statement of your own free will, you couldn't remember whether or not you had seen him on the night of April the 2nd, 1932?

A. That's right.

Wilentz had scored a point on Kloppenburg, but he immediately gave the man an opportunity to repair his credibility by asking:

Q. What caused you to change your mind and come to this court and swear differently from the statement you gave to the police?[23]

With this question Wilentz violated two maxims of cross-examination: (1) Never ask a question when you don't know the answer, and (2) Don't ask open-ended questions. The cross-examiner wants to maintain control of the flow of information. Asking open-ended questions on subjects you know nothing about surrenders control of the flow of information to the witness and gives the witness carte blanche to make up plausible explanations. Kloppenburg could have said that he was nervous when questioned at the Bronx District Attorney's office and simply forgot, but had his memory jogged after the interview. Instead Kloppenburg gave the implausible explanation:

Q. But none of these things that you now remember, none of them did you remember when you were talking to the police in September or to the District Attorney in October, 1934.

A. Yes, I remembered them, but I was not sure.[24]

---

[23] Trial Transcript 3371.

[24] Trial Transcript 3374.

Even today with computer-assisted indexing and storing of data, in a complex case essential material can get overlooked or its significance can go unrecognized. In 1935, given the size of the Lindbergh Kidnapping Case, it is understandable that Wilentz overlooked a golden opportunity to destroy the April 2 alibi. Detective Claude Patterson of the New Jersey State Police had determined that on April 2, 1932, Hauptmann's gas and electric had been cut off, and he had written a full report. The service had been cut off on March 29, 1932, and Hauptmann had requested that it be restored on April 4, 1932. [25] Kloppenburg said he could remember the night because they joked about the previous day being April Fool's Day, but he said nothing about them having their music night in pitch dark.

The essence of an alibi is to prove that the defendant was somewhere else when the crime occurred. Proof that someone else was at the scene of the crime isn't strictly alibi evidence, but it certainly supports direct alibi evidence. Reilly attempted to support the April 2 alibi with such evidence. Philip Moses, a New York taxi driver, testified that he was working the night of April 2 and had been in the neighborhood of St. Raymond's Cemetery after 8:00 p.m. He had driven to the cemetery on Balcom Avenue near the rear part of the cemetery. Reilly asked what he had seen at the cemetery. Before he had gotten to Tremont and Waterbury avenues he noticed a brand new green car, lower part dark green and upper part a shade or two lighter. He then drove three blocks south to Balcom where three men hailed him. The men huddled and then jumped in the taxi, and Moses drove them two blocks past the cemetery gate. The men jumped out and met a fourth man. The four men got into a gray

---

[25] Mark W. Falzini, *Their Fifteen Minutes: Biographical Sketches of the Lindbergh Case* (Bloomington, IN: iUniverse, 2008), 169–170.

car, and Moses pushed the gray car back to the other side of the cemetery. The event with the four men had happened after eight o'clock on April 2. Moses reported what he had seen to the police in October 1934 after Hauptmann had been arrested.

Wilentz began his cross-examination by showing Moses had been giving autographs in Flemington. The page in an autograph book Moses had signed was received in evidence as State's Exhibit S–292. It read "A star witness in the case. Philip Moses."[26] Wilentz then turned to a map of the cemetery Reilly had used with Moses. Using the map, Wilentz asked Moses about Whittemore, the street where the ransom was paid. Moses told Wilentz, "As far as I'm concerned, I wasn't there."[27] Moses had said that he had seen four men at St. Raymond's the evening of April 2, but it had not been at the location on Whittemore where Condon said the payment was made. If Wilentz had not effectively neutralized Moses with this line of cross-examination, Moses had almost certainly neutralized himself by doing Will Rogers impressions from the witness stand. The other members of the defense team had disapproved of Reilly's plan to call Moses, and their disapproval was well-founded.[28]

Reilly called Benjamin Heier to testify that he had been at St. Raymond's Cemetery on the evening of April 2. Heier had called for a young lady about 7:30 p.m. He was not familiar with the Bronx, but after viewing Exhibit S–174, the map of the cemetery, he recalled being on Tremont Avenue. He had parked opposite the cemetery wall. Heier and his date had been across from the wall for about two hours when they heard a man hit the sidewalk as

---

[26] "Star Witness Sets Courtroom Laughing, *NYT*, February 6, 1935.
[27] Transcript, 3498.
[28] "Star Witness Sets Courtroom Laughing, *NYT*, February 6, 1935.

if he had jumped. It would have occurred between 9:30 and 10:00 p.m., and Heier said he got a good look at the man. When shown Exhibit D–39,[29] a photograph of Isidor Fisch, Heier said there was a strong resemblance.

Wilentz asked Heier about operating a cabaret. Heier said that his brother operated the cabaret but used his name because he was better known. Wilentz asked Heier if he had been convicted of a crime, and Heier asked what a conviction meant. Judge Trenchard asked Heier if he had been convicted of a crime, to which Heier asked if a suspended sentence was a conviction. Trenchard asked again about a conviction, and Heier admitted he had been convicted. Heier admitted that he had read in the newspapers about the ransom being paid at St. Raymond's on April 2, but he had not told the police about having been there that night. When asked the address of the woman he had been with at the cemetery, Heier refused to answer. Heier told Wilentz that the woman had died in August of 1932, but, before dying she had married someone else. Heier told Wilentz that after he had read about the ransom payment and about the Fisch story, he did not report what he had seen to any authorities because he had forgotten it. Wilentz pressed Heier and asked what street he had parked his car on. Heier didn't know the name of the street and admitted he had not gone back to the cemetery to locate the name of the street.[30]

Near the end of his cross, Wilentz asked Heier about his certainty about who he had seen at the cemetery. "You are not positive, are you?" "No," replied Heier.[31] Not content to stop on a high point, Wilentz continued for

---

[29] While it was discussed with witnesses, the court reporters' official index of exhibits does not show a D–39. This omission appears to be an error by the court reporters.

[30] Transcript, 3582.

[31] Transcript, 3617.

several more pages before ending his cross-examination. As he had with other witnesses, Wilentz had allowed the witness to remain on the stand and retell his story several times. When his testimony ended, Heier got off the witness stand and walked over to where Hauptmann was sitting to ask Hauptmann for an autograph. Hauptmann began to comply with Heier's request, but before he could sign his name to the card Heier had given him, an officer shooed Heier away.[32]

Wilentz rebutted Heier's testimony in two ways. First, he gave Isidore Fisch an alibi for the night of the ransom delivery. On the evening of April 2, Fisch was at the home of Otillia Hoerber transacting business. Hoerber could state the date with certainty because she gave Fisch a document dated and signed by her. Wilentz had the document marked as S–308 for identification but did not offer it into evidence.[33] Neither Wilentz nor Reilly asked Hoerber to explain what sort of business was being transacted. Second, he gave Heier an "alibi." Joseph J. Farber testified that at about the time of the ransom delivery, he was involved in an automobile accident with Heier miles away from the cemetery.[34]

Most observers of the trial agreed that Reilly's new witnesses were not very good. Author A. Scott Berg summed them up in this language: "So impeachable were many of the other defense witnesses, it was often difficult to keep track of who was on trial." Even Hauptmann was so disturbed by the quality of Reilly's witnesses that he asked Lloyd Fisher, "Where are they getting these witnesses from? They're really hurting me."[35] Reilly's

---

[32] Russell B. Porter, "Café Man Swears Fisch at Cemetery; Five More Witnesses Fail to Appear," *NYT*, February 2, 1935.
[33] Transcript, 4272–4279.
[34] Transcript, 4087–4092.
[35] Berg, *Lindbergh*, 328.

summation cleared up the mystery of where he was getting the witnesses:

> [W]e sent an appeal out through the radio and through the news and in the theaters: "If there is any soul on God's earth that knows anything about this case, please come forward and tell us."[36]

There is nothing wrong with sending out a public plea for assistance in a criminal investigation, but in such a high profile case any potential witnesses answering the call require careful vetting to weed out the kooks and crazies. Apparently the only vetting Reilly did was to find out what the witnesses had to say and then put them on the stand. As soon as the witnesses were revealed to the prosecution, Wilentz put his army of investigators onto the task of digging up dirt on them, and in many cases they didn't have to dig deep at all. The other members of the defense team were appalled by Reilly's tactics, but he was lead counsel until such time as the Hauptmanns relieved him of command.

4c. ALIBI: November 26

Cecile Barr identified Hauptmann as the man who purchased a ticket from her to Lowe's Sheridan's Square theater on the evening of November, 26, 1933, using money that was found to be a ransom bill. Proving Hauptmann had passed that bill would not, by itself, prove he was the kidnapper, but it would impeach his story that he had not received the ransom money from Fisch until the next month. In an attempt to discredit

---

[36] Transcript, 4775.

Barr's testimony, Reilly asked Hauptmann if he remembered the 26th of November every year, and Hauptmann replied that it was his birthday. Reilly turned to November 26, 1933. Hauptmann said he had never been to that theater, although he had an idea of where it was. Hauptmann estimated the theater to be twelve to fifteen miles from his home. Reilly asked if he was ever in that territory in his life, and Hauptmann replied no. "So you couldn't, could you, have handed a bill to this woman?" "No, sir."[37] Reilly also asked Anna Hauptmann about November 26th, 1933, Hauptmann's last birthday as a free man. Anna said that on the evening of November 26th there had been a birthday party at her house. Also attending the party were Maria Mueller, her niece, Paul Vetterle, and Isidor Fisch.[38] November 26th had been a Sunday, and her young son Manfred had just been born on November 3rd. Maria Mueller was the godmother of Manfred Hauptmann.

Reilly called Maria Mueller[39] and asked if she remembered being at Anna Hauptmann's house on November 26, 1933. She said that when she arrived only Anna was there, but later Paul Vetterle, Hauptmann, and Isidor Fisch came. Paul Vetterle was from Mueller's hometown in Germany and had brought a present for Mueller's daughter from her mother. Vetterle had arrived about 3:30 p.m. and about four o'clock Hauptmann had arrived. Sometime after that Fisch had come. She said that she had left between 9:30 and 10:00 p.m. Hauptmann had not left the home while she was there. She left with Hauptmann, Vetterle and Fisch. Hauptmann would always take her home. Wilentz challenged Mueller on the

---

[37] Transcript, 2485.

[38] Transcript, 2920.

[39] The court reporters varied between spelling Mueller and Muller for this witness.

time she had come home, suggesting that her husband would say it was six o'clock and that they had had supper together. Mueller would not agree to that. Wilentz then challenged Mueller on who had been at the Hauptmann house that evening. Referring to her statement to the authorities, Wilentz said, "And then you were asked: 'Was there anybody up there?' And your answer was 'No'." Mueller contended that she had corrected that statement immediately.[40] Wilentz asked several questions about her recollection of the time she had left the Hauptmann house trying to show she was being very precise about it being 9:30 p.m. or after. Wilentz returned to an argumentative format. Asking about her saying 9:30 or after, Wilentz asked, "And that is after you have heard the story of Miss Cecilia Barr, that Hauptmann was down there around 9:30?"[41] To Wilentz it didn't matter what her answer would be, he had made this statement-argument to the jury.

Paul Vetterle told Reilly that he had known Anna Hauptmann all his life and that they had gone to school in the same school house. He remembered being at the Hauptmann home on November 26, 1933. He had arrived about three o'clock or half past three. Other people there were Anna, Hauptmann, Maria Mueller, and Isidor Fisch. They had spent the evening talking about Germany and how Maria's family was at home. Isidor Fisch arrived about seven o'clock. At ten o'clock Hauptmann had driven Vetterle, Mueller, and Fisch to the 225th Street station for the train. During cross-examination Wilentz asked an argumentative question. "As a matter of fact, Mrs. Muller [sic] and you all left about six o'clock, didn't you." Vetterle persisted that it was ten o'clock.[42] In order

---

[40] Transcript, 3507.
[41] Transcript, 3508–3509.
[42] Transcript, 3409.

to properly ask that question, Wilentz would have needed a good faith basis for believing that Vetterle and the others had left earlier than they testified, and when Vetterle denied leaving at 6:00, he should have been prepared to offer rebuttal testimony supporting his contention. Instead Wilentz released the witness without pursuing the departure time.[43]

The defense also tried to weaken Cecile Barr's testimony by offering witness Joseph T. Tartell, who testified he was a frequent patron of the Sheridan Square Theater where Barr worked. He testified that he knew her as the cashier at the window. Pope then attempted to offer testimony that Barr was unable to recognize Tartell when he had presented a $5.00 bill to her. Wilentz repeatedly objected to the questioning, and finally Pope withdrew Tartell as a witness.[44]

5. SCIENTIFIC EVIDENCE

As part of the attack on the investigation, the defense tried to overcome the forensic evidence presented by the prosecution experts. John M. Trendley attacked the handwriting evidence, Erastus Mead Hudson sought to weaken the fingerprint investigations, and the wood evidence was countered by Stanley Seal, Hugh Orr, Charles DeBisschop, and Ewald Miekle. Because Hudson's testimony was so closely allied with the next topic, we will deal with it there.

---

[43] Transcript, 3405–3410.
[44] Transcript, 3511–3519.

5a. The Ladder

Did Hauptmann construct the ladder found on the grounds of the estate the night of the abduction? The indictment did not allege that Hauptmann had used a ladder in the commission of the crime, but the prosecution case theory contended that Hauptmann built the ladder from supplies he had on hand and used it to enter the nursery on the second floor. There were a number of attacks open to the defense beginning with questioning whether the ladder was used at all. The evidence suggesting that a ladder was used included holes in the mud just below the nursery window which corresponded with the bottom rails of the ladder and "ladder marks" on the side of the home above the holes in the mud. There was mud found in the nursery at the window above where the holes and the ladder marks were found. There were several pieces of mud on the nursery floor leading away from or back to the window.

The defense could make a strong argument by pointing out the difficulty of entering and leaving the nursery window using the ladder, which had been built in three separate sections that would collapse and "nest" in the bottom section. The third section made the ladder too tall for the nursery window, but two sections put the top of the ladder thirty inches below it. A burglar would have to stand on the very top of the ladder to open the shutters and climb into the nursery. Leaving with the child, the burglar would have to climb out the window backwards and use his feet to feel for the top of the ladder while holding the child. Fisher asked Schwarzkopf about the ladder dimensions to emphasize these points for the jury.

When discovered on the grounds, the ladder had a fracture where the two bottom sections were joined. The prosecution theorized that the ladder cracked under the additional weight of the child being carried down. The defense countered that Hauptmann, a professional carpenter, would not have designed and constructed such a flimsy ladder. The defense could also argue that the kidnapper, carrying a thirty pound child and a forty pound ladder, would have left more footprints in the soft mud from the house to the place where the ladder was discovered.

The defense had to attack Arthur Koehler's integrity and his opinion that the ladder included one rail from Hauptmann's attic. Koehler also testified that the wood in the ladder bore tool marks identical to those made by a wood plane found among Hauptmann's tools. The defense would want to ignore that Koehler had testified twelve years earlier in the horrific "Christmas Bombing" murder case in Wisconsin[45] and a number of times in civil trials. They would want the jury to think that Koehler was a "novice" expert or that there was no such thing as a wood expert. During the prosecution case, Frederick A. Pope had tried to prevent Koehler from giving an opinion on the wood by objecting:

> We say that there is no such animal known among men as an expert on wood; that it is not a science that has been recognized by the courts; that it is not in a class with handwriting experts, with fingerprint experts or with ballistic experts. That has been reduced to a science by the courts. The witness probably may

---

[45] In this case John Magnuson stood charged with mailing a bomb to James A. Chapman which injured Chapman and killed his wife Clementine. "Professor Arthur Koehler of the United States Forestry Products Lab at Madison established the fact that the sawdust taken from the defendant's workbench was of white elm. This would not have been significant had not the defendant denied that he had ever worked in elm wood in his shop in his life. He admitted having worked on oak. Under the microscope it appeared that the sawdust came from hemlock, oak, and white elm. That part of the wooden covering of the bomb which remained was white elm." Magnuson v. State, 187 Wis. 122, 203 N.W. 749, 751 (1925).

> testify as an experienced carpenter or something like that, but when he attempts to qualify and express opinions as a wood expert, that is quite different.[46]

Pope called four witnesses to attack the wood evidence. Stanley Seal, a Flemington wood pattern maker, questioned whether the markings on wood could be identified because markings made by planes differ due to the angle at which the planes are held when they are used. To illustrate his point, Seal did some demonstrations using Hauptmann's plane. Under cross-examination by Wilentz, Seal admitted that the nicks made with Hauptmann's plane during the demonstration were the same when used at the same angle. "You can tell it is the same nick?" Seal answered, "Yes, you could tell it is the same nick."[47] Not content to leave well enough alone, Wilentz later undermined his point by asking, "In other words, you have used Mr. Hauptmann's plane and, in using it on your piece of lumber here, 61, after using it, each side which you used with Hauptmann's plane shows nicks from the plane, doesn't it?" Seal replied, "Shows nicks, but not alike."[48]

Pope next called Hugh Orr, a graduate of Massachusetts Institute of Technology. Orr said that he had testified previously in his area of expertise. Wilentz asked to question Orr on his expertise on plane markings on wood. Orr said that he had not testified on variations in grain, on weight or strength of lumber, or the study of defects in lumber. Orr conceded that his expertise lay in the field of architecture. When asked directly about whether he had ever made a study of marks made by particular tools on wood or lumber, he replied "No, sir."[49]

---

[46] Transcript, 2202.
[47] Transcript, 3926.
[48] Transcript, 3927.
[49] Transcript, 3930.

After the questioning by Wilentz, Judge Trenchard stated in the presence of the jury, "I don't think he has qualified."[50] After a few more questions, Trenchard said, "Well, Mr. Pope, you evidently undertook to qualify this gentleman as an expert and I think you have failed to do that."[51] Wilentz had essentially neutralized Orr.

Pope then called Charles J. DeBisschop, a general contractor, who built boats and wrecked houses. DeBisschop said that he had substantial experience matching up grains in wood. When Wilentz questioned him about his qualifications, DeBisschop said that he had matched grains in separate pieces of lumber for thirty years. He testified that he could look at two pieces of lumber and determine whether they once had been one piece. Because Koehler had said he identified the mill where the ladder lumber originated by the saw knife cuts, Wilentz asked DeBisschop whether he had ever done that. "I have not," he answered.[52] Trenchard asked Pope whether he thought DeBisschop had qualified as an expert. This question put Pope in an embarrassing position. Having previously said that there was no such animal as a wood expert, he was now offering DeBisschop as a wood expert. Pope temporized: "Well, that depends upon what you mean by 'as an expert.' I didn't think that even the State's great witness qualified as an expert."[53]

Pope said he called DeBisschop more as a practical or highly specialized technical expert. Trenchard permitted the jury to hear DeBisschop, leaving it up to them to determine how much weight they would give his testimony. On direct examination DeBisschop tried to undermine Koehler's testimony which tied Rail 16 to the

---

[50] Transcript, 3935.
[51] Transcript, 3937.
[52] Transcript, 3958.
[53] Transcript, 3961.

attic board by showing that they had identical growth rings. DeBisschop displayed two pieces of lumber that had come from two different buildings. One piece was forty-seven years old, the other was five to six years old. Despite the difference in the age of the two pieces, DeBisschop said the two pieces matched on the ends. DeBisschop repeated the demonstration with other lumber pieces. Pope then asked him about the comparison of the ladder rail and the attic board. DeBisschop testified that they were "an entirely different board."[54]

Under cross-examination by Wilentz, DeBisschop questioned the drawing Koehler had made showing how the grains on the ladder rail and the attic board would have met. He said that the drawing was made just to connect the pieces, not to truly illustrate the grain flow. DeBisschop also challenged that the two boards were originally one piece because of the placement of knots—testifying that the bottom of the tree, the butt cut, would have more knots than a piece from higher up the tree. DeBisschop said that a board nailed down to joists could not be removed without leaving marks every sixteen inches where it had been attached to the joists. The attic board did not have any such marks. However, under cross-examination by Wilentz, he conceded that the attic board could have been nailed down. "So far as you know, it had been nailed down to joists?" DeBisschop replied, "It might have been."[55] Wilentz challenged DeBisschop on his ability to determine whether a nail had been used previously. Producing a nail, Wilentz asked if DeBisschop could determine whether it had been used before. DeBisschop said that the nail had not been used previously. "Would you be surprised to learn that it had

---

[54] Transcript, 3978.
[55] Transcript, 4017.

been one nail taken from the attic board, S–226?" DeBisschop answered, "I would be awful surprised."[56]

Ewald Miekle, a millworker who had worked as a carpenter, testified as the final defense witness on the subject of the wood. After establishing the witness' familiarity with planes having nicks from usage, Pope asked about the ladder rail and the attic board. Wilentz objected to Miekle giving an opinion on this subject, but Trenchard was inclined to permit the question. Wilentz asked to test Miekle's expertise.

> **Q:** But you don't match the pieces for identity, to see whether or not the two pieces came from the same board originally?
>
> **A:** I wouldn't try it.
>
> **Q:** No, you wouldn't try it and you wouldn't try it because you haven't practiced that, have you, you haven't made any study or made any attempt to find out?
>
> **A:** Not technical.
>
> **Q:** Well, technical or otherwise, you have never tried to find out whether two pieces of wood, separated when they came to you, were ever at any one time the same board, have you?
>
> **A:** No, I have not.
>
> **Q:** Nor have you ever made any study or any practice of trying to ascertain whether or not two pieces of board, once disconnected, had ever come from the same tree?
>
> **A:** Never had occasion to.[57]

Koehler had testified that there was a piece missing from between the ladder rail and the attic board. Pressed on whether a match could be made if a piece between

---

[56] Transcript, 4022.
[57] Transcript, 4052.

them were missing, Mielke said he didn't think anybody could make such a match. Wilentz had now contrasted Mielke's lack of expertise compared to Koehler, and he ended his cross-examination. Pope tried to rehabilitate Mielke on the match questions, but Wilentz objected and Trenchard sustained the objection. Pope showed Mielke the ladder rail and the attic board and asked if they had been part of the same board. Mielke replied that they were not. Pope turned to the plane. Mielke said that the marks on the wood would depend on the angle at which the plane was held. Mielke then noted that one of the two boards was thinner than the other. Wilentz attempted to impeach Mielke using DeBisschop's testimony. Mielke testified that the attic board was from higher on the tree. "And, you didn't hear the last gentleman testify that that couldn't be so because it had more knots in it, and he numbered them—you were sitting here and heard that testimony, didn't you?" Mielke realized his dilemma. "I wouldn't want to go back to that testimony now and swear to it."[58] Wilentz then reaffirmed that Mielke had only examined the boards for five minutes, and ended his questioning. The defense had scored some points on the wood testimony, but Wilentz had also been able to challenge it on a number of points.

5b. The Handwriting

Albert S. Osborn, one of the leading questioned document examiners in the United States, had testified at the habeas corpus hearing in the Bronx that Hauptmann wrote the nursery note. The defense team needed to counter or neutralize that opinion by better impeachment

---

[58] Transcript, 4086.

or by producing their own experts. The questioned document examiners called by the prosecution had assisted the defense claim Hauptmann was not the author of the nursery note when they testified that the note looked like a disguised handwriting. On the other hand, the fact that the prosecution had secured some of the leading questioned document examiners in the country presented the defense with a problem.[59] They could not match these experts with witnesses of equal reputation despite Fisher's promise in opening statement that the defense would produce competent handwriting experts to show clearly that "there can't be any doubt in any of your minds that that is not the handwriting of Bruno Richard Hauptmann."[60] The defense only called John M. Trendley to the stand. Trendley said that he had testified as a questioned document examiner in nearly 400 trials including the Molineux murder as well as a number of other prominent trials.[61]

Assistant Attorney General Joseph Lanigan began a voir dire of Trendley's qualifications. "Mr. Trendley, you are an imitator of handwriting, are you not?" Trendley responded, "Yes, sir."[62] In the Rice case Trendley had produced nine fake signatures of William Marsh Rice in

---

[59] When John Magnuson was convicted in the December 17, 1922 bombing death of Clementine Chaptman in Wisconsin, where wood technician Arthur Koehler testified, there were also questions about handwriting on the bomb package. Three questioned document examiners including Albert S. Osborn and John F. Tyrrell testified. The effect of their testimony was noted by the Wisconsin Supreme Court, referring to them as "probably the three most eminent and reputable handwriting experts in the United States." Magnuson v. State, 187 Wis 203, N.W. 749, 751 (1925). The third Magnuson questioned document examiner, Jay F. Wood, did not testify in the Hauptmann trial.

[60] Transcript, 2385.

[61] Transcript, 3167.

[62] Transcript, 3168.

an attempt to show the handwriting experts could not tell the difference. Trendley admitted that his forgeries were not accepted as genuine. Trendley testified that he had been frequently mistaken in his opinions. "Oh, I have, yes, I don't claim to being an authority over everybody."[63] Lanigan continued his questioning by asking whether Trendley had ever testified to one opinion in the morning and then reversed himself on the afternoon of the same day. Trendley had no recollection of ever having done that.

> **Q:** All right. Now, let me refresh your recollection. I quote from the record of [Olmer against the Southern Manganese Company] and I ask you if in that case you were asked the following questions and made the following replies:
>
> > "**Q:** Now, Mr. Trendley, do you ever recall testifying in a case where you first gave one side an opinion that the signature was genuine and then without realizing it, you gave the other side an opinion that it was a forgery?
> >
> > "**A:** I do.
> >
> > "**Q:** Do you recall testifying in such a case as that?
> >
> > "**A:** Yes, sir.
> >
> > "**Q:** Have you ever done that more than once?
> >
> > "**A:** That is about all I remember. That was a case where I examined the paper in the Probate Courtroom on a dark rainy day and afterward I had a photographic copy taken of it in the light and I saw it, but I didn't testify that way. I didn't testify in that case.

---

[63] Transcript, 3170.

> "**Q:** You gave two different opinions about the same handwriting in the same case, is that right?
>
> "**A:** Yes.
>
> "**Q:** So you were not always certain about your opinion?
>
> "**A:** No, I can be mistaken."
>
> "**Q:** Is that correct?
>
> "**A:** That is right.[64]

Lanigan then asked about other instances where Trendley had changed his opinion during a trial. Trendley admitted that in another case he had testified without looking at the evidence, saying it was an unusual circumstance. Lanigan led Trendley through other testimony of his where he had changed his opinion on the witness stand and got him to say, "I shouldn't have answered a lot of things that the jury would take as my final word on it."[65] Lanigan then asked whether any of the State's handwriting experts had ever been deceived by Trendley's forgeries. Trendley said they had not. Lanigan then challenged Trendley as an expert in the Hauptmann case. Trenchard allowed Trendley to testify, saying his mistakes were up to the jury to decide; but the jury would hear Trendley's testimony against the backdrop of Lanigan's attack.

After Reilly reviewed Trendley's examination of the ransom correspondence, he asked Trendley if he had an opinion as to whether Hauptmann had written them. "In my opinion he did not," Trendley replied.[66] Instead of attacking all the handwriting evidence point by point,

---

[64] Transcript, 3170–3171.

[65] Transcript, 3184, citing the transcript in the Hugh W. Thomasson case from St. Louis.

[66] Transcript, 3200.

Reilly chose two aspects of the evidence to serve as proxies for all the evidence—the nursery note and the testimony of a single handwriting examiner—Albert S. Osborn. Reilly led Trendley through words and letters that were in the nursery note but which were not on Osborn's charts and demonstrative evidence. Osborn's charts had no "Dear Sir!," no capital *H* or *a-v-e*, no *5* followed by four *0*'s from the ransom demand, no "redy," no letter *y*, no dollar sign, no "in," no "bills," and none of the letters *A-f-t-e-r* from the word "After". Reilly's tactic was clever because the jury could easily see these things were missing from Osborn's charts. Reilly next attacked the photographs of the handwriting the State's experts used in their testimony. "Is it possible that the lines can be shortened or made longer by the use of the camera?" Trendley said, "Well, yes, they can distort it."[67] Trendley said that a different slant to the handwriting could be obtained by the way a negative was printed. Reilly and Lanigan had several testy exchanges over Trendley's testimony.

Under Lanigan's cross-examination Trendley admitted he had offered his services to the defense after only seeing reproductions of the handwriting in the newspapers and before he had seen the actual evidence. Trendley told Lanigan that he had not prepared any charts because the prosecution would not permit him free access to the handwriting evidence. Trendley asked Lanigan, "How could we when you wouldn't surrender nothing?"[68] Lanigan clearly demonstrated that Trendley had made only a cursory examination of the originals, but his examination also suggested that the state had unfairly denied Trendley adequate access to them. Trendley said he wouldn't accept any dictated handwriting made in a police station, referring to the compelled writings Hautpmann made.

---

[67] Transcript, 3209.
[68] Transcript, 3255.

Trendley testified that the nursery note and four lines of the second note had been written left-handed. Lanigan confronted Trendley with an apparent contradiction in his testimony as to whether he found certain words such as "gut," "Public," and "anything" distinctive. Having earlier said these were not distinctive, Trendley now said, "It stands out with the others" prompting Lanigan to ask, "Which answer do you want to stand now?"[69] Reilly asked a few questions on redirect examination and then released Trendley.

Reilly had tried to turn Osborn's strong, persuasive charts into a weakness. Now the jurors would view those charts knowing about all the words, letters, and markings that Osborn had left out of them. If the jurors had a reasonable doubt that Hauptmann had written that note, they might find that Hauptmann had not been the original abductor and was therefore not the one who caused the death of the Lindbergh child.

6. THE SHODDY POLICE INVESTIGATION

Despite their best efforts, the police found no fingerprints in the nursery or on the ladder. Leaving no stone unturned in their quest to develop evidence, they called on Dr. Erastus Mead Hudson. Dr. Hudson graduated from the College of Physicians and Surgeons in New York and had practiced medicine, but he became interested in fingerprint chemistry during his service in the Navy. Dr. Hudson had made a study of fingerprints, and he was familiar with a more advanced method than the one customarily used by the police. While the police usually developed fingerprints by using a powder that adheres to

---

[69] Transcript, 3269.

a waxy secretion in fingers, Hudson used a chemical process. Latent fingerprints contain sodium chloride. Silver nitrate will chemically combine with sodium chloride and change into silver chloride. When exposed to light, silver chloride darkens, bringing out the detail of the fingerprint. On March 13, 1932, almost two weeks after the kidnapping, Major Schoeffel of the New Jersey State Police had enlisted Dr. Hudson to assist in efforts to find fingerprints. Dr. Hudson first tried to develop fingerprints of the Lindbergh baby on toys and books he had played with at the house. After developing the child's fingerprints, Hudson turned his efforts to the ladder. Dr. Hudson, Trooper Frank Kelly, and Sergeant Kubler sprayed silver nitrate on the entire ladder and took it out into the bright sunlight. The effort proved both a success and a failure. Numerous latent prints were identified, but none belonging to Hauptmann. Dr. Hudson would not testify as a prosecution witness.

The defense called Dr. Hudson in an effort to show that the police botched the fingerprint investigation. Wilentz did not object when defense attorney Frederick A. Pope proffered Dr. Hudson as an expert. Wilentz would have looked foolish had he attempted to claim that a man recruited by the police to lift fingerprints wasn't an expert. Pope began Hudson's testimony by describing how Hudson's methods differed from the usual police methods and telling how he had been successful in lifting fingerprints from the ladder. Hudson said that after they had sprayed the ladder and exposed it to sunlight "fingerprints began to come out all over the ladder."[70] He estimated that at least 500 prints and print fragments developed on the ladder. He said that the ladder was very clean, and from his examination of it one could expect fingerprints to be obtained at least six months to a year

[70] Transcript, 3792.

after they were placed on the ladder. Pope asked what opinion Hudson would have if Hauptmann's fingerprints were not found on the ladder that the State contended Hauptmann had built. Hudson answered that there would be fingerprints on the ladder from each time the maker touched or moved it. He also said that if the maker had worn gloves each time the ladder was touched, there would be no fingerprints. Wilentz, realizing that Hudson's testimony could raise doubts, attempted several technical objections to the questions Pope was asking. Judge Trenchard permitted the questions.

Hudson and Kelly had made detailed measurements of the ladder, and Pope directed him to ladder Rail 16. Hudson said that he recalled only one nail hole in Rail 16 when he examined it, but his notes did not have any mention of nail holes in the rail. Hudson's testimony about the nail holes seemingly assisted the defense contention that the ladder's integrity had been compromised.[71] As it turned out, the defense had planted the seeds of Hudson's destruction when they broached the subject of nail holes in Rail 16. On cross Wilentz challenged Hudson's testimony concerning the nail hole. Hudson appeared to become evasive in his answers, somewhat frustrating Wilentz. When shown a ladder rail, Hudson said he didn't remember the nail holes. Wilentz persisted and presented Hudson with Rail 16. He pointed out one nail hole in Rail 16, and Hudson identified it as the nail hole he saw. Wilentz then pointed out two more nail holes in Rail 16. "No, sir; that nail hole wasn't there. Those two holes were not there when I saw the ladder."[72] Wilentz showed Hudson a photograph of Rail 16 (State's

---

[71] Arthur Koehler had testified about the four nail holes in Rail 16 and how they aligned with the holes in the joists in Hauptmann's attic. Transcript, 2211.

[72] Transcript, 3826–3827.

Exhibit S–294 for identification) and had him recognize nail holes in it. Wilentz then asked Hudson whether he would be mistaken about his testimony about the one hole if the photograph had been made in March, 1932. Hudson replied that under that premise he would say yes. Hudson then retreated from this answer saying that police reports about the rail from 1932 would not change his testimony. Under further questioning from Wilentz, Hudson became evasive again. He told Wilentz that he had no idea what the photograph S–294 depicted, and he would not state that the rail in the photograph had discoloration from the silver nitrate solution. He would not directly answer Wilentz' questions.[73]

Wilentz then showed Hudson a photograph of the ladder which Hudson admitted had some discoloration or pattern on the wood. Hudson admitted that the earlier photograph of the ladder did not show discoloration. Wilentz was trying to get Hudson to concede that photographs showing the nail holes in Rail 16 had to have been taken before Hudson applied silver nitrate to the rail. After the silver nitrate was applied, the discoloration would remain on the wood for a long time; so if photographs showed the nail holes in an unstained Rail 16, Hudson's recollection of the single nail hole would be wrong. As Hudson left the stand, Wilentz asked if he had written Lloyd Fisher a letter of congratulations on the course of the trial. Hudson answered, "Not in reference to this trial."[74]

In rebuttal Wilentz called Corporal George G. Wilton of the New Jersey State Police to testify that he photographed Rail 16 before Dr. Hudson had finger-printed the ladder, and that Rail 16 had four nail holes in it. Wilentz offered the photographs into evidence as

[73] Transcript, 3833–3840.

[74] Transcript, 3875.

Exhibits S–264 and S–265. [75] Harold S. Betts, an employee of the U.S. Forestry Service, also testified that he examined the ladder before Dr. Hudson treated it with silver nitrate. When he saw the ladder, Betts recorded in his notes the fact that he saw four nail holes in Rail 16.[76]

During the prosecution case, the defense had tried to raise reasonable doubt by attacking the integrity of the investigation of the murder. Lloyd Fisher had promised the jury in his opening statement that the defense would show that no case in history was as badly handled as this case. The defense called law enforcement officers Thomas H. Sisk, Russell H. Snook, John E. Keykora, E. Paul Sjostrom, Louis Kubler, Frank A. Kelly, and H. Norman Schwarzkopf in an attempt to show weaknesses in the investigation. Snook told Fisher that he couldn't say he had exchanged fingerprint information with Dr. Hudson, but he thought that some of the prints on the ladder could have been identified. Sjostrom told Fisher 68 photographs of fingerprints or marks were given to him. He could not identify any of the prints as belonging to Hauptmann. Kubler testified that he eventually found 120–125 fingerprints on the ladder and that he didn't know that Hudson was told there were over 500 prints found. Kelly testified he attempted to get fingerprints from markings on the window, but he was not successful. He did not recall discussing nail holes in the ladder with Dr. Hudson. Keykora had tried to locate the ransom money box at St. Raymond's Cemetery without success. Reilly asked him if Dr. Condon had been examined by psychiatrists.[77] Keykora could not answer that. Schwarzkopf recounted the demonstration with a duplicate ladder which broke under a weight of 180 pounds. The child

---

[75] Transcript, 4110–4121.
[76] Transcript, 4122–4128.
[77] Reilly used the antiquated term "alienist" instead of "psychiatrist."

weighed thirty pounds, suggesting the abductor weighed about 150 pounds. In all this law enforcement testimony the defense had really only established that the police had not used Dr. Hudson more in the investigation and that the officers differed on whether Hudson had demonstrated the silver nitrate process on the actual ladder or a separate piece of wood.

7. REASONABLE DOUBTS

The defense of reasonable doubt is available in every criminal case in American courts. The key word is "reasonable." Every jury in a criminal case receives instructions from the judge on how to go about deliberations. Some states define "reasonable doubt" for juries, but some do not. Both prosecutors and defense attorneys can make the job of the jurors more difficult by using words other than "reasonable" in their arguments to those jurors. Defense attorneys may argue that the prosecution's case "doesn't add up" or "doesn't make sense," but those terms are not found in the jury instructions. Prosecutors may argue "we've proved this case" without going on to explain why that proof takes the jury beyond a reasonable doubt. The juries are then left to decide in their own minds whether they have any doubts; whether those doubts are reasonable; and whether those doubts exist about a material element in the case. On the issue of reasonable doubt, Justice Trenchard instructed the jury that:

> Reasonable doubt is a term often used, probably pretty well understood, but not easily defined. It is not a mere possible doubt, because everything relating to human affairs and depending on moral evidence is open to some possible or imaginary doubt. It is that state of the

> case which, after the entire comparison and consideration of all the evidence, leaves the minds of the jurors in that condition that they cannot say that they feel an abiding conviction to a moral certainty, a certainty that convinces and directs the understanding and satisfies the reason and judgment of those who are bound to act conscientiously upon it.[78]

The prosecution alleged, and therefore had to prove beyond a reasonable doubt, that the crime occurred in Hunterdon County. Only the courts in the county where the crime occurred have authority to conduct the trial. The Mercer County line was just a few hundred feet behind the Lindbergh house. If the jurors were not sure the death occurred during the actual abduction from the nursery, they may have doubts that it occurred before the baby crossed the Mercer County line to the place where the body of the child was later found. If they were not convinced beyond a reasonable doubt that the death of the child occurred in Hunterdon County, they would have to acquit Hauptmann. With this in mind, the defense wanted to clearly establish the proximity of the county line so they could argue these doubts in summation.

Was the decomposing body of a child found in the woods off Mt. Rose Road actually that of the Lindbergh baby? The prosecution alleged that Hauptmann murdered Charles A. Lindbergh, Jr. and therefore would have to prove beyond a reasonable doubt the body was that of the Lindbergh baby. This particular issue would be a tough one for the defense because Anne Morrow Lindbergh, the child's mother, testified to the identity of the baby by connecting the garments found on the body to the child. Further identification of the body came from the father, Charles Lindbergh, a national hero and Bessie Gow, the

---

[78] Transcript, 4499.

child's nursemaid. Charles E. Willamson had testified the face of the body looked like the child. He testified that while the body was dark, the hair was light and curly. There were crime scene photographs of the body of the child, but the defense did not want the jury to see those photographs because the gruesome depictions of the body of the child could inflame the jurors and prejudice them against Hauptmann. If the defense hotly contested the issue of identity, the photographs might become "necessary"[79] to prove the identity. In addition, the defense did not want any witness to dwell on the condition of the body—i.e., that it was badly decomposed and partially eaten by animals. Lindbergh had identified his son on the second day of the trial, and Bessie Gow had identified the body as the Lindbergh baby on the fourth day of the trial. Wilentz sought to put to rest any question of the identification of the Lindbergh child by calling Dr. Charles H. Mitchell to the stand on the twelfth day of the trial, January 17. Mitchell testified that he had compared the body to an ante-mortem photograph of the Lindbergh baby and said that he was very much impressed that it was the same child. During cross-examination of Dr. Mitchell, Reilly did not pursue the issue of identity, instead focusing on the cause of death. The State had alleged murder, and Reilly wanted to question that. Later on the 17th, Wilentz responded to rumors that the body may have been a child from the nearby St. Michael's Orphanage by calling Elmira Dormer, the custodian of the orphanage, to show no

---

[79] "[G]ruesome photographs will often be excluded because the required showing of unusual probitiveness cannot be made. This is because there is no legitimate need for the gruesome photographs of a homicide victim's corpse that the prosecutors usually seek to introduce." One of the factors used to determine whether the photographs were necessary for the jurors is whether the facts are disputed by the defendant. State v. Lafferty, 749 P.2d 1239 (Utah, 1988).

children were missing. Dormer testified that when the Lindbergh child had been abducted on March 1 and when the body had been found on May 12, all of her children were accounted for at the orphanage. Wilentz asked Dormer, "Are these books the books of attendance of your school?" Dormer replied, "Yes, sir." Wilentz then turned to the defense.

> **WILENTZ:** if there is any dispute about the attendance I will offer them. If there isn't, I won't.
> **REILLY:** There is no dispute.
> **WILENTZ:** There is no claim that the child came from the orphanage?
> **POPE:** No.
> **WILENTZ:** Am I to understand that there is no claim that this child came from the orphanage?
> **FISHER:** I thought your proposition was if we didn't dispute the attendance you would not offer them.
> **WILENTZ:** If there is any claim about it, I will offer them.
> **REILLY:** I will say now that there has never been any claim but that this was Colonel Lindbergh's child that was found there. However, I am glad you brought the lady here because I want to ask her a couple of questions about the terrain.[80]

Reilly's statement went beyond the acknowledgement that no child was missing from the orphanage. He conceded that the body was the Lindbergh child—something the State had to prove beyond a reasonable doubt before the jury could convict Hauptmann. His concession on identity caused a stir in the defense camp. Author Anthony Scaduto wrote that Fisher, after hearing Reilly's concession, "[S]hot up straight now and shouted at Reilly, 'You are conceding Hauptmann to the electric

---

[80] Transcript, 1580.

chair.'"[81] The transcript does not reflect any such comment by Fisher during this moment of the trial. The *New York Times* reported that Fisher got up and stormed out of the courtroom when Reilly made the announcement, but it said nothing about Fisher shouting as he did so. As the *Times* reported:

> [I]t was learned that Reilly is not getting on well with his associates. According to friends of the other attorneys, they have all been considerably disappointed by the manner in which Reilly has been conducting the case. The concession of the identity of the baby was a disputed point of procedure among defense counsel and Mr. Fisher is reported to have told Mr. Reilly "You're conceding this man to the electric chair."[82]

Although Fisher had better judgment than to say such a thing in the hearing of the jury, he had no qualms about letting the media know how he felt: "We have neglected to take advantage of the most important point in the defense case." The defense team was evenly split over this particular ploy, with Rosecrans approving the maneuver but Pope and Fisher opposing it.[83] On this issue, it seems that Reilly and Rosecrans had sound tactical reasons for conceding identity. The jury had heard Lindbergh, Bessie Gow, and Dr. Mitchell identify the body as the Lindbergh child. They had seen unique circumstantial evidence in the size of the homemade undershirt and the silk thread used in making it when Anne Morrow Lindbergh identified the shirt as her child's. Now there was no dispute about children missing

---

[81] Anthony Scaduto, *Scapegoat: The Lonesome Death of Bruno Richard Hauptmann* (G. P. Putnam's Sons: New York 1976), pp. 149–50.
[82] "Defense in a Rift on Reilly Methods," *NYT*, January 18, 1935.
[83] "Body Found Near Hopewell Is Not Lindbergh Baby?" *Associated Press, Sarasota Herald-Tribune*, February 21, 1935, page 5.

from the orphanage near where the body was found. If the defense continued to contest the issue of identity, Wilentz could recall Anne Morrow Lindbergh, have her face the photographs of the mutilated body of the child, and identify it as her son. Reilly did not want the jury to be haunted by the image of Anne Morrow Lindbergh breaking down on the witness stand as she identified photographs of the decomposed, animal-ravaged body of her son. Justice Trenchard would instruct the jury that they should not permit sympathy and prejudice to enter their deliberations, but they would find it difficult to do so after seeing the image of the grief-stricken mother identifying the decomposed body of her son.

The defense had to test the reasonableness of the prosecution theory that Hauptmann knew where to go and when to go to the Lindbergh house to commit the crime. They emphasized Hauptmann's unfamiliarity with the Lindbergh house and the family routine. Their task was made easier because the baby's cold caused the Lindberghs to alter their routine. How could Hauptmann have known about this unless he had inside information? The necessity for Hauptmann to have inside information worked two ways for the defense. First, what is the reasonableness of an insider reaching out to a German carpenter a good distance away to commit the crime of the century? Second, how could the insider notify Hauptmann, who had no telephone, about the abrupt change of routine? Reilly asked Elsie Whateley whether she had heard the child cry out. She had not. Reilly then established that the child was familiar with her, Bessie Gow, Anne Morrow Lindbergh, Lindbergh, and Whateley's husband. He was setting up the following argument: (1) If a stranger had entered the nursery, the child would have been startled and would have called out. (2) He did not call out. (3) No member of the staff would have startled the child. (4) A member of the staff removed the child from the room. Reilly was a master of innuendo—

phrasing his questions to make suggestions that he could later use as a basis for arguing reasonable doubt.

Reilly asked Mrs. Whateley if Violet Sharpe had ever mentioned George Payne or whether Whateley's husband had ever mentioned Payne. He asked if an insurance man had ever visited the house. Whateley said no. Reilly had her say that her husband had been out of her sight for some time. Reilly asked Bessie Gow about living in Detroit, wanting to suggest that the notorious Purple Gang had been involved in the crime. Gow admitted to Reilly that she had told people that the Lindberghs would be staying at their home beyond the weekend before the abduction. Reilly asked about the phone call Gow had received the evening of March 1 from Englewood, New Jersey. In an argumentative question Reilly asked, "Don't you know it was from Hopewell?"[84] Reilly returned to the child being comfortable enough with the household staff to not cry out if one of them had gone in his room. "The child was not accustomed to strangers, was it?" Gow answered, "No, not strangers."[85] Reilly wanted to show that Hauptmann could not have known where the nursery was. "It wasn't generally known where the baby nursery was, was it?" Gow replied it was not.[86] How could Hauptmann have known where the nursery was in the house? How did he know when to enter the nursery? There was no outcry by the child during the abduction. Did the child know and trust the person who took him from his crib? Did the dog not bark because there was no "stranger" in the house? Wilentz asked Elsie Whateley if the dog had barked that night between 7:30 and 10 o'clock, and she said no, saying the dog had been at the far end of the house in her sitting room in his basket. Bessie Gow told Reilly that anything

---

[84] Transcript, 303.
[85] Transcript, 309.
[86] Transcript, 312.

Mr. or Mrs. Whateley did would not excite the dog. She said that the dog would bark when strangers came to the house. Reilly could now argue that there were no strangers in the house that night because the dog didn't bark. Through skillful questioning Reilly had suggested that either Mr. Whateley had abducted the child or someone inside had assisted the kidnapper.

8. OTHER SUSPECTS

If Hauptmann was in New York when the crime occurred, then who committed the kidnapping? The defense had no legal obligation to answer this question, but as a practical matter it would help the alibi defense if they could. They tried to do just that by offering a number of witnesses who testified that they saw suspicious activities and people at the time of the abduction. While some of these witnesses contradicted each other in their accounts of who appeared to be involved in the abduction, the jury heard a number of witnesses talking about someone other than Hauptmann being involved in the crime or suspicious activity.

The defense produced three separate witnesses to tell the jury that on March 1, 1932, they had seen cars with ladders either in the passenger compartment or attached on the outside, one very near the Lindbergh estate and two near Princeton. None of these cars could be connected with Richard Hauptmann. It might have been a coincidence that the two Princeton witnesses saw cars with ladders, but the car seen by the third witness was not only very close to the scene of the crime, it was also close in time to the abduction.

Lou Harding and William Brevoort Bolmer were working near Princeton on March 1st when they saw cars with ladders. Harding was constructing a sidewalk, and

Bolmer was operating a gas station. Harding testified that between 2:30 and 3:00 o'clock in the afternoon in Princeton, a dark blue suburban type car with two men pulled up behind him and asked directions to the Lindbergh estate. While explaining how to get to the estate, Harding stood at the passenger window and noticed that the rear seats in the suburban had been removed. On the floorboard he could see a seven to eight foot ladder partially covered by a three foot pasteboard box. Harding testified that upon learning of the abduction the next day he immediately reported what he had seen and was taken to the Lindbergh estate where he saw the same ladder leaning up against the side of the house. Reilly then showed Harding the ladder which had finally made its way into evidence.

> **Q:** I show you the State's Exhibit S–211, the ladder. Was the ladder that you saw in the car on the Princeton Road that afternoon of March 1st, 1932, a ladder of that description?
>
> **A:** It was something kind of like that....
>
> **Q:** Your best recollection is that it was a ladder of this description?
>
> **A:** Yes. Something about like that.[87]

Wilentz asked Harding whom he had spoken to at the Lindbergh estate, but Harding could not remember. Wilentz asked a few questions about Harding's work history. "Have you ever been convicted of a crime?" Harding replied, "Yeah."[88] Harding admitted to being convicted of assault and battery in 1931. While it is permissible for attorneys to use prior convictions of certain crimes to impeach the credibility of a witness, the

---

[87] Transcript, 3137.
[88] Transcript, 3142.

attorneys are not usually permitted to go into the details of the convictions. Wilentz pursued Harding on his conviction. "On a woman?" Wilentz asked. "No," Harding answered.[89] Wilentz then got Harding to admit he had been convicted of a second offense. Wilentz returned to Harding's having been at the Lindbergh estate. When asked again whom he had spoken to, Harding identified an officer seated in court; it was Sergeant Kelly of the New Jersey State Police. Wilentz then asked argumentatively, "Don't you know, as a matter of fact, that Sergeant Kelly never spent one minute on the Lindbergh case?"[90] Wilentz returned to Harding's description of the ladder he had seen in the car. Harding stated that he couldn't tell anything about the ladder, just that it was a ladder. The more Wilentz questioned Harding about the ladder, the more certain Harding became in his testimony. Harding finally estimated the ladder he had seen in the car was eight to ten feet long—longer than the ladder sections at the Lindbergh estate. There is an old maxim about cross-examination: "When you strike oil, stop boring." Wilentz did not stop boring. His continued questioning about the length of the ladder caused Harding to retreat from his estimate of length. "I wouldn't swear definitely to how long the ladder was."[91] While he could argue the credibility of Harding's testimony, Wilentz had lost the advantage of the earlier estimate of the ladder's length.

In rebuttal Wilentz called Patrolman William Konietzko of the Princeton Township Police. Konietzko testified that he was the officer who dealt with Harding, and that Harding had never said anything about the two men in the car having a ladder. On cross-examination

---

[89] Transcript, 3142.

[90] Transcript, 3149. This was not Frank A. Kelly who had been part of the investigation.

[91] Transcript, 3160.

Reilly established that Konietzko was completely dependent upon his memory of what Harding said because he wrote no report. Reilly also got Konietzko to admit that his memory was only "fair."[92]

Under the questioning of Frederick A. Pope, William Brevoort Bolmer testified that he was a 1914 graduate of Princeton in Civil Engineering, and that in 1932 he operated a service station at the corner of the road from Hopewell to New Brunswick and the road from Somerville to Princeton. Pope drew Bolmer's attention to the latter part of February, 1932, and asked if anyone had come to his service station that caused him to take particular notice of them. Bolmer said he had seen a dark green Ford Model A coupe. He testified that the Ford had been to his station three or four times previously. He testified that the last time he had seen the car was about 1:15 a.m. on March 1, 1932, when he noticed a poor looking ladder attached to the car. "It took me quite a while to know that it was a ladder," Bolmer said.[93] When asked to describe the ladder to the jury, Bolmer said the jury could easily see what he had seen if they looked at the ladder in the courtroom, adding, "I saw that ladder."[94] Bolmer said he could see the ladder from the lights on the gas pumps, and he could see that a man and a woman were in the car. When asked if Hauptmann was the man, Bolmer said positively not. Bolmer tried to describe the man in the car, but Wilentz objected. Judge Trenchard permitted the testimony. Bolmer described the man he had seen as having dark hair and smooth faced. Pope showed Bolmer a photograph, Defendant's Exhibit 39, and asked Bolmer to compare the person in that

---

[92] Transcript, 4201–4202.
[93] Transcript, 4036.
[94] Transcript, 4036.

photograph with the man seen at the service station.[95] He could not identify D–39, and he said he would not be able to identify the woman in the car.

Wilentz asked if Bolmer had reported what he saw to the New Jersey authorities, and Bolmer replied that he had not. On redirect examination, Bolmer told Pope that he had not reported it because the ladder he saw in the news accounts was extended and the ladder he had seen on the car was nested. At the time he didn't think it was the same ladder. Now, having seen the ladder in court, he said it was the same ladder. Wilentz would have to re-cross Bolmer. Wilentz asked if the ladder he had seen on the car was a sectional ladder, and Bolmer answered that it was a sectional ladder, nested with three sides slid together. Wilentz pressed Bolmer on sectional ladders, prompting the following exchange:

> **A.** You can't tangle me up.
>
> **Q.** You are a little too anxious.
>
> **A.** I am willing to tell the truth.
>
> **MR. POPE:** I object to the Prosecutor scolding the witness.
>
> **THE COURT:** [speaking to the witness] I have already cautioned you that when there is an objection you are to keep quiet and be kind enough not to be so free with your talk.
>
> **THE WITNESS:** Yes, sir.
>
> **THE COURT:** Simply answer the questions. Now you understand that, don't you?
>
> **THE WITNESS:** May I ask, tell you something, sir?

---

[95] The list of exhibits in the official trial transcript at page 4684 does not reflect a D–39 either for identification or admitted into evidence. Reilly had shown D–39 to Hans Kloppenburg who could not identify the person in the photograph. Transcript, 3359. There appears to be no record of who or what was shown in D–39.

THE COURT: No, not unless counsel see fit to have you do so.[96]

This exchange did nothing to enhance Bolmer's credibility with the jury. Wilentz concluded his cross-examination by highlighting the discrepancies between Bolmer's testimony and Lou Harding's: Bolmer saw a man and a woman; Harding saw two men. Bolmer saw a Model A Ford; Harding saw a Dodge. Bolmer's Model A had the ladder tied to the side; Harding's Dodge had the ladder in the back seat.

Sebastian Lupica could testify that he saw a man with a ladder at the entrance to Lindbergh's estate. He could also say the man was not Hauptmann, but he would have to admit that the man looked like Hauptmann. Both the prosecution and defense realized that Lupica's testimony was a two-edged sword. If called for the state, Lupica could give testimony helpful to the prosecution case theory, but he was adamant that the man he had seen near the Lindbergh estate on March 1 was not Hauptmann. If called by the defense, Lupica would say the man he had seen was not Hauptmann, but he could be forced to admit that he had said that the man looked like Hauptmann. Wilentz elected not to call Lupica as a state witness, preferring to cross-examine him. Admissions wrung from Lupica as he testified for the defense would be more persuasive than weak assertions made by Lupica testifying as a prosecution witness. The defense gambled that calling Lupica would help them more than it hurt.

Fisher conducted the direct examination of Lupica. The Lupica family lived about a mile north of the Lindbergh estate. Lupica attended the Princeton Preparatory School and had to pass the Lindbergh estate gate on his way home from school. Fisher quickly established that

---

[96] Transcript, 4046–4047.

the prosecution had used Lupica before the Grand Jury and had subpoenaed him for the Hauptmann trial. Lupica testified that on the way home from school on the evening of March 1, he had stopped at his mail box, which was at the Lindbergh gate house. While reading his mail, he noticed a car come around the bend on the wrong side of the road and park at the entrance to a corn field. Lupica told Fisher that the road there was wide enough for the car to have passed him on the correct side. Lupica then pulled up the road and passed the car on the driver's right side. He said that as he passed the car, he noticed two sections of a ladder lying across the front seat of the car, extending from the windshield onto the rear glass. Lupica said the ladder was the nearest thing to him in the other car. Fisher asked if he had gotten a look at the driver. Lupica said that the driver was a man with a dark coat on, wearing a black, dark fedora hat, and was 35–40 years old. He characterized the driver as having thin features. Lupica had gone to the Lindbergh estate the next day to report what he had seen. At the estate Lupica saw three sections of a ladder, not two; but the ladder sections at the estate were "strikingly the ladders that [he] had seen the night before."[97]

Lupica told the police that he had seen the man the afternoon before between 5:30 and 6:00 o'clock. He had not known the type of car the man was driving until the police drove him around to look at cars. He picked out a green 1929 Dodge but he testified that the car he had seen was black or dark blue. Lupica would later tell the police that the car had a New Jersey tag with an "L" representing Mercer County. Lupica had given an interview to the *Daily Mirror* which reported that he had identified the driver as Hauptmann. Lupica said the *Mirror* had misquoted him, and he had written a letter to the city editor asking for a correction. Lupica testified that he had

[97] Transcript, 3339.

told no one he could definitely recognize Hauptmann as the man he had seen in the car and went on to say that he could not identify Hauptmann as the driver. Lupica told Fisher that Captain Lamb of the NJSP told him he would not be called for the State because they had other witnesses who were more positive.

Under cross-examination by Wilentz, Lupica admitted he had seen photographs of Hauptmann's Dodge in the newspapers. He said Hauptmann's Dodge was not a 1929. He admitted his glance at the ladder was fleeting because he had not seen it until he was passing the car. He told Wilentz that he had been paid for the two news articles, adding that the articles were not his statement. Wilentz noted that the article in the *Daily Mirror* said it was by Ben Lupica, and Lupica agreed.

> **Q.** And the very first sentence was, was it not, "I saw Bruno Richard Hauptmann for an instant in the courtroom"—that's the second one. Let me give you the first one first ... "Bruno Richard Hauptmann is the same man that I saw at the foot of the lane leading to the Lindbergh home only a few hours before poor little baby Lindbergh was killed and murdered," that's what appeared in that article?
>
> **A.** That is right.[98]

Wilentz read on in the article about the car being a black Dodge sedan that had a ladder inside the car, and Lupica agreed. Wilentz then reminded Lupica that he, Wilentz, had asked him what he meant by saying in the article that he had identified Hauptmann when he couldn't tell the police he remembered positively. Lupica remembered that. Wasn't Lupica warned not to give any

---

[98] Transcript, 3351.

further statements to the newspapers? Lupica answered yes. Lupica was reminded further that if his statement was merely that the man he saw that night resembled Hauptmann, that was all the Attorney General would permit him to say. Again Lupica agreed. Wilentz was poised to make his persuasive point.

> **Q:** Yes. And you said then, did you not, to the Attorney General in the presence of Prosecutor Hauck and five or six other people that the man you saw in the court room in the Bronx, Hauptmann, that the man you saw on the night of March the 1st resembled Hauptmann?
>
> **A:** That Mr. Hauptmann has a resemblance to him.
>
> **Q:** Yes. Didn't you say so?
>
> **A:** (No answer.)
>
> **Q:** And you have always said that he resembled Hauptmann, haven't you?
>
> **A:** Yes, it is the truth.
>
> **Q:** And you say so today, don't you, Ben?
>
> **A:** Yes.[99]
>
> . . .
>
> **Q:** You told everybody in the world that the man you saw on March the 1st in an automobile with a ladder on it looked like Hauptmann, isn't that right?
>
> **A:** He has a resemblance, yes.[100]

Knowing how valuable this testimony would be against Hauptmann, Wilentz closed his questioning of Lupica saying, "I am very much obliged to you, sir."[101]

Fisher saw the damage Lupica had done to the defense case, perhaps recalling that he had told the jury in

---

[99] Transcript, 3352–3353.
[100] Transcript, 3353.
[101] Transcript, 3353.

the defense opening statement that the defense would produce the man who has always been considered by the State Police of New Jersey to have been the last man and the only man to actually see the kidnapper. Would the jury think that Lupica had actually seen Hauptmann? The car and the man were very near the Lindbergh gate on the evening of the abduction. He had described the car and the man in detail, front, inside, and back of the car. He had closely observed the radiator on the front of the car and the lack of trunk and the one spare tire on the rear. He described the man driving and the hat and clothing he was wearing. He noticed the tag and one letter of the tag number. The car was similar to the car Hauptmann owned at the time. Fisher would have to question Lupica about his vantage point to maximize the exculpatory information (things that didn't match Hauptmann or the car) while minimizing the inculpatory information (things that did match Hauptmann and the car.) In Lupica's case, he had seen a man park a car about 50 yards ahead of him on the wrong side of the road facing him. As Lupica drove toward that car to pass it on the driver's right hand side, he could observe the car, the man, and as he passed he could see the ladder inside. Fifty yards is 150 feet. When Lupica started driving toward the Dodge, he would only have a few seconds to see the car, the man, the inside and rear of the car.

If either side emphasized Lupica's fleeting vantage point, they would not only weaken Lupica's unfavorable testimony, they would also weaken his favorable testimony. Neither Fisher nor Wilentz wanted a detailed analysis of Lupica's vantage point. They both got what they wanted. For Wilentz, Lupica always said the driver resembled Hauptmann, who owned a dark blue Dodge

DD Sedan manufactured in late 1930.[102] Lupica put the man who resembled Hauptmann at the Lindbergh gate on March 1 with a ladder in the car just hours before the abduction. For Fisher, Lupica denied that the man he had seen was Hauptmann and asserted that the car was a 1929 model with New Jersey tags. Lupica placed the man who wasn't Hauptmann in the same place at the Lindbergh gate. It would be up to the jury to decide whether Lupica had weakened or strengthened the evidence of Hauptmann's identity as the kidnapper.

The defense called Peter H. Sommer in an attempt to show that the abduction was an "inside job" and that Hauptmann wasn't involved. They wanted to cast suspicion on Violet Sharpe and Isidor Fisch. Sharpe would be a rich target for the defense because she had become distraught under repeated police interrogation and had committed suicide rather than be interviewed again. Sommer identified himself as a fingerprint expert working with the Building Management & Supply Division, Department of Public Welfare, New York City. In the early evening of March 1, 1932, he was in Fairview, New Jersey, giving fingerprinting instruction to police officer William Ackerman. Going home after the training, Sommer took the 42nd Ferry. In the trolley on the way to the ferry, Sommer saw two men sitting directly in front of him, one about 5'9" and the other 5'4". The trolley arrived at the ferry between midnight and 12:30. Reilly showed Sommer a photograph which had been marked for identification as Exhibit D–5. Sommer said he had seen the man in the photograph on the ferry boat. Reilly had originally showed D–5 to Bessie Gow who did not recognize anyone in the

[102] Order for Dodge Brothers Motor Vehicle from Williamsbridge Motors, Inc., 3510 White Plains Avenue, Bronx, NY, March 3, 1931, signed by Richard Hauptmann.

photograph.[103] No one on the defense team ever identified who was in D–5, so when Sommer recognized the man from the ferry, that man's identity was never revealed and the exhibit was never placed into evidence.

Sommer told Reilly that when the ferry boat reached New York, the man he recognized and another man assisted a lady with a baby onto a trolley. The woman was very nervous. Reilly showed Sommer Exhibit D–7 for identification, and Sommer said the woman in the photograph strongly resembled the nervous woman he had seen. It is not clear what Reilly showed Sommer as D–7, since the official index of exhibits describes Exhibit D–7 for identification as "Sheet of standard handwriting of Dr. Condon made on cross-examination."[104] Sommer described the baby as about two years old, blond, and dressed in a one piece nighty. Sommer said he had reported what he had seen to the police the next day, and he had been accompanied to the police station by Joseph Dutt and Carl Joerg.

After listening to an opposing witness testify, the trial lawyer must consider what cross-examination questions would assist the case, advance the case theory, or whether to even cross-examine at all. Sommer had said that the woman depicted in the photograph D–7 resembled the nervous woman he had seen with the baby "very strongly," but that woman was never identified and the jury was never shown that photograph. Sommer said that he had seen the man in photograph D–5 on the ferry boat, but the man was never identified and that photograph was never shown to the jury. He had described the baby as being blond and about two years old. For that to have been the Lindbergh baby, its killers would have to have taken the body of the child back to New Jersey from New

---

[103] Transcript, 329.
[104] Transcript, 4683.

York to deposit it where it was found. Sommer had not been shown Exhibit S–6, the ante-mortem photograph of the Lindbergh child to see if it resembled the baby he had seen. Had Sommer's testimony been that damaging to the State's case against Hauptmann? If so, wouldn't a surgical cross-examination on just these points have been the better decision? Wilentz thought otherwise. Sommer's testimony covers sixty-two pages of transcript, most of which was cross-examination.

Wilentz, no doubt, did not believe Sommer. However, a lengthy, detailed cross-examination could make the jurors believe that Sommer was more important than he had really been—more damaging to the State's case than it appeared. The Attorney General's strategy, of course, was to string the testimony of Sommer out to the end of the day, which was a Friday, so that his army of detectives would have the entire weekend to investigate Sommer. In this instance, however, the investigation failed to turn up any really damaging evidence. On cross-examination, Wilentz asked Sommer why he had not reported what he had seen after Hauptmann had been arrested. Sommer admitted he had not told Fawcett what he had seen, had not told anyone during the habeas corpus hearing in the Bronx, and had not told anyone after Hauptmann arrived in New Jersey for trial. Wilentz handed Sommer Exhibit D–33, a photograph of Fisch, for identification, but Sommer said the photograph was too blurred to recognize anyone. He would not give an opinion. Wilentz then handed Sommer another photograph and asked, "How about this one: is this too blurred?" Sommer answered, "No, that is a pretty good picture."[105] Sommer would not identify the man in the second photograph either. Wilentz asked that the photograph be marked for identification, and the court

---

[105] Transcript, 3283.

reporter designated it as S–287. The Index of Exhibits for the trial reflects that S–287 for identification was "Photograph shown to witness Peter H. Sommer on cross-examination"[106] but does not identify anyone in the photograph. Sommer told Wilentz that he had seen photographs of the woman in the newspapers about a year after the crime but certainly before the trial began. He had seen photographs of the man before January 1, 1934, in a newspaper. Wilentz then locked him down on the time when he had seen the photographs—that it was before January 1, 1934. Wilentz then asked, "Why, don't you know that the picture of that man never appeared in any newspaper in this world until after September, 1934?"[107] Having made such an assertion, Wilentz was obliged to offer some proof that the photo had never appeared in a paper before September, 1934. He offered no such proof.

By the time Sommer was released from the witness stand, the jury was well familiar with his story, perhaps to the point of giving it more credibility. Wilentz had even established that Sommer had testified for the prosecution in the Hall-Mills case, a notorious murder case which occurred just a short distance from Flemington and was certainly familiar to the jurors. Wilentz raised issues about Sommer being a "professional witness" who had received money for his testimony rather than for what he knew. Sommer conceded an inconsistency on dates in testimony in other cases, and it may have appeared that he had changed testimony in order to receive his expenses. Pope objected. Trenchard asked Wilentz if he was examining Sommer on a collateral matter—proving Sommer made inconsistent statements in another case. Wilentz admitted it was collateral, and Trenchard

---

[106] Transcript, 4682.
[107] Transcript, 3329.

reminded Wilentz that he could not impeach Sommer on collateral matters. Wilentz then began to re-hash the testimony about the man and the woman, and finally Sommer was excused. The weekend investigation had turned up only a minor inconsistency, and it was so minor that Trenchard ruled it inadmissible. In this particular instance, Wilentz would have done better to conduct a brief cross-examination.

The defense called Joseph Dutt and Carl Herman Joerg to testify that they accompanied Sommer to speak with the police on March 2, corroborating Sommer's testimony. Their testimony didn't corroborate what Sommer had seen on March 1, only that he had gone to the police on March 2. This corroboration technique was popular with the defense team.

Anna Bonesteel took the stand to give testimony which would further arouse suspicion about Violet Sharpe and her possible connection to the crime. Bonesteel operated a restaurant in Yonkers at the ferry. She said that she knew Sharpe about two or three months and had seen her and some other women about an hour or so on the evening of March 1. Sharpe left the restaurant between 8:30 and 8:45 p.m. and ran to a car about 200 feet from the restaurant. On cross-examination Bonesteel admitted she had not seen a baby and actually knew the women with Sharpe better than she knew Sharpe. Although Bonesteel's testimony placed Sharpe in New York on the evening of the abduction, it put her in Bonesteel's restaurant at the approximate time that the abduction was occurring in New Jersey.

Violet Sharpe, a servant at the Englewood residence of Anne Morrow Lindbergh's mother, had been a major distraction from the outset of the investigation, engaging in behavior that clearly indicated she had something to hide. Because she told conflicting stories concerning her whereabouts on the night of the kidnapping, investigators jumped to the conclusion that she was hiding her involvement in the kidnapping and acted accordingly. The police interrogated her repeatedly, with each interrogation more intense than the last. Sharpe became more and more distraught as the interrogations continued until she became hysterical under questioning. A physician was summoned and he put a stop to the interrogation. Sharpe was determined to never be questioned again, but the police were just as determined to continue to apply pressure to her. On June 10, 1932, Inspector Harry Walsh of the NJSP arrived at the Morrow residence to take her to his office for further questioning. When she was told that Walsh wanted to question her again, Sharpe again became distraught and ran upstairs to a closet and retrieved a container of silver polish containing cyanide. She drank the polish and died.

Violet's guilty secret turned out to be something that would not raise an eyebrow today, but it would ruin a young lady's reputation in that day and age. She had gone to a roadhouse with a young man she had just met. In order to dispel any suspicions in the minds of the jury, Wilentz had to air Sharpe's dirty laundry in rebuttal. Ernest Miller, testified that at 8:00 p.m. on the night of the kidnapping he met Sharpe at the Morrow residence and took her to the Peanut Grill. They spent the evening at the roadhouse and Miller took her back to Englewood, getting her to the Morrow residence between 10:30 and 11:00 p.m. It had been a double date, and the couple who went to the Grill with Miller and Sharpe also testified. George Marshall, the night watchman at the Morrow residence testified that Sharpe left the residence around 8:30 p.m. and returned around 11:00 p.m.

The final witness for the prosecution was Elizabeth Morrow, the grandmother, who testified that Sharpe served her supper at 7:00 p.m. Sharpe then left the residence and returned at approximately 11:00 p.m. Trial advocacy manuals teach that a forensic presentation should have a strong beginning and a strong ending.[108] Starting the case with the testimony of Charles Lindbergh, the most famous man in America, had given Wilentz a strong witness to begin his case. The defense attack on Violet Sharpe gave him an opportunity to use another strong witness to end his case—Lindbergh's mother-in-law Elizabeth Morrow, the grandmother of the victim and the widow of a United States Senator.

---

[108] See, e.g., Ronald Clark, George R. Dekle Sr., and William S. Bailey, *Cross-Examination Handbook: Persuasion, Strategies, and Techniques* (Frederick MD: Wolters-Kluwer, 2014), 70–72.

8

Summing Up the Case

In Chapter 3, we outlined fifteen things the prosecution needed to prove in order to get a conviction:

(1) That the victim was Charles A. Lindbergh, Jr.
(2) That the victim was dead.
(3) That the death resulted from the criminal agency of another human being—Justice Trenchard characterized the criminal agency as a "felonious stroke."[1]
(4) That the crime occurred on March 1, 1932.
(5) That the killing occurred in Hunterdon County, New Jersey.
(6) That the killer was engaged in the commission of a common law burglary when he caused the death of the victim.

In order to prove the commission of a common law burglary, the prosecution had to prove that the killer

(7) broke and entered
(8) the dwelling of Charles A. Lindbergh, Sr.
(9) at night
(10) with intent to commit petit larceny of the child's sleeping suit.

---

[1] Transcript, 4499, 4500.

The prosecution had to prove intent to commit petit larceny by proving that the killer actually committed petit larceny, which means that he would also have to prove that the killer:

(11) took, stole, and carried away
(12) the property of another
(13) of some value
(14) with intent to permanently deprive the owner of the property.

Finally, the prosecution would have to prove that

(15) Bruno Richard Hauptmann was the killer.

The defense readily admitted the first four elements, but they contested almost everything else. The two most troublesome elements were (5) that the killing occurred in Hunterdon County, New Jersey, and (15) that Bruno Richard Hauptmann was the killer. The fact that the body was found in a neighboring county gave rise to a presumption that the killing occurred in that county.[2] In order to combat the presumption, Wilentz put great stress on the broken ladder and the fact that the death was "instantaneous."[3] If the baby died instantaneously after falling from the ladder on the side of the Lindbergh home, then the death certainly occurred in Hunterdon County. Because the jury likely would be unsympathetic to such a technical defense, Wilentz could anticipate that he would not need to give overwhelming evidence that the killing occurred in Hunterdon County.

The central fact in issue was element (15), the identity of the killer, and the prosecution had to build their

---

[2] Transcript, 4502.
[3] Transcript, 4337.

summations to insure that the jury would decide that issue in their favor. The first task in devising a summation is deciding what specific arguments to make. The prosecution identified and made at least 40 arguments supporting the proposition that Hauptmann was the killer. Below is a list of those arguments followed by the trial transcript page number where the arguments were first voiced. Arguments which were first made during Wilentz's rebuttal final argument are in brackets. The arguments have been arbitrarily grouped according to their nature, and they have been abbreviated to simply state the initial fact from which a chain of inferences could be argued to the conclusion that Hauptmann was the killer.

Eyewitness Testimony Linking Hauptmann to the Killing

1. Millard Whited saw Hauptmann near the Lindbergh residence. 4341.
2. Charles Rossiter saw Hauptmann near the Lindbergh residence. 4341–4342.
3. Amandus Hochmuth saw Hauptmann near the Lindbergh residence. 4347.
4. Benjamin Lupica saw a man fitting Hauptmann's description near the Lindbergh residence. 4347–4348.
5. John Condon identified Hauptmann as the man who received the ransom. 4349.
6. Charles Lindbergh identified Hauptmann as the man who received the ransom. 4349.
7. Hildegarde Olga Alexander saw Hauptmann tailing John Condon. 4348.
8. Joe Perrone identified Hauptmann as the man who gave him a ransom note for Condon. 4349.
9. Cecile Barr took a five dollar ransom bill from Hauptmann. 4353.

10. Walter Lyle took a $10 ransom bill from Hauptmann. 4352.

Handwriting Evidence Linking Hauptmann to the Killing

11. The nursery note was written by the same person who wrote the ransom correspondence. 4345–4346.
12. Hauptmann wrote the nursery note. 4345–4346.
13. Hauptmann wrote the ransom correspondence. 4345–4346.
14. Hauptmann's first ransom letter and the nursery note were written on the same piece of paper torn in two. 4346.
15. Hauptmann's first ransom letter to Lindbergh mentioned the nursery note's instructions not to call the police and mentioned its $50,000 ransom demand. 4345–4346.
16. Hauptmann's ransom correspondence bore the same symbol as the nursery note. 4345–4346.
17. Hauptmann's ransom letter to Colonel Breckinridge mentioned the nursery note's instructions not to call the police and mentioned its $50,000 ransom demand. 4345–4346.
18. Paper of the type used in the ransom correspondence was found in Hauptmann's home. 4455.

Financial Evidence Linking Hauptmann to the Killing

19. Hauptmann had approximately $50,000 in unexplained wealth after the ransom. 4351.
20. Hauptmann spent money extravagantly after the ransom delivery. 4353.

21. Hauptmann lost money heavily in the stock market after the ransom delivery. 4353.
22. Hauptmann had over $14,000 of ransom money when he got arrested. 4350.
23. Hauptmann had a $20 ransom bill in his pocket when he got arrested. 4352.
24. Hauptmann admitted to passing 12–15 ransom bills. 4424.
25. No ransom bill was ever recovered after Hauptmann's arrest. 4424.

Scientific Evidence Linking Hauptmann to the Killing

26. Rail 16 of the ladder came from Hauptmann's attic. 4343–4344.
27. Rails 12 & 13 of the ladder came from the Bronx lumberyard where Hauptmann worked. 4342–4343.
28. Hauptmann's plane was used to plane the ladder. 4394.
29. Two of Hauptmann's saws made cuts the width of the saw cuts in the ladder. 4345.
30. Hauptmann was missing a chisel of the size and type found at the Lindbergh home. 4344.
31. Hauptmann's missing chisel was the size of the chisel that cut the notches in the ladder. 4344–4345.

Things Hauptmann Did Which Indicate his Guilt

32. Hauptmann wrote John Condon's address and phone number on a board in his closet. 4348.

33. Hauptmann lived in the Bronx, near the two cemeteries and the lumber yard. 4350.
34. Hauptmann lied repeatedly about the ransom money in his possession. 4352.
35. Hauptmann quit his job shortly after ransom delivery. 4351.
36. Hauptmann had the sleeping suit worn by little Charles on the night of the kidnapping. 4347.
37. [Hauptmann knew the baby was dead before they discovered the body ("Will I burn?")]. 4388.
38. Hauptmann tried to disguise his handwriting after his arrest. 4353.
39. Hauptmann was limping shortly after the kidnapping. 4348.
40. [In Germany Hauptmann broke into a home by crawling through a window]. 4367.

Deciding what to say is just the beginning of the process. Next they must decide how to arrange their arguments so as to have the maximum persuasive effect. Since ancient times trial lawyers schooled in the methods of Classical rhetoric have used a standard format for the arrangement of their arguments,[4] and it appears that the prosecution used that format insofar as possible in a modern courtroom. The six parts of a Classical forensic speech are:

1. The Introduction, in which the speaker attempts to render the audience attentive, receptive, and well-disposed.[5]
2. The Statement of Facts, giving a narration of the facts of the case which is lucid, brief, and worthy of belief.[6]

---

[4] *Rhetorica ad Herennium*, I:iii:4.
[5] *Ibid*, I:iii:6.
[6] *Ibid*, I:ix:14.

3. The Division, in which the speaker identifies what the parties agree upon and where they disagree and establishes the main issues.[7]
4. The Confirmation, where the jury is told why they should resolve the main issues in the prosecution's favor.
5. The Refutation, where the opponent's arguments are answered.[8]
6. The Conclusion, where the speaker sums up the arguments and ends the speech.[9]

In Hauptmann's case, the prosecution made two summations to the jury and the defense made one. The prosecution opened the summation, then the defense summed up, and the prosecution made a rebuttal summation. In such a case the structure of the summation naturally divides itself into two parts, with the prosecution giving the Introduction, Statement of Facts, Division, and Confirmation in the first summation and saving the Refutation and Conclusion for the rebuttal. Anthony M. Hauck, Jr., the Prosecutor of the Pleas in Hunterdon County, gave an opening summation, which closely followed the Classical format.

His Introduction, some 231 words in length, divided into three parts. He began by thanking the jurors for their service and congratulating them on their patience. This is a common way for trial lawyers to begin their argument to a jury. By such an opening they hope to ingratiate themselves to the jury and render the jurors attentive, receptive, and well-disposed. The second portion of Hauck's Introduction, a brief description of the procedure for the making of summations, is also a common component of the Introduction used by many modern lawyers. In the final part of his Introduction, he explained how Wilentz became

---

[7] *Ibid*, I:x:17.
[8] *Ibid*, I:x:18.
[9] *Ibid*, I:xxx:47.

involved in the case. He said that he had called on the Attorney General for assistance in the prosecution because of the limited resources of his office.[10]

Hauck's Statement of Facts consumed 1,713 words, succinctly laying out the facts of the case.[11] The Division, consisting of 783 words, dealt with the three most troublesome issues in the case—whether the prosecution had proved the crime occurred in Hunterdon County, whether the prosecution had proved a burglary, and whether the prosecution had proved that Bruno Richard Hauptmann was the killer. Hauck concluded his Division by identifying the most important issue: "Now, you might say to me—and I will say to you, Bruno Richard Hauptmann, who sits in this very court room, did all of these things. We have proved conclusively and overwhelmingly that he has done these things."[12] In the Confirmation, Hauck gave 35 of the 40 arguments listed above.[13] After making his arguments, Hauck concluded his summation by explaining that Reilly would speak second and Wilentz would close for the state. He then appealed to them to do their duty in the case and ended his remarks by saying, "Remember, we are not required to have a picture of this man coming down the ladder with the Lindbergh baby; but we have shown you conclusively, overwhelmingly, beyond a reasonable doubt, that Bruno Richard Hauptmann is guilty of the murder of Charles A. Lindbergh, Jr. Thank you."[14] Hauck's summation lasted a mere 45 minutes.[15]

---

[10] Transcript, 4331–4332.
[11] Transcript, 4332–4338.
[12] Transcript, 4341.
[13] Transcript, 4341–4353.
[14] Transcript, 4354.
[15] Transcript, 4687; Matthew 7:1 (KJV); Russell B. Porter, "Reilly Accuses Servants, Charges Police Frame–up in His Final Plea to the Jury," *NYT*, February 12, 1935.

The Confirmation formed the heart and soul of Hauck's summation. Here was where he made the arguments showing that Hauptmann indeed killed the Lindbergh baby. For best effect, the arguments should be arranged in some sort of logical order. Hauck could have arranged his arguments chronologically or topically. He could have either followed the chronology of the events as they unfolded in real time during the investigation of the case, or he could have followed the chronology of the actual presentation of the evidence at trial. He could have arranged the arguments under an assortment of topics. One set of possible topics has been used to arrange the arguments at the beginning of the chapter. Hauck's argument roughly followed the chronology of the presentation of the prosecution's evidence. The *New York Times* printed his entire summation with captions inserted to show its structure. Combining the *Times* captions with the parts of a Classical speech, we have the following outline:[16]

- I. Introduction
- II. Statement of Facts
    - a. Corpus delicti
    - b. Discovery of kidnapping
    - c. Manner of the kidnapping
    - d. Death of child in fall from ladder
- III. Division
    - a. Proof that murder occurred in Hunterdon County
    - b. Proof of burglary
    - c. Proof of identity
- IV. Confirmation
    - a. Koehler's examination of the ladder
    - b. Linking the ladder to the attic

---

[16] "Hauptmann's Guilt Overwhelmingly Proved, Declares Hauck for Prosecution," *NYT*, February 12, 1935.

c. The ransom correspondence
d. The handwriting evidence
e. Helpful admissions from defense witnesses
f. Condon's testimony
g. Hauptmann's sudden wealth
h. Hauptmann's arrest
i. Hauptmann's speculation in the stock market

V. Conclusion

Hauck did a workmanlike job of arguing the case. His style was not flashy, but the content and structure of his argument showed him to be a capable prosecutor who delivered a clear, concise, and credible presentation. Often when a prosecution team presents a case, they divide the opening and closing summation between the best teacher, who speaks first, and the best motivator, who speaks last. The first prosecutor gives the opening summation assuming a professorial air, outlining the evidence and arguments in a matter-of-fact fashion. The second prosecutor gives the closing summation as though making an altar call at a tent revival. This is exactly how Wilentz and Hauck did their summations.

If we were to fault Hauck's performance, we would have to say that his presentation was a little too matter-of-fact, and he could have arranged his arguments more persuasively. With the right arrangement of his arguments, he could have used both verbal and visual techniques to drive home his points. One of the most powerful rhetorical tools is the tricolon, a three part presentation which renders arguments vivid, memorable, and persuasive.[17] Tricolons are more powerful if they either rhyme or alliterate, as demonstrated by Julius Cae-

---

[17] Richard A. Lantham, *A Handlist of Rhetorical Terms*, 2nd ed. (Berkley: University of California Press, 1991), 154.

sar's letter to the Roman Senate announcing his victory over King Pharnaces II of Pontus—*veni, vidi, vici* (I came, I saw, I conquered). The suggested opening statement set out in Chapter 4 made use of two alliterative tricolons, either of which could have served as headings under which to arrange the arguments. The first tricolon was "kidnapper, killer, conman," and the second was "ladder, letters, and loot." Using the second tricolon as a framework for his points, Hauck could have structured his Confirmation somewhat like this:

> Ladies and gentlemen, the evidence of Hauptmann's guilt falls into three categories—Ladder, Letters, and Loot. Hauptman built the ladder and used it to kidnap and kill little Charles Lindbergh, He conned the Lindberghs with the ransom letters, and he wound up with all the loot.
> Let's first look at how the Ladder proves Hauptmann's guilt. …
> Now let's look at the Letters. …
> Finally, what does the Loot tell us? …

Under the Ladder, Hauck could have started with Amandus Hochmuth, who saw Hauptmann with the ladder at the entrance to the Lindbergh estate. With Hochmuth, he could have discussed the other witnesses who put Hauptmann in the vicinity. Then he could close out the Ladder segment with a discussion of Koehler's findings. In the Letters section he could argue the evidence of the ransom correspondence, the handwriting examinations, Condon's testimony, and the evidence of the board in the closet bearing Condon's address and phone number. The Loot section would contain the arguments arising from the tracing of the ransom money, the discovery of the money in Hauptmann's garage, his sudden wealth, extravagant spending, and adventures on the stock market. Some arguments might not readily fit under one of the three sections, but with a little effort they can be shoehorned into one section or the other. When he got to the end of his summation, Hauck could then have used a visual aid to summarize and drive home his points. He could have made his points much more memorable with something as simple as a flip chart with three pages each containing a bullet pointed list of arguments under the headings of Ladder, Letters, and Loot.

Writers on rhetoric have long recognized that human beings are persuaded by three types of appeals: to logic, to character, and to emotion. Aristotle described these three appeals with the tricolon *logos*, *ethos*, and *pathos*.[18] In his summation Hauck appealed heavily to logic, for the most part ignoring appeals to character and emotion. In a case like the kidnapping and killing of a baby belonging to a beloved American icon, there is little need to voice appeals to character and emotion. Simply stating the facts of the case without elaboration is sufficient to conjure up a strong appeal to these latter two elements. Hauck had done a good job but not a great one. The next day Reilly would have his opportunity to argue to the jury.

Defense attorney Reilly delivered his closing summation on the thirtieth day of the trial, arguing for four hours without notes.[19] Author P. J. O'Brien characterized Reilly's start of the summation as "his usual Bible-quoting, flag-waving routine."[20] Reilly's summation, like any good speech, required a strong beginning to seize the attention of the jurors; a middle where he would clearly outline the points of his argument; and a strong finish where he would appeal for the desired verdict in the case.

---

[18] Edward P.J. Corbett and Robert J. Connors, *Classical Rhetoric for the Modern Student* (New York: Oxford University Press, 1999), 32.

[19] Russell B. Porter, "Reilly Accuses Servants, Charges Police Fame–up In His Final Plea To Jury," *NYT*, February 12, 1935.

[20] O'Brien, *The Lindberghs*, 266.

He would need to avoid Lloyd Fisher's mistakes in the defense opening statement of talking in the arcane terms of the indictment and referring to legal pleadings such as bills of particulars.

A good summation has a theme, and Reilly's theme was "David Harum horse sense." This theme should have resonated with the jury because it was a reference to a popular novel by Edward Noyes Westcott[21] which had recently been made into a Will Rogers movie. Horse sense was Reilly's term for the ordinary common sense which jurors are allowed to use in their deliberations. To strengthen his argument, Reilly would need to stress that common sense could lead to reasonable doubts and reasonable doubts should lead to an acquittal, but he often neglected to make that important connection for the jurors. Although the law limits appeals to emotion in criminal trials, Reilly understood that he would have to depend on emotion because the jury had the power to sentence his client to death.

Reasonable doubt is the focus of criminal defense summations, and that was the key to Reilly's argument. He argued three topics in an attempt to raise reasonable doubt: (1) The extreme severity of the punishment called for extreme care. (2) The possibility that others were guilty gave rise to a reasonable doubt. (3) The quality of proof was insufficient to erase all reasonable doubt. We will label these topics (1) The Finality of Punishment; (2) The Fiendish Plot; and (3) The Failure of Proof. Reilly made several arguments supporting each topic: Under Finality of Punishment he argued (a) the forbidding of judgment by the Bible, (b) the fear of wrongful judgment, and (c) the fact of wrongful judgment. Under the Fiendish Plot topic, Reilly spun a conspiracy theory which accused

---

[21] Edward Noyes Westcott, *David Harum: A Story of American Life* (New York: D. Appleton and Company, 1899).

disloyal servants, key witnesses, unavailable suspects, and unknown suspects. Under Failure of Proof he argued: (a) The authorities were both incompetent and corrupt—We will call this argument "The Bungled Investigation." (b) The eyewitness identifications were either mistakes or lies—"The Unbelievable Witnesses." (c) The expert witnesses were incompetent and untrustworthy—"The Bad Experts." (d) The prosecution theory required Hauptmann to be both an evil genius and a bungling incompetent—"Both Mastermind and Fool?" (e) The state could prove neither cause of death nor venue—"The Botched Proof."

The lack of notes to support his argument led to a disjointed argument filled with unnecessary repetitions, and his jumping back and forth among his points weakened his delivery. We will attempt to bring order to the chaos of Reilly's disjointed argument by bringing all his arguments on a single topic together. The result may not make a stronger argument for Hauptmann's acquittal than Reilly actually delivered to the jury, but it should make a more coherent one.

The Finality of Judgment

The Forbidding of Judgment

Reilly began his argument by attempting to engage the feelings of the jurors. Deciding Hauptmann's fate would be an emotional one during deliberations, and Reilly had to play upon that emotion.

> I believe in approaching this case that I do it with a great feeling of responsibility. I wish to give you a text from St. Matthew: "Judge not lest ye be judged," and ask of you in the consideration of this case that you

> bring into your hearts and into your consciences the feeling that you are weighing that which you cannot give back, if you take away—life.[22]

In modern American criminal practice trial lawyers cannot make religious references. The jurors must decide the case on the law and the evidence, and they cannot allow feelings of sympathy or religious beliefs to affect their decisions. The lawyers should not argue in any way to divert the jurors from following their oaths to rely solely on the law and the evidence. Reilly would later employ a similar diversion when he argued that the State's experts were being paid with New Jersey tax money.[23] While trying to fan the flame of possible emotion in one direction, Reilly tried to extinguish the effect of any possible emotion in another by arguing that the jury should not be influenced or distracted by any public sentiment against Hauptmann.

> But the State stands here and says, "Kill Hauptmann. Close the pages. Let everybody else sink into oblivion and security. Kill the German carpenter."[24]

Reilly told the jurors they would have to put aside any feelings about Hauptmann's nationality and would have to follow the Constitution, the laws, justice, and decency. Reilly told them that the public sentiment created a problem for Hauptmann upon his arrest—the burden of guilt had shifted to him, and he would have to prove his innocence. In light of what Fisher had said in the opening statement, Reilly seemingly endorsed Fisher's assuming the burden of proving Hauptmann innocent. Reilly talked about the mobs wanting

---

[22] Transcript, 4687.
[23] Transcript, 4722.
[24] Transcript, 4715.

Hauptmann killed, as mobs have done for two thousand years in hysteria and afterwards discovered that the person killed by the mob vengeance wasn't guilty at all. These remarks provide a segue into the next argument we will consider.

The Fear of Wrongful Judgment

It is relatively common in criminal cases, especially heinous crimes, for attorneys to argue that the crime was atrocious, but it would be equally atrocious for an innocent person to be convicted. During the trial Reilly had conceded the identity of the body as that of Charles Lindbergh, Jr. Reilly's concession of the baby's identity allowed him to make that argument.

> So I say at the very beginning that this is the crime of the century and it is the worst crime and the lowest type of crime ever committed, to my knowledge, or according to any of the books I have read. But it is not the defendant who is guilty of it.[25]

Reilly's decision to characterize the case as the "crime of the century" and "the worst crime and the lowest type of crime ever committed" proved to be a blunder when the case was appealed. Wilentz followed Reilly's argument with a fiery argument including statements of his personal beliefs about Hauptmann's guilt, statements that the New Jersey Court of Errors and Appeals described as "vituperative characterizations of the defendant, given his guilt," and intimations that the jury would be guilty of a crime in failing to convict. However, the New Jersey court reasoned that because

[25] Transcript, 4690–4691.

Reilly had begun his argument by saying "this is the crime of the century" and because Reilly had offered his own personal beliefs in Hauptmann's innocence, he had invited the Attorney General's comments. Since Wilentz was responding to an argument made by Reilly, they refused the defense plea to overturn the guilty verdict.[26]

Reilly praised the Lindberghs and their fine home in Hopewell and added that the jury could not be swept off its feet because the Lindberghs were involved if there was no evidence. "But Bruno Richard Hauptmann never drove a nail in that house; Bruno Richard Hauptmann was never on those grounds; Bruno Richard Hauptmann was never standing on any road near Princeton, nor did any man, no matter who he was, see him standing on any road February 17th, 18th and 19th."[27] Hauck had told the jury that the State was not required to produce a photograph of Hauptmann coming down the ladder, but Reilly argued they were entitled to more than that to sentence Hauptmann to death on circumstantial evidence.

> What you and I want is somebody who is going to come in here and say, "I saw Hauptmann do something; I saw Hauptmann do something in connection with the murder,"—not having possession of ransom money or other money that New York County or Bronx County is interested in.[28]

---

[26] State v. Hauptmann, 115 N.J.L. 412, 180 A. 809 (Ct.Err. & App., 1935).
[27] Transcript, 4691.
[28] Transcript, 4717.

The Fact of Wrongful Judgment

Reilly cautioned the jury about sentencing Hauptmann to death on circumstantial evidence, telling them "Circumstantial evidence is no evidence."[29] Circumstantial evidence is good evidence and often used in criminal cases, but as Justice Trenchard would later tell the jury, "In order to justify the conviction of the defendant upon circumstantial evidence, it is necessary not only that all of the circumstances concur to show that he committed the crime charged, but that they are inconsistent with any other rational conclusion."[30] Reilly needed the jury to believe that the circumstantial evidence failed to rule out the rational conclusion "We might be making a mistake." He attempted to weaken the circumstantial evidence by referring to a specific case the jurors would recognize.

> You can't bring back life. You can't pay back a debt after a man has gone to prison for life by saying, "Well, I made an honest mistake." Many a respected citizen of this county has been placed on trial, wrongfully. Right in this courtroom 19 years ago in the Wyckoff case, the prosecutor then cried to heaven for the blood of a man, tried before this very distinguished jurist who is now on the Bench, I believe, and defended by Judge Large, who is part of the prosecution—circumstantial evidence, they cried for the blood of that man, they cried for the blood of that man.[31]

Wilentz objected to Reilly's reference, and Trenchard sustained the objection as not being part of the evidence, but Reilly had gotten his point before the jury. William H. Wyckoff had stood trial in Flemington in February,

---

[29] Transcript, 4715.
[30] Transcript, 4512.
[31] Transcript, 4715–4716.

1916, for the murder of his uncle Richard J. Wyckoff and the uncle's housekeeper, Catharine Ann Fisher. Wyckoff was acquitted, and in December, 1916, William McLoughlin and Montford Udell, alias Charles M. Hawkins, stood trial in the same courthouse for those murders. The prosecution had called the wrong man a murderer, and the right people turned up later. The jurors would be familiar with the Wyckoff case, which even received coverage in The *New York Times*.[32] Some of them may have even known the wrongly accused man.

The Fiendish Plot

Good trial lawyers often analyze their cases by asking, "If this is true, what else must be true?" Reilly used this technique in preparing his disloyal servant defense. If it is true that only a very few people knew that the Lindberghs had changed their plans and chose to remain in Hopewell the night of March 1, then it must also be true that (1) Hauptmann did not know the Lindberghs were in Hopewell on the night of the kidnapping, and (2) Hauptmann could not have committed the kidnapping. It must also be true that (3) if the kidnapper was one of the very few people who knew where the Lindberghs were, and (4) if the servants were among those very few people, then (5) the servants must have committed the kidnapping. Of course, this conspiracy theory ignores the possibility that the kidnapper just guessed correctly; or that the kidnapper had done surveillance prior to the crime. The argument targeted improbabilities in the prosecution case theory and also tried to avoid the impact of the ladder evidence.

---

[32] "Wyckoff Murder Trial On," *NYT*, December 17, 1916.

> Colonel Lindbergh was stabbed in the back by the disloyalty of those who worked for him, and despite the fact that he courageously believes that there was no disloyalty in the servants' quarters, I say now that no one could get into that house unless the information was supplied by those who worked for Colonel Lindbergh.[33]

Reilly ridiculed the language of the kidnap note that "We have planned this for a year." The kidnapping could not have been planned for a year because the Lindberghs had just begun moving into their new home in Hopewell and did not normally spend Monday and Tuesday nights there. Reilly argued that no one in the world knew about the change of plans to keep the child there Tuesday night except Lindbergh, Anne Morrow Lindbergh, the Whateleys, Betty Gow, and Red Johnson. Reilly contrasted them with Hauptmann, who was away in the Bronx without a phone, and could not possibly have known this change of plans. Reilly then broadened the ring of knowledge to suggest that the Morrow staff may have learned of the change of plans.[34] Of course, he had one particular Morrow employee in mind—Violet Sharpe, whom he described as sophisticated and worldly. Reilly directly connected Sharpe to the conspiracy, blaming her suicide on her participation in the crime. "She didn't do it because she feared she would lose her job. She did it because the woman from Yonkers, Mrs. Bonesteel, told the truth. [Sharpe] was at the ferry with a blanket and she was at 42nd Street with a child and that child was the Colonel's child."[35] Reilly also stated directly that the butler Whateley did not die of natural causes. "The man that was there with the dog, the man that had charge of the ground floor, he is stricken while

---

[33] Transcript, 4694.
[34] Transcript, 4696.
[35] Transcript, 4748–4749.

his wife is off to Europe—dead in two days. Sharpe—'bring her downstairs; I want to ask her something.'—Dead."[36] Reilly jumped in and out of the conspiracy argument, and this argument format probably took a toll on juror retention.

Oliver Whateley and Violet Sharpe were convenient targets because they were dead, but Reilly also took aim at a more dangerous target. "Now, the Colonel can have all the confidence in the world he pleases in Betty Gow. I have none."[37] Reilly was treading on thin ice by including Gow. The jury may have found her to be credible—even likeable, and they may now discount Reilly's argument. Reilly's personal lack of confidence in Gow was irrelevant. It is how the jurors felt about Gow, not how Reilly felt about her. In modern practice, it is objectionable for a trial attorney to express personal feelings and beliefs for that very reason.

Reilly pointed out that the dog didn't bark at a stranger in the house and noted that the butler controlled the dog's movements that night. He did not remind the jurors that the Lindbergh's house was large and the dog was at the far end of the house away from the nursery. Reilly would later argue that just as there was no bark from the dog, neither was there an outcry from the child when taken from the crib. Had a stranger taken the child, the child would have been startled. Therefore, argued Reilly, the child was comfortable with the one who removed him because it was no stranger. "I don't know anything about these people, but I say the circumstances point absolutely along a straight line of guilt toward that butler and the servants who were disloyal to Colonel Lindbergh."[38]

---

[36] Transcript, 4750.
[37] Transcript, 4695.
[38] Transcript, 4697.

Reilly then attacked the reasonableness of the prosecution's theory that Hauptmann climbed the ladder to the nursery. "You have got to place Hauptmann in that room; because the State says that's the way the crime was committed; Hauptmann was in that room."[39] He argued that a man couldn't come to a strange house with a ladder and place it up against the wall and run up the ladder, push open a shutter, and walk into a room that he had never been in before. That's what the State wanted them to believe. Returning to his theme, Reilly told the jurors:

> This is the scenario they have written. But it doesn't ring true to common sense, the common sense view of things. That is why they pick a jury, not composed of lawyers or judges—for the common sense view.[40]
>
> And they'd have you believe that he had gloves on—30 inches below this window sill. Now he has to reach up. There is no need of any chisel. He reaches up and he finds that the shutters are just closed together. He opens the shutters, one back and the other back. Now how long do you suppose two loose shutters would stay back with a gale howling? They would be banging, banging, banging, back and forth. But nevertheless, with those shutters banging back and forth and a gale blowing, this man has to take himself by his two hands, and I don't see how he could get above the second section of the ladder, because he would have to hold on to the side of it, and he would have to hold on to the wall as he went up, to steady himself; but finally he is on the top rung now, and he is reaching three feet through the air, gripping the bottom of the window sill, of a house he had never been in, of a house where he doesn't know who is inside the room—and any fool would know that a Colonel of the United States Army

---

[39] Transcript, 4698.
[40] Transcript, 4700.

> would have a gun somewhere around and put a bullet through your heart.[41]

Reilly argued that Hauptmann would have been in a room that was absolutely dark where there were toys, furniture, table and chairs, and across the room was a crib. He would have to navigate without bumping into anything. The child would cry out when the stranger put a hand on him. Hauptmann would have to swing himself out the window with a twenty-five or thirty pound child in the darkness and be able to find the top rung of that ladder three feet below the window. Reilly pointed out that the return down the ladder would be much more difficult because of the kidnapper having the child. He used a photographic exhibit of the ground around where the ladder stood to show there was no disturbance from someone falling from the ladder into the soft mud. Reilly capped off this argument with the statement, "That ladder was a plant and nobody went up that ladder that night, if it was ever up against the house." [42] The problem Reilly had just created for himself and for Hauptmann, is that he had just made the disloyalty theory much more involved. In addition to an employee slipping the child out of the house to someone who had been alerted to take the child and the butler controlling the dog, the plot included planting a ladder at the scene to suggest that the kidnapping had been a burglary. But if there was no ladder for Hauptmann and the child to fall from, what was the explanation for the fatal blow to the child's head? Reilly may have thought that removing the ladder had little effect on how the child was killed. If the jury thought that the child had fallen from the ladder to its

---

[41] Transcript, 4701.
[42] Transcript, 4703.

death, it would still be a death in the perpetration of a burglary for Hauptmann.

Arguing that the ladder was a plant could be viewed as conceding that wood evidence was strong, and the conspiracy against Hauptmann required planting evidence strong enough to convict him. Continuing with the ladder being a plant, Reilly said there was no mud on the ladder, and, if there was no mud on the ladder, why was there mud in the nursery? Why did the kidnapper take the ladder and the baby? Why would he pay any attention to the ladder after he had the baby? The man on the ladder would fall, wouldn't he? And if he did, why was there no impression of his fall in the soft mud at the bottom of the ladder?

> You can't get away from these physical facts. There is nothing in the mud that indicates Hauptmann or anybody else fell in that mud and there is nothing in the mud that indicates the baby fell in the mud—nothing.[43]

Reilly could have also asked at this point, "Do you have a reasonable doubt about Hauptmann or anyone falling in the mud that night as the State leads you to believe? If so, you must find my client not guilty." Reasonable doubt is the legal standard, and the jury should be constantly reminded of that. Reilly would have been better off not offering any explanation for the ladder—leaving the jury to wonder about its connection. Now the prosecution could call attention to the fact that Hauptmann, found to have over $14,000 in ransom money in September, 1934, also could be tied to the construction of the ladder that someone supposedly planted at the scene before anyone even knew that Hauptmann existed.

---

[43] Transcript, 4704.

At this point Reilly's disloyalty conspiracy theory involved three people: the butler Whateley, who controlled the dog; Gow, who left the ransom note on the window sill; and Violet Sharpe, who took the child to New York. But where did the baby go? Gow, Whateley, and Violet Sharpe were around for police interrogation, so there had to be a plan for someone to be taking care of the child during the negotiations. The conspiracy theory had to expand to account for all the reasonable possibilities. This may account for why Reilly took the risk of including Gow in the conspiracy—so that he could include Red Johnson. Gow tipped off Johnson as to the baby's whereabouts, and Johnson kidnapped the child and left the ladder. The signal to Johnson was made through the phone call with Gow.

> [A]nd all of a sudden comes the signal, "The coast is clear, they are at dinner." The telephone call from Red Johnson that she had only left two hours before....[44] No, that baby came down those stairs, and all the circumstances and inferences they talk about the ladder, don't ring true according to good common sense.[45]
>
> Was there any effort made to bring him back? Ask yourselves that question. Why was the man that talked to Betty Gow while the Colonel was eating his dinner allowed to remain in the safety of Denmark?[46]

Reilly told the jurors they had to put Hauptmann in that room through evidence and not guesswork. Reilly said the state's theory was the ladder broke and that the child received a blow on the head which caused instantaneous death. "Well, unfortunately you can't convict anybody of disorderly conduct on theories, much less murder in the first

---

[44] Transcript, 4707.
[45] Transcript, 4713.
[46] Transcript, 4708.

degree."[47] He should have explained this point more. The burden of proof is the same in small crimes as it is in the most serious crimes. The theory of the State was unreasonable and would be unacceptable in one of the smallest of crimes. Reilly compared the State's theory to a moving picture scenario. How long would the note have stayed there with a gale howling? There was mud on the floor of the nursery, but Lindbergh and Whateley had gone outside to look for the baby. Lindbergh went back up to the nursery and walked around. It is just as consistent that the mud came from Lindbergh's shoes. The suitcase right below the window wasn't damaged from anyone stepping on it coming in the window. "I will leave it to you whether his body wouldn't have forced his leg right through that suit case."[48] When his turn came to sum up, Wilentz answered this argument by standing on the suit case—it didn't collapse—and announcing that he weighed 160 pounds.[49]

If Gow had taken the baby from the crib and there had been no ladder entry to the room, there would be no stranger's fingerprints in the nursery. Reilly would have to explain that. He broadened the planning of the conspiracy. Reilly argued that Frank A. Kelly, the fingerprint technician, should have been able to find fingerprints of Anne Morrow Lindbergh, Bessie Gow, and the baby all around the room, but Kelly found only partial prints or smudges which could not be identified. Reilly would have to account for this lack of evidence.

> But if somebody had been instructed, some of the disloyal servants of Colonel Lindbergh had been instructed, that by taking a handkerchief and wiping around the crib or anything else that they touched, fingerprints would be wiped off—and somebody must

[47] Transcript, 4709.
[48] Transcript, 4712–4713.
[49] Transcript, 4408.

> have done it, because Kelly did not get a fingerprint of anybody in that room.[50]

Defense attorneys, when arguing against the reasonableness of the prosecution's case, must be careful about the reasonableness of their own arguments. Was the wipe down of the nursery a step too far? Shortly after suggesting that the conspiracy included wiping down the nursery, Reilly attacked the quality of the police investigation.

> Now Kelly comes in and Kelly says, "I am the fingerprint expert of the State Police. I went all over the room, looking for fingerprints. I didn't find one." … Now here is where the bungling of your State Police begins; and don't think they didn't bungle it.[51]

Reilly later pointed out that his fingerprint expert, Erastus Mead Hudson, had found hundreds of fingerprints on the ladder that had not been found by the police. Why not attribute the lack of fingerprints to Kelly's bungling instead of a conspiratorial wipe down of the bedroom?

Reilly further widened the disloyalty conspiracy by trying to show a connection between Dr. John Condon and Red Johnson. He told the jurors that he didn't know anything about Condon's background. He had asked Condon why he had been transferred from one school to another. "I tried to get into his past life. It was objected to." The suggestion was that there was a reason for the Condon transfers, but it was improper for Reilly to argue something that had excluded by objection.

> Between the 1st and the 2nd, before [Condon] put his ad in the paper, nobody asking him to, he says he is around investigating the background of Red John-

---

[50] Transcript, 4713.
[51] Transcript, 4714.

> son…And here comes the answer right back. Now doesn't that indicate to you, ladies and gentlemen, somewhere a person was waiting for the signal from the *Bronx News*?[52]

Reilly pointed out to the jurors that all the important ransom negotiations occurred when there were no other witnesses to support Condon's account of them. He said that Wilentz had described Condon as a patriotic gentleman of the old school and added that he didn't share that opinion of Condon. "Condon stands behind something in this case that is unholy, and I will bear it out, I think, by his testimony and by his actions."[53] As Reilly attacked Condon, he told the jurors that Wilentz would defame the defense witnesses.

> You will hear the General tomorrow when he says, 'Oh, Lupica,' and he will defame him. But he was studying for Princeton. You will hear the General defame the man from the gas station [William Brevoort Bolmer], a graduate of Princeton, who says he saw that ladder in a car with a man and a woman; but because he is a defense witness you will hear him defamed and yet the boy who was studying and the man that graduated, one studying for and one graduated from the same college that one of the distinguished gentlemen sitting at the prosecution table graduated from. So there is no criterion because you are on the side of the defense you must be defamed and because you are for the prosecution you must be glorified.[54]

Reilly's final co-conspirator was Isidor Fisch, who had to be included because he was the one who gave Hauptmann the ransom money. Reilly argued that no one

---

52 Transcript, 4732.
53 Transcript, 4727.
54 Transcript, 4728.

person could have planned the kidnapping, taken care of the child, written notes, and run around different states. The kidnapping was the work of a gang bent on an evil undertaking. By involving so many people in the conspiracy, Reilly ran the risk of attacking some witnesses whom the jury found credible. They may have liked Bessie Gow. They may have found Dr. Condon quaint but truthful. There had been audible gasps from the spectators when Reilly began his attack on Condon.[55] The jury must have heard this also. How would that affect their reception of this argument? Reilly may have been better off depicting Condon as a willing dupe instead of a coconspirator. He had no such problem with the butler, Whateley, who was dead at time of trial, or Red Johnson, who was in Denmark. Violet Sharp and Isidor Fisch were also conveniently dead, and the jury would have to gauge the plausibility of the disloyalty conspiracy on Gow and Condon. How credible was their testimony? While Condon could have been a dupe, Gow would have to have been a key player in the conspiracy. Reilly noted how convenient it was for Gow to have found the thumbguard in an area that had been searched by many people. He asked the jury if they believed that. It would have been better to ask if they had reason to doubt that. Framing the issue as "who's telling the truth?" rather than "do you have reason to doubt?" lowers the prosecution's burden of proof.

---

[55] O'Brien, *The Lindberghs,* 267.

The Failure of Proof

The Bungled Investigation

The argument that the police are corrupt or inept generally works better in an urban setting where the jurors are less likely to be acquainted with the individual police officers. Because most of Reilly's practice was in New York City, such an attack would have been almost second nature to him. He may have blundered by making the argument in Flemington. Reilly said that Colonel Schwarzkopf bungled the case within fifteen minutes by not turning out bloodhounds and other dogs to search for the baby and leaving the fingerprints to Kelly alone. "Would you send for the greatest fingerprint men you could possibly get—New York, Philadelphia, Washington or anywheres else immediately."[56]

Reilly found fault with the collection handwriting samples from Hauptmann. He condemned the police for requiring Hauptmann to write samples using language and words from the ransom notes and argued that the spelling variations had been dictated, also, to bring Hauptmann more in line with the ransom notes. Continuing to the writing on the closet board that the prosecution insisted was Dr. Condon's address and 1932 phone number, Reilly said that, like the ladder, the closet board was a plant. Faulting the New York police for this plant, Reilly said it was the worst example of police crookedness that he had seen in a great many years. Reilly next challenged the assertion that Hauptmann had admitted that the handwriting on the closet board was his. Reilly contested what had seemed to be a straightforward admission to the Bronx District Attorney and which

---

[56] Transcript, 4715.

appeared to be confirmed at the habeas corpus hearing. As to Hauptmann admitting he had written the address and phone number, Reilly argued "Now he didn't [say] anything of the kind." Reilly quoted Hauptmann from the habeas corpus transcript: "It looks like my handwriting." But the very last answer he gave was, "I can't say whether it is or whether it is not my handwriting."[57] The problem for Reilly was that Hauptmann readily admitted writing some of the other information on the closet board. The police would have had to have found that writing and added the Condon information to it to frame Hauptmann. The forgery would have to be good enough for Hauptmann to be unsure about it. Reilly noted that the officer who went into the closet and found the writing was a German, Inspector Bruckman. Bruckman could get a pretty fair imitation of German Hauptmann's figures and handwriting.

Reilly moved to fingerprints and the ladder. When Reilly questioned whether there had been four nail holes in Rail 16 of the ladder, reminding the jury that Hudson, the defense fingerprint expert, had only found one, Reilly displayed the close-up photographs of the rail the police said were taken back in March of 1932. Reilly argued that the photographs were made much later than March 1932. The police officer who took the photographs could not account for the photographic plate. Reilly mentioned the wood expert, Koehler, but he was careful not to mention the detailed notes and measurements Koehler had made of the ladder and which included the four nail holes. Koehler made these notes and measurements not knowing how they would compare with the attic joists of a man who would not be brought into the case until September of 1934.

---

[57] Transcript, 4763–4764.

Reilly contrasted Hudson with Koehler. He told the jury that Hudson wouldn't commit perjury for President Roosevelt and asked the jury to view Koehler's testimony against their horse sense. Reilly described Koehler as a lumber cruiser. Speaking of Koehler, Reilly said, "He never testified in his life before—he said so—in a case like this."[58] Reilly had forgotten or simply ignored Koehler's mention of testifying in the Magnuson murder case in Wisconsin over a decade earlier. The prosecution had not highlighted it beyond Koehler's mention in his qualification, and the defense apparently had not researched it. Reilly argued that Koehler's reputation was at stake in his testimony—he was a great man from Washington. Reilly said Koehler was testifying for glory, vanity, preferment, and advancement. DeBisschop, on the other hand, was not paid any money, not even carfare. "Koehler was wrong many times. He was wrong on his measurements. They look alike; they are alike; they are absolutely the same."[59] Reilly argued that Pope had found errors in Koehler's measurements. Reilly asked the jury what they were going to do with that kind of testimony. The case was too perfect, Reilly argued. What he was really saying is that the evidence was too strong, a dangerous argument. One man couldn't have planned it. Certainly a mastermind wouldn't be so foolish as to rip a board out of his attic leaving the other half there. Reilly returned to planted evidence. "No, I'm afraid this board was prepared for this trial. I am pretty certain that these pictures were prepared."[60]

Reilly's argument became more complex and unstable. He initially argued that the ladder was a plant to suggest a burglary. This point would have logically

---

[58] Transcript, 4771.
[59] Transcript, 4775.
[60] Transcript, 4776.

required Red Johnson or some accomplice to drop it there. Reilly then argued that the ladder was changed to add three additional holes to match Hauptmann's attic, and further that the photographs of the ladder were made long after the ladder was discovered on March 1. Reilly charged that the police were out to frame Hauptmann and pin it on him if they tore his house to pieces or tore down his garage. "Now, Hauptmann didn't build the garage and didn't build the house, and whoever built the garage, of course, put some lumber in it. So, we have them finding a brace, an arm brace from the garage, and then you have them coming in and tearing up a board from the attic."[61] But Hauptmann had built the garage before the kidnapping.[62] Reilly questioned how the police removed the attic board. Mocking the detective, Reilly said, "all I had to do was to reach in with my hand or something and pull it up. The nails came right out."[63] It was not reasonable Reilly continued. There was not a mark of a hammer, pinch bar—not a mark of anything.

The Unbelievable Witnesses

Reilly challenged Lindbergh's identification of Hauptmann by voice after hearing "Hey, Doctor!"[64] because of years of hearing aircraft motors, but he did not want to run the risk of spending too much time attacking the great Lindbergh. It was better to treat Colonel Lindbergh, the American hero, as a victim. He had no difficulty, however, in attacking the truthfulness of

---

[61] Transcript, 4768–4769.
[62] Lloyd C. Gardner, *The Case That Never Dies: The Lindbergh Kidnapping* (Princeton: Rutgers University Press, 2004), 405.
[63] Transcript, 4769.
[64] Transcript, 4740.

Millard Whited, the man who said he saw Hauptmann skulking around the Lindbergh residence in February before the kidnapping, by arguing that he was an out-and-out liar.[65] Reilly described Cecile Barr, the Sheridan Square ticket seller, as a notoriety hunting young woman trying to get her picture in the paper. He compared witnesses like Barr to the good, honest people at Hauptmann's birthday party—hardworking, industrious people; no crooks, no convicts. Mrs. Hoff saw Isidor Fisch and Budreau at her house. Fisch wanted to leave bundles at her house, but she declined. "Why would this mother come down here to commit perjury for a man she doesn't know?"[66] Reilly switched to Anna not having seen the box in the kitchen closet. Reilly argued that the State contends that because Anna didn't climb to the top shelf of the kitchen closet, she wasn't telling the truth.

Reilly told the jury that the State was accusing every defense witness of perjury because they had come there to help a man unjustly accused of crime. If they testified for Hauptmann, the State believed they must be perjurers. But Reilly sarcastically said Cecile Barr was no perjurer—she could remember every five-dollar bill she ever saw when she was in the ticket booth. Turning to the witnesses who testified that Whited's reputation in the community was bad, Reilly argued that they had been belittled and degraded because they were people from Sourland Mountain, because they were not well dressed.

Speaking of Hildegarde Olga Alexander, the woman who said she had seen Hauptmann watching Condon at the Fordham Station of the New York Central, Reilly said, "But they bring this dizzy young lady from the Bronx who is looking for a movie contract or something and she tells the impossible story—plant number 999."

---

[65] Transcript, 4693, 4785.

[66] Transcript, 4783.

He said that Alexander was a liar, and the State knew it as soon as she left the stand. "Now, why plant people in this case?"[67]

Reilly questioned Joe Perrone's testimony about being hailed by Hauptmann to deliver a note to Condon. Reilly said it was unreasonable to believe that Perrone or any cab would have been on Gun Hill Road. He asked what Hauptmann or anyone else would be doing in the middle of Gun Hill Road and in the middle of Bronx Park. How would the New Jersey jurors be able to appreciate this reference? Reilly argued that there had to be a friendship between Condon and Perrone. Perrone said he could identify Hauptmann at eight o'clock in the night from only the light from a street light "and you know how dull they are,"[68] Reilly added.

The Bad Experts

Reilly then turned his attention to the handwriting evidence. "It is not my intention to take the handwriting of each and every one of these experts. Expert evidence, his Honor will charge you, I believe, is nothing more nor less than opinion evidence. What does opinion evidence mean? Opinion evidence means this: that this man says 'I think it is this' and another man says 'I think it is that.' "[69] Reilly pointed out to the jury that the law gave them a perfect right to disregard expert evidence altogether and use their own common sense in considering the matter. Reilly had an advantage in the fact that the jury had heard hours and hours of direct examination and cross-examination about the handwriting analysis. They

---

[67] Transcript, 4781.
[68] Transcript, 4737.
[69] Transcript, 4720.

would not likely retain much of that testimony nor would they be inclined to have much of it read back to them during deliberations. What worked against Reilly and Hauptmann, however, were the demonstrative exhibits prepared by the prosecution witnesses. A glance at these exhibits provided effective comparisons of the ransom note writing and the writings known to have been written by Hauptmann. Clark Sellers had prepared a particularly effective exhibit by cutting and pasting together letters from the ransom notes to create almost an identical replica of Hauptmann's personal signature.

When confronted by an opposing expert witness, attorneys often resort to the "fee attack"—pointing out that the expert witness is receiving payment for the work done on the case. The "fee attack," by itself, is not that effective. It only works when the jury perceives that the witness is being paid an exorbitant fee. Reilly tried to make the fee issues more persuasive by noting that "they expect to be paid and paid well—out of your pockets."[70] It is normally impermissible to make an argument like this that appeals to juror bias on how their taxes are spent, but there was no objection. Reilly spent less time on what may have been a more effective argument. Only the nursery note would put Hauptmann in that nursery the night of March 1. The nursery note was connected to the rest of the notes by the handwriting, the continuity of content, and the time sequence. The prosecution experts, however, testified that the nursery note contained disguised writing—that it wasn't the way Hauptmann regularly wrote. Reilly argued that the opinions that Hauptmann had written the disguised nursery note boiled down to a comparison of the word "is" in the nursery note and Hauptmann's known writings.

---

[70] Transcript, 4722.

> I think you will agree with me that to take one word, "is" out of all those lines and compare that "is" to one "is" of Hauptmann's and say then that because that "is" in your opinion looks something like an "is" that he wrote, that is pretty slim evidence, opinion evidence, guesswork evidence, to put a man in a nursery of a house he knew nothing about it.[71] ... If this is disguised handwriting where is there any standard by which it can be examined with that certainty with which you will send a man to his death or with that certainty with which you would send a man away for life imprisonment? One "is," one "is."[72]

Reilly turned his attention to the medical examiner who didn't belong to any professional associations, made no report of his findings beyond filling out a simple form, participated in no inquest, and did not give the care and attention one would expect to be given to the child of Colonel Lindbergh. "There isn't a doctor living that can tell when that poor unfortunate baby died, or what it came to its death from."[73] Reilly argued that the fracture in the child's skull could have come from being probed by the officer's stick. Reilly would not take the doctor's word in an accident case, much less a case of life and death. Again, Reilly improperly gave his personal opinion on the credibility of a witness.

Reilly attacked the testimony about Hauptmann's finances, showing the State had alleged that Hauptmann had spent $35,000 of the ransom money; and, when added to the money found in his garage, the sum equaled the $50,000 ransom. "And how will you feel? And how would I feel if, when that money is found, because it

---

[71] Transcript, 4722.
[72] Transcript, 4723.
[73] Transcript, 4747.

must be some place[?]"[74] Reilly asked. He pointed out that the State finance expert said Hauptmann had lost $5,000. "They would have you think that he was spending Lindbergh money down to the day of his arrest, and yet when you look at the accounts, as you will, you will see that in July, 1933, when Isidor Fisch gave him the last $4,500 to balance the account, from July 2nd, I think it was, 1933, down to the day of his arrest, this defendant didn't put a dollar into his Wall Street account excepting one or two small dividend checks that came in that were credited to his account."[75]

Both Mastermind and Fool?

Several times Reilly argued that the prosecution made differing points about Hauptmann as a criminal. "[I]n one breath they say, 'Hauptmann, you are a mastermind; you are clever; you are not wearing gloves; you are wearing gloves; you are shinning up poles and coming down poles', and all this thing; and the next thing they say, 'You are a dummy; you are talking for an hour and a half with Condon.' "[76]

The Botched Proof

Lloyd Fisher had re-read the indictment to the jurors, repeating the accusatory and arcane language. Reilly instead paraphrased the indictment and explained his theory:

---

[74] Transcript, 4753.
[75] Transcript, 4755.
[76] Transcript, 4757.

> Now it says this, in plain language, but it is the pattern by which you must go; it says first that this defendant alone on the 1st day of March, and that doesn't mean the 2nd, 3rd, the 4th, the 5th, it means the 1st and the 1st only, in the township of East Amwell, nowhere else, not Mercer County, not the Bronx, not Niagara Falls, East Amwell alone and only therein, did willfully, feloniously, and with malice aforethought kill the young Lindbergh baby.[77]

Venue lies in the jurisdiction where the crime was committed, and the prosecution must prove that court has the authority to try that case by proving the crime was committed in its jurisdiction. Hauptmann was being tried in Hunterdon County and the indictment had also alleged that the crime had been committed in the township of East Amwell. A witness or witnesses would have to establish that the murder of the Lindbergh baby had occurred in East Amwell in Hunterdon County beyond a reasonable doubt. Testimony from the engineer, Walter E. Roberts, established that the distance from the rear paved porch of the Lindbergh home to the Mercer County line was 870 feet and the body of the child was found in Mercer County. It was reasonable to believe that the murder occurred in Mercer County. Reilly did not vigorously argue the prosecution's failure to prove venue to the jury. The defense probably reasoned that (1) the jurors would not acquit Hauptmann on such a legal technicality—"yes we think the prosecution has proved Hauptmann murdered the child but he really did it in another county so we must acquit him;" and (2) in the case of a conviction, a good record had been created for the appellate argument that venue had not been established beyond a reasonable doubt.

---

[77] Transcript, 4688–4689.

The cause of death would become an issue with other arguments Reilly wanted to make, but it was up to the State to prove the death was murder. The child's death and the cause of death had to be proved by direct evidence, and the State looked to the medical examiner for the cause of death. The best the doctor could say was the child received a blow on the head. Whenever this child received that blow, death was instantaneous. Reilly asked what "whenever" means. "That doesn't mean March the 1st, 1932. That doesn't mean March the 1st, 1932, by falling off a broken ladder. That doesn't mean March the 1st, 1932, in the township of East Amwell."[78]

Reilly concluded his argument with flattery, telling the jurors they were people "from sturdy stock ... notorious for its square-shooting" who "all believe[d] in the Golden Rule." He referred to his high ethical standards and then told the jury, "I believe this man is absolutely innocent of murder." Because the evidence was conceded that Hauptmann had ransom money in his possession when arrested, Reilly added, "Whatever other charge there is against him in the Bronx will be disposed of."[79] In modern practice trial attorneys are not permitted to offer their personal opinions and beliefs to a jury, but in 1935 that prohibition was not well settled and did not often raise objections. Reilly ended his conclusion by mentioning Colonel Lindbergh. "And I feel sure, in closing, even Colonel Lindbergh wouldn't expect you and doesn't expect you to do anything but your duty under the law and under the evidence. May I say to him, in passing, that he has my profound respect and I feel sorry for him in his deep grief, and I am quite sure that all

---

[78] Transcript, 4710.
[79] Transcript, 4786.

of you agree with me, his lovely son is now within the gates of heaven."[80]

Reilly had not walked the jury through the elements of the crime of murder as the State had alleged. He had not attacked the facts and evidence in a point-by-point fashion. He argued that the evidence was too perfect—a concession about and an explanation for the strength of the evidence. The strength of the evidence relied upon a conspiracy by a large number of people using planted evidence. There were so many plants that Hildegarde Olga Alexander was "plant number 999." If the jury had doubts that so many people could come together and fashion a fabricated case against a man, all they had to fall back upon was the strength of the State's case against Hauptmann—a case that Reilly had said was "too good." The purpose of closing argument or summation is to tell the jury what the evidence means, not to just repeat the evidence that the jury has heard over the several weeks of a trial. Reilly rambled at times, and his argument suffered from a lack of organization to help focus on the specific issue of whether, over 4000 pages of testimony, the State had proved beyond a reasonable doubt that Hauptmann had committed the crime and should be found guilty.

He didn't argue the facts and evidence from the "if this is true, what else must be true" standpoint. He raised but he didn't walk the jury through the reasonable inferences that could be drawn from the case. The State's experts were hired guns, the other witnesses were seeking fame or importance, the significant evidence was faked and planted, and the defense witnesses were honest people seeking justice. Reilly did not argue to the jury about a recommendation of mercy that would spare Hauptmann from the death penalty if the jury were to convict. Had he raised any doubts in the minds of the

---

[80] Transcript, 4786–4787.

jurors, he could have raised the life or death aspects of their deliberations. He did not remind them that they would determine whether Hauptmann walked free, spent the rest of his life in prison, or died. It was their decision.

Wilentz, when his turn came to sum up, began with a brief Introduction in which he made flattering remarks to the jury, referred to his high ethical standards, and spoke of his duty as Attorney General.[81] He then launched off into a Refutation which consumed 73 pages of transcript[82] and ended his summation with a Conclusion 62 pages long.[83] During his argument, Wilentz made a telling remark: "I have never prosecuted a murder case in my life, I have never prosecuted anybody, I don't want to do it again; but I am not altogether unacquainted with court practice."[84] He may not have been altogether unacquainted with court practice, but he was certainly unacquainted with how a prosecutor should argue a case to a jury. During the course of his summation, Wilentz made a number of objectionable arguments. We will by no means recount all of his objectionable arguments, but we shall discuss a few of the more egregious ones.

Reilly had begun his appeal by lifting a Bible in the air and reminding the jury of the Biblical injunction "judge not that ye be not judged,"[85] and then gone on to attack the character of almost every witness who testified for the prosecution. Of the 100 pages of transcript that his argument consumed, only ten made a logical argument for acquittal based on the defense presentation.[86] Wilentz

---

[81] Transcript, 4358–4359.

[82] Transcript, 4359–4431.

[83] Transcript, 4431–4492.

[84] Transcript, 4382.

[85] Russell B. Porter, "Reilly Accuses Servants, Charges Police Frame–up in His Final Plea to the Jury," *NYT*, February 12, 1935.

[86] Transcript, 4687–4777 (appeal to character and emotion), 4777–4787 (appeal to logic).

was glad to point out this disparity when he summed up: "They spent twenty minutes talking about the defense witnesses. All day on this floor yesterday, talked about everything in the world except the defense's case. For twenty minutes from 4:10 to 4:30, counsel talked about the defense witnesses, all of them, and that is all they were worth."[87] Wilentz answered Reilly's scripture with a quotation of his own: "And he that killeth any man shall surely be killed … Shall surely be put to death."[88]

During his summation Reilly said, "Public clamor is not going to have, in the squares of Flemington, a man drawn to his death or life imprisonment because the mob wants it."[89] Wilentz responded by saying, "it seems to me that if there is such a clamor so far as they are concerned, there must be a good basis for it."[90] Later in his summation he returned to the subject of public clamor and said:

> [I]f there is a clamor from the people of this country for this man's conviction, regarding which I don't know anything, except as referred to by counsel, I have sufficient faith in the American people to know that it is their honest belief and conviction that he is the murderer.[91]

There are multiple problems with such an argument. First, Wilentz is suggesting to the jury that a fact outside the evidence (the public clamor) is a good reason to convict the defendant. Second, Wilentz committed the *argumentum ad populum* fallacy by arguing that Hauptmann was guilty because a majority of Americans

---

[87] Transcript, 4378.
[88] Trial Transcipt, 4360.
[89] Transcript, 4699.
[90] Transcript, 4359.
[91] Transcript, 4488.

believed him guilty. As Anatole France is supposed to have said, "If a million people think a foolish thing, it is still a foolish thing."

Wilentz seemingly attempted to make the jury angry with Hauptmann by blaming him for the inconvenience they had suffered by being sequestered: "I know how it must be with you; weeks and weeks locked up. But that is not my fault. That is not the Court's fault. Everything that has happened in this courtroom, men and women, everything, you may lay to the door of the gentleman sitting over there between the guards."[92] It goes without saying that a prosecutor should never suggest to a jury that they should be angry with a defendant for exercising his Constitutional right to a trial by jury.

When he answered Reilly's attempt to show that the kidnapping was the work of a gang rather than of Hauptmann acting alone, Wilentz attacked Reilly's character and the character of the other defense lawyers: "Now all this talk about others is clearly the effort of an experienced criminal lawyer to confuse and befuddle a jury. ... There is nobody at that [defense] table that doesn't feel he is guilty; I don't care what they say."[93] It is proper to say that an argument is confusing and befuddling, but not to say that opposing counsel is intentionally trying to confuse and befuddle. Criticism of an opponent's summation should be aimed at the argument, not the arguer. Nor may a prosecutor suggest that the defense team is hypocritical because they are defending a man whom they believe to be guilty. First, no lawyer is allowed to express his personal opinion as to the merits of a case which he is litigating.[94] The fact that

---

[92] Transcript, 4361.

[93] Transcript, 4363.

[94] Rule 3.4(e), American Bar Association Model Rules of Professional Conduct.

someone sincerely believes a proposition is no guarantee that the proposition is true. Second, Wilentz was no mind reader. He couldn't know what the defense lawyers believed. Third, he was appealing to "facts" outside the evidence. Fourth, defense counsel's opinion whether a client is guilty or innocent is irrelevant.

In his summation, Reilly had capitalized on gaps in the evidence and things left unexplained by the evidence and had offered those matters as reasons to acquit. Wilentz responded by asserting that Hauptmann could answer the questions and implying that Hauptmann had done something wrong by not supplying the answers. "There may be some questions you can't answer, but there sits the man that can answer them."[95] The burden of proof in a criminal case always rests on the prosecution; the defense need prove nothing. Although there are rare occasions when the prosecution can talk about a defendant's failure to produce evidence,[96] a prosecutor cannot suggest that the defendant has done something wrong by not coming forward with evidence.

Wilentz then launched off into a virulent personal attack on Hauptmann's character. He asked, "Who would be the type of person that would take a child like that and murder it?" He proclaimed that a lion or tiger or venomous snake would never stoop so low, and then he described the person who would do such a thing: "He wouldn't be an American. No American gangster and no American racketeer ever sank to the level of killing babies."[97] He then described the man who would commit such a crime.

---

[95] *Ibid.*

[96] For example, when the defendant claims an alibi and says his wife was with him, the prosecution may call attention to the fact that the defendant failed to call his wife as an alibi witness. Daughtrey v. State, 325 So.2d 456 (1st DCA), cert. denied 336 So.2d 600 (Fla. 1976).

[97] Transcript, 4366.

It would have to be someone who would break into a prominent citizen's home, who would "hold up women at the point of a gun, women wheeling baby carriages, … an animal lower than the lowest form in the animal kingdom, public enemy Number One of this world, Bruno Richard Hauptmann."[98] Yes, a person who would kidnap and kill an infant is a bad person, but the fact that someone is a bad person doesn't mean that he has kidnapped and killed an infant. The only portion of this argument that is possibly relevant is the reference to Hauptmann's breaking into a house back in Germany, and Wilentz did not even mention the relevant fact that Hauptmann entered the home by using a ladder to crawl through a window. Wilentz hadn't finished his assault on Hauptmann's character with these words. He would later tell the jury that Hauptmann was the lowest sort of animal, "no heart, no soul," with only the appearance of humanity.[99] "If I had my choice," he said, "I wouldn't get in the same room [with Hauptmann], I wouldn't become contaminated, I wouldn't want to breathe the same air."[100]

Reilly made several arguments about unfair tactics by both the police and prosecutors. In answering Reilly's accusation that the police had framed Hauptmann, Wilentz said, "there are more crooks amongst the lawyers than there ever will be amongst policemen, and the sooner we all take notice of that the better off we will all be."[101] This argument was, of course, aimed at suggesting that the defense attorneys were the true villains instead of the police. In answer to Reilly's complaint that the defense team was not allowed sufficient time to examine the ransom notes, Wilentz told the jury that of all the

---

[98] Transcript, 4367–4368.
[99] Transcript, 4425.
[100] Transcript, 4460.
[101] Transcript, 4373.

handwriting experts summoned by the defense "only one man would dare walk in this courtroom to say it wasn't Hauptmann. … Why aren't those other experts here? You know the reason. They wouldn't dare say it is not Hauptmann's, because, of course, they are Hauptmann's."[102] Again referring to facts not in evidence, Wilentz recruited the uncalled defense experts as prosecution witnesses by suggesting to the jury that they agreed with the prosecution experts. It may well be true that they agreed with the prosecution experts, but that fact doesn't make it proper for Wilentz to make the claim in summation. Reilly had made a common defense complaint about the state having far more resources than the defendant and spending far more money than the defense could afford. Wilentz replied by making the preposterous assertion, "Why, I think they [the defense] have probably spent more money than the State has."[103]

Wilentz then answered an accusation by Reilly that the prosecution had concealed a phonograph recording of Condon mimicking Cemetery John's voice. Reilly suggested that the prosecution didn't play the recording because it sounded nothing like Hauptmann. In reply Wilentz asserted that the defense had an opportunity to play the recording themselves but didn't do so because they were afraid of it, and the prosecution didn't play the record because "[w]e couldn't produce the record. It wasn't admissible from us."[104] In response to Reilly's accusation of police bungling, Wilentz replied that Charles Lindbergh had expressed his happiness with the investigation by testifying, "I think New Jersey has a good State Police."[105] In response to Reilly making an

---

[102] Transcript, 4379.
[103] Transcript, 4380.
[104] Transcript, 4390.
[105] Transcript, 4410.

issue about the police only recovering one of the child's thumb guards, Wilentz said, "The gentleman over between the two guards [Hauptmann] can tell you where the other one is."[106] When Reilly questioned the truthfulness of the witness Joe Perrone, Wilentz responded by accusing Reilly of untruthfulness: "I want to tell you that is a masterpiece, to stand up with that massive sincerity, making believe he means it … and say to you 'Do you believe that trash about Perrone?' "[107] Wilentz concluded his remarks about Reilly's attack on Perrone by saying that after his summation, Reilly had made "an apology to Colonel Lindbergh."[108] It made absolutely no difference at all that Reilly may or may not have said something to Lindbergh during a court recess.

In defending against Reilly's attack on Doctor Mitchell's autopsy, Wilentz said, "I have seen some good lawyers in cases that tried to get away from the facts and started off on that line of insinuations [but] I have never seen that before, never before in my life, and if I live to be a million years old, never again will I hear the number of insinuations, and unfair ones, that I have heard in this case."[109]

Wilentz told the jury that the crime of killing the Lindbergh baby "would shrink into absolute insignificance in comparison to the crime that would be committed if this man were freed. That would be the crime of the century."[110] If, on the other hand, the jury were to convict Hauptmann "this jury can, by its verdict, do one thing for the Colonel, for Anne, for the country—

---

[106] Transcript, 4414.
[107] *Ibid.*
[108] Transcript, 4418.
[109] Transcript, 4421–4422.
[110] Transcript, 4403.

we can make the children a little safer, we can make women a little happier."[111]

On appeal, the defense complained of these and other statements, contending that they were so prejudicial Hauptmann should be granted a new trial. The New Jersey Court of Errors and Appeals agreed that the remarks were improper but refused to reverse the case. In explaining their decision, the Court said:

> As may be surmised, the summation on both sides was lengthy. That by Mr. Reilly, of the New York bar, for the defense, covers one hundred pages of the printed case; that by the attorney-general, one hundred and thirty-five pages. From this latter counsel for plaintiff in error have extracted a number of passages, which, as they claim, amounted to illegal and unconstitutional abuse of the rights and privileges of an arguing advocate and charge error on the part of the trial judge in failing to intervene and restrict the speaker to his legitimate line of argument. Some are expressive of a belief in defendant's guilt on the part of prosecuting officers; some are vituperative characterizations of defendant, given his guilt. One or more intimate that the jury would be guilty of a crime in failing to convict. But we find no legal error properly raised. Throughout the lengthy summation it was at one juncture, and one only, that defense counsel interposed with an objection that the state counsel was going outside the evidence. We shall return to this presently. With that exception the four lawyers representing defendant and employed by him, said nothing by way of protest.[112]

---

[111] Transcript, 4488.

[112] State v. Hauptmann, 115 N.J.L. 412, 416, 180 A. 809, 814 (Ct.Err. & App., 1935).

The one objection made by the defense dealt with remarks made by Wilentz about the recording made of Condon's voice as he imitated the voice of Cemetery John. Reilly had complained about being denied access to a recording of John Condon imitating the voice of Cemetery John: "I produced evidence that Condon repeated as best he could the voice he heard and it was made on a Victrola record and I challenged them to produce it and they admitted they had it and they don't bring it in here. … Now why? Because … the voice is not the defendant's, even the imitation of it."[113] Wilentz replied by saying that the recording was available to the defense to play if they wanted the jury to hear it and went on to say, "I would have loved if you had heard the story all over again, Condon telling about this conversation, 'Will I burn if the baby is dead? Are you German, John? No, I am Scandinavian. …' "[114] Reilly objected that Wilentz was quoting from a recording that was not in evidence. Wilentz replied that he was quoting from John Condon's testimony about his conversation with Cemetery John. The Court of Errors and Appeals ruled:

> But quite plainly, what the attorney-general was quoting was from the testimony of Condon, not from a phonograph record. The obvious construction to be placed upon the remarks of the attorney-general was that the defense were afraid to call for and produce the phonograph record because they felt that if produced and played before the jury it would be found to repeat what Dr. Condon had testified to in regard to his interview with the defendant at the cemetery. … We agree with the trial judge that counsel was within his rights in challenging the failure of the defense to call

---

[113] Transcript, 4743.
[114] Transcript, 4387–4388.

> for the record as due to fear of what it might and probably would show.[115]

It is hard to understand why the four experienced lawyers sitting at the defense table made only one objection during the course of Wilentz's summation. Had they objected early and often, they could quite probably have prevented most of the inflammatory remarks by Wilentz. In many jurisdictions today, such an argument by a prosecutor would earn a reversal even if the defense attorney failed to object. The rationale of those modern cases is that, regardless of whether an objection is made, the trial judge must intervene when an attorney is committing an act so egregious that it amounts to "fundamental error" or "plain error."[116] Under such a standard, a modern appellate court could very well find the argument to be fundamental error and reverse Hauptmann's conviction. Unfortunately for Hauptmann, New Jersey law did not recognize the concept of fundamental error until 1949,[117] a full 13 years after his execution.

One possible explanation for the failure of the defense to object is that Wilentz and Reilly had a gentleman's agreement that both men could say whatever they wanted in summation without fear of objection. Such arrangements were not uncommon in some jurisdictions years ago, and court reporters would not even record the summations when such understandings were reached. Three things suggest that Wilentz and Reilly had such an agreement: (1) Wilentz did not object to the many improper comments made by Reilly. (2) When Reilly

---

[115] State v. Hauptmann, 115 N.J.L. 412, 419–420, 180 A. 809, 816 (Ct.Err. & App., 1935).
[116] See, e.g., Morgan v. State, 464 So.2d 1306 (4th DCA Fla., 1985).
[117] State v. De Paola, 5 N.J. 1, 73 A.2d 564 (1950).

objected to an argument by Wilentz, he responded by saying that he had not interrupted during Reilly's summation.[118] (3) The placement of Reilly's summation[119] in the transcript after both the Attorney General's summation[120] and Justice Trenchard's instructions on the law[121] suggest that Reilly's summation was included by the prosecution after they learned that the defense had asked to include a transcript of the prosecution summations. It appears that the other members of the defense team did not approve of Reilly's agreement with Wilentz, and when Anna Hauptmann fired Reilly after the conviction, they decided to include a complaint about the prosecution argument. Had Reilly remained lead counsel throughout the appellate process, the summations may very well have been excluded from the record on appeal.

---

[118] Transcript, 4388.
[119] Transcript, 4687.
[120] Transcript, 4358.
[121] Transcript, 4498.

9

Verdict and Aftermath

When Justice Trenchard entered the courtroom on the morning of February 13, he found a standing-room-only crowd.[1] On this, the 32nd day of the trial, the jurors were tired, having endured hundreds of witnesses and exhibits and listened to long opening statements and summations by the prosecution and defense. Their time of passive listening was nearing its end. They would soon receive the case, discuss it among themselves, and try to reach a just verdict. But first, they would have to suffer through one more speech. Justice Trenchard had to give them their instructions on the law applicable to the case. He wanted no disturbances while he performed this vital task, so he ordered the standing spectators out of the courtroom and had the doors locked. Nobody would be permitted to enter or leave the courtroom during the instructions.[2]

In the modern American courtroom, judges face severe limitations on what they can and cannot say. They cannot comment on the nature and quality of the evidence; they cannot point out significant issues; they cannot speak to the credibility of witnesses; they can only inform the jury of the applicable law and the procedures they must follow in deciding their verdict. This was not the case in early Twentieth Century New Jersey. Under New Jersey law,

---

[1] George Waller, *Kidnap*, 547.
[2] Demaris, *The Lindbergh Kidnaping*, 141.

> ... it is always the right, and in many cases the duty, of the trial judge to express freely the impressions made on his mind by the evidence, thus giving the jury the benefit of his judicial experience, and suggesting to them points of weakness or strength that they might otherwise overlook, provided always the ultimate decision of disputed matters of fact is fairly left to them.[3]

Trenchard obviously thought the prosecution had a strong case, and he was joined in this opinion by the justices of the Court of Errors and Appeals.[4] If he gave the jury his honest appraisal of the evidence, he ran the risk of appearing to advocate for the state. Author P.J. O'Brien, who attended the trial, would later write "[I]t was the consensus of those in the courtroom that the charge was 'exceedingly' strong against the defendant, but everyone, even Hauptmann's own attorneys, admitted it was fair."[5] Hauptmann's attorneys may have admitted outside the courtroom that Trenchard fairly instructed the jury, but making such an admission on the record wasn't going to help Hauptmann in the least. They voiced strenuous objections to his instructions, and they later complained of his instructions when they appealed the case.

Many chroniclers of the trial agree with O'Brien that the charge was "exceedingly strong against the defendant," but they disagree with his assessment that it was fair. Gregory Ahlgren and Stephen Monier complain that Trenchard "basically instructed them [the jury] to convict Hauptmann, and they did just that."[6] Lloyd Gardner

---

[3] State v. Overton, 85 N.J.L. 287, 294, 88 A. 689, 691 (Ct.Err. & App., 1913).

[4] They wrote that the evidence "inescapably led" to a guilty verdict. State v. Hauptmann, 115 N.J. L. 412, 330, 180 A. 809, 826 (Ct. Err. & App., 1935).

[5] O'Brien, *The Lindberghs*, 291.

[6] Gregory Ahlgren and Stephen Monier, *Crime of the Century: The Lindbergh Kidnapping Hoax* (Boston: Branden Books, 1993), 261.

writes that "Judge Trenchard's charge to the jury was really like a debate rebuttal speech to Reilly's summation."[7] Ludovic Kennedy finds no fault with the wording of Trenchard's charge but complains about the inflection of Trenchard's voice when he gave it.[8] The instruction that brought much criticism of favoritism by Trenchard against Hauptmann regarded the defense theory that the crime was gang-related. Trenchard charged the jury:

> It is argued by defendant's counsel that the kidnapping and murder was done by a gang, and not by the defendant, and that the defendant was nowise concerned therein. The argument was to the effect that it was done by a gang, with the help or connivance of some one or more servants of the Lindbergh or Morrow households. Now, do you believe that? Is there any evidence in this case to support any such conclusion?[9]

In its opinion affirming Hauptmann's conviction, the New Jersey Court of Errors and Appeals thoroughly discusses the defense complaint about Trenchard's purportedly erroneous comments on the testimony. Justice Charles W. Parker, author of the Hauptmann appellate opinion, cites the long standing tradition of judicial comment to jurors: "The [defense] brief under this point ignores one of the most thoroughly settled rules in our New Jersey criminal jurisprudence. That rule is that 'it is always the right and often the duty of the trial judge to comment on the evidence and give the jury his impressions of the weight and value, and such comment

---

[7] Gardner, *The Case that Never Dies*, 355.
[8] Kennedy, *The Airman and the Carpenter*, 337.
[9] Transcript, 4507.

is not assignable for error so long as the ultimate decision on disputed facts is plainly left to the jury.' "[10]

The test, then, is whether the judge makes it clear to the jury that it can follow or disregard the comment. Early in the instructions he said:

> In the determination of all questions of fact, the sole responsibility is with the jury. You are the sole judges of the evidence, of the weight of the evidence, and of the credibility of the witnesses. Any comments that I may make upon the evidence will be made, not for the purpose of controlling you in your view of the facts, but only to aid you in applying the principles of law to the facts as you may find them. You must not consider what I say concerning the evidence as being accurate, but you must depend upon your own recollection.[11]

Trenchard followed this warning up with no fewer than ten reminders of the jury's independence[12] and ended the

---

[10] State v. Hauptmann, 115 N.J. L. 412, 180 A. 809 (Ct. Err. & App., 1935).
[11] Transcript, 4498.
[12] Those warnings were:

> "There is evidence from which you may conclude, if you see fit, that ..." Transcript, 4500.
> "... you may possibly conclude that ..." Transcript, 4501.
> "...from the evidence you may conclude, if you see fit, that ..." Transcript, 4502.
> "...The evidence justifies the inference, if you see fit to draw it, that ..." Transcript, 4503.
> "The weight of the evidence to prove the genuineness of handwriting is wholly for the jury. ..." Transcript, 4507.
> "... if you believe that he did, although he now denies it, you may conclude ..." Transcript, 4508.
> "... the defendant denies that he was the man who was paid the ransom money, and there is other testimony which, if credible and believed by you, supports his statement." Transcript, 4508.
> "There is evidence from which you may conclude, if you see fit, that ..." Transcript, 4509.

instructions by telling the jurors that they had the duty to exercise their own independent judgment in arriving at a verdict.[13] These repeated comments satisfied the appellate court that Trenchard had instructed the jury fairly.

The tradition of judicial comment during instructions in New Jersey is often traced back to a case decided by the New Jersey Court of Errors and Appeals in 1869. In that case Peter Castner and Daniel Sliker got into a fight at a bar, and during the fight Castner put out both of Sliker's eyes. Sliker sued Castner for battery and got a judgment against him. Castner appealed the case, complaining that the trial judge had instructed the jury improperly when he told them:

> If you believe that the loss of the plaintiff's eyesight was the result of an intentional act on part of the defendant, I cannot perceive how you can hesitate to find in favor of the plaintiff. To take away the eyesight of an adversary, could only be justified by imminent danger of great bodily harm. It is difficult to imagine how, under the ordinary conditions of a private combat, such extreme violence could be justified. In this case there did not appear to be the faintest excuse for resorting to so dire a necessity, and *if,* consequently, *you agree with me*, that none of the necessities of self-defence existed at the occurrence in question, to justify the resort to such an act, and that the defendant wilfully and knowingly inflicted that incurable wound, you will find a verdict against him.[14]

[Emphasis in original.]

"... if a reasonable doubt of guilt is raised, even by inconclusive evidence of an alibi, the defendant is entitled to the benefit of that doubt." Transcript, 4510.

"There is evidence from which you may conclude, if you see fit, that ..." Transcript, 4514.

[13] Transcript, 4515.

[14] Castner v. Sliker, 33 N.J.L. 507, 511 (Ct. Err. & App., 1869).

In affirming the judgment for the plaintiff, the court wrote "It is the right and duty of a judge to comment upon the evidence, and in cases where he thinks it required for the promotion of justice, to give his views upon the weight of it, provided he leaves it to them to decide, upon their own views of it. This is too well settled by repeated decisions, to be now called into question."[15] The use of the conditional language "if … you agree with me" reminded the jury the decision on the verdict was theirs.

Justice Trenchard was well aware of the law concerning judicial comment on the evidence. In addition to his duties as a trial judge and Supreme Court justice, he sometimes sat on the Court of Errors and Appeals, and in 1909 he wrote the court's opinion in a bigamy case where the defendant complained that the trial judge had improperly commented on the evidence. In dealing with the complaint, Trenchard wrote:

> Whatever the rule may be in other jurisdictions, it is entirely settled in this state that the judge may call attention to any matter affecting the credibility of a witness, and may comment on the testimony, and intimate an opinion to its weight, whenever he thinks it necessary for the promotion of justice, so long as he fairly leaves the jury to determine the facts and draw their own conclusions as to the credibility of the witnesses and the weight of the testimony.[16]

Trenchard lived up to these words when he instructed the Hauptmann jury. He said what he thought about the evidence, but he repeatedly reminded the jury that they were free to disregard him. He also made comments favorable to Hauptmann: "As I have said, the defendant denies that he was the man who was paid the ransom

---

[15] *Id* at 512.

[16] State v. Warady, 77 N.J.L. 348, 349, 72 A. 37, 38 (Sup.Ct., 1909).

money, and there is other testimony which, if credible and believed by you, supports his statement."[17] Perhaps his most defense-friendly comments came when he discussed circumstantial evidence:

> The evidence produced by the State is largely circumstantial in character. In order to justify the conviction of the defendant upon circumstantial evidence, it is necessary not only that all of the circumstances concur to show that he committed the crime charged, but that they are inconsistent with any other rational conclusion.
>
> It is not sufficient that the circumstances proved coincide with, account for and therefore render probable the hypothesis that is sought to be established by the prosecution. They must exclude to a moral certainty every other hypothesis but the single one of guilt, and if they do not do this, the jury should find the defendant not guilty.
>
> And when the case against the defendant is made up wholly of a chain of circumstances, and there is reasonable doubt as to any fact, the existence of which is essential to establish guilt, the defendant should be acquitted.
>
> But the crime of murder is not one which is always committed in the presence of witnesses, and if not so committed, it must be established by circumstantial evidence or not at all.
>
> And where the essential facts and circumstances are proved, which cannot be explained upon any other theory than that the defendant is guilty of the crime charged against him, such evidence should be considered as satisfactory and convincing as that of the most direct and positive character.[18]

---

[17] Transcript, 4508.
[18] Transcript, 4512–4513.

Trenchard's comments on the evidence may be perceived as unfair, but they were neither unlawful nor legally inappropriate. Since the Lindbergh case, New Jersey courts have continued to allow judicial comment on the evidence, but they have come to be more circumspect about the practice. *State v. Swint*, decided in 2000, gives evidence of this trend by holding that "Judges are, and should be, reluctant to comment extensively on the facts developed during the trial. When they do, they run the risk of being perceived by the jury, as well as the parties, as an advocate."[19] As a consequence, contemporary trial judges make only sparing comments on the evidence, except where the evidence is complex or the potential for confusion great.[20]

Trenchard spoke for an hour and ten minutes, concluding his instructions at 11:13 AM. He had the jury room inspected to insure that no recording devices had been hidden in it, and then allowed the jury to retire and consider their verdict. He cleared the courtroom of all spectators who were not members of the press, and retired to his chambers to await the verdict.

When the jury retired to deliberate they asked for a magnifying glass so they could thoroughly examine all the tangible evidence in the case. After carefully examining the evidence they took a ballot without discussion. On the first ballot they voted 7 for guilty as charged without recommendation of mercy to 5 for guilty as charged with a recommendation of mercy. They then discussed the case. In all, they deliberated for some 11 hours over two days. The second ballot was 9–3 for guilty as charged without a recommendation of mercy. On the third ballot it was 10–2, and on the fourth it was 11–1. Finally on the fifth ballot they voted unanimously

---

[19] State v. Swint, 328 N.J.Super. 236, 248, 745 A.2d 570, 584 (2000).
[20] State v. Beigenwald, 106 N.J. 13, 44, 524 A.2d 130, 146 (1987).

to find the defendant guilty without recommendation of mercy.[21] Oddly enough, it had taken so long to get a unanimous death recommendation because some of the jurors thought death was too lenient a punishment for Hauptmann. Shortly before Hauptmann's execution juror Verna Snyder told a reporter, "I wanted to give him life imprisonment because I thought death was too good for him. The only reason I finally gave in was because he might get out some day if he got life."[22]

Some insight into the jurors' evaluation of the case against Hauptmann might be found in an interview given by juror Liscom Case. "My summing up will be simple," he said, "Hauptmann was in court because he was caught with a lot of the ransom money. The handwriting evidence, presented by men we could see were honest and sincere, left us no doubt as to his connection with the ransom notes. Then came the wood story. Wood in a Bronx lumber yard got into the ladder found at Colonel Lindbergh's home in Hopewell. Hauptmann had worked in that lumberyard. Hauptmann had bought wood from that lumberyard. Pieces of it turned up in the ladder. Wood in the ladder proved to have come from the attic of the house in which Hauptmann lived. Can you blame us for our verdict?"[23] It appears that the jurors were convinced by the triad suggested in Chapter 3—Ladder, Letters, and Loot.

Once the jury had agreed, they advised the bailiff that they had arrived at a verdict. According to the custom of Hunterdon County, whenever a jury arrived at a verdict, they would ring the courthouse bell to signal the end of deliberations. Undersheriff Keith Barrowcliffe ran up-

---

[21] "CCC Juryman Last to Vote for Death," *NYT*, February 15, 1935.

[22] Kenneth T. Downs, "Bruno Jurors Standing Pat," *Reading Eagle*, February 29, 1936, https://news.google.com (accessed March 20, 2015).

[23] Schrager, *The Sixteenth Rail*, 262–263.

stairs to the courthouse bell tower to ring the bell.[24] This was the sign for the various parties to assemble in the courtroom for the formal publication of the verdict. Hauptmann was brought into the courtroom at 10:30 AM. As he waited to hear his fate, Fisher leaned over to him and said, "This is only the beginning. Don't show a sign because if you do it will count against you." Hauptmann remained stoic as Foreman Charles Walton announced the verdict—guilty as charged without recommendation of mercy. The judge pronounced sentence, and Hauptmann was whisked back to his cell, where his self-control deserted him. He fell on his bunk and sobbed.[25]

Fisher had told Hauptmann the truth when he said the verdict was only the beginning. When a death penalty is pronounced, the lawyers contest appellate and post-conviction litigation every bit as hard as the trial itself. The battle over Hauptmann's guilt or innocence continued for the next 14 months. It was fought in the courtroom, the newsroom, and even more exotic locations, and it continues to rage to this day. Hauptmann himself fired the first salvo of this battle shortly after pronouncement of sentence. Sheriff John H. Curtis, at Fisher's request, allowed newsman Russell B. Porter to interview the condemned man in his cell. Hauptmann maintained his innocence and asked for donations to finance the expenses of his appeal.[26] Some took advantage of the plea to send small checks made out to Hauptmann. He would endorse the checks, they would be deposited to his defense fund, and the makers of the checks would get Hauptmann's autograph for a pittance.[27]

---

[24] "Bell at Courthouse Announces Verdict," *NYT*, February 14, 1935.

[25] Craig Thompson, "Hauptmann in Cell Falls in Collapse," *NYT*, February 14, 1935.

[26] Russell B. Porter, "Hauptmann Asks Public for Funds to Finance His Appeal," *NYT*, February 15, 1935.

[27] Waller, *Kidnap* (New York: Dial Press, 1961), 580.

When he left the courthouse after the publication of the verdict, jury foreman Charles Walton told reporters, "No one will ever learn from us what went on in that jury room."[28] His prediction proved not quite as accurate as Fisher's. It was not long before he sang another tune. On April 30, 1935, Walton announced that the jurors had agreed to write a book about their experiences, with each juror contributing a chapter.[29] The book never saw publication, but they were able to sell their stories to a newspaper which published them as a serial.

Hauptmann himself tried to raise more money for his appeal by writing his autobiography. At first prison officials refused him permission to release the biography, but eventually they relented.[30] Hauptmann couldn't get his book published either, and he eventually sold it for a low figure to a New York newspaper.[31]

Relations among the defense team had never been rosy during the trial, and they ruptured beyond repair in the post-trial litigation. The first problem came when Reilly wanted to delay filing Hauptmann's appeal papers until Wilentz returned from the vacation he took after the verdict was announced. Fisher wanted to file the paperwork immediately, and he took his complaint to both Hauptmann and the press. Hauptmann gave Fisher permission to proceed immediately, and Fisher gave the press an earful of complaints about Reilly's performance at the trial. In talking about Reilly's decision to delay filing the necessary paperwork, Fisher said:

> Mr. Reilly has not conferred with any of us, and I think it is an outrage. There is no sense to this. When our man is scheduled to die March 18, to think that we

---

[28] "CCC Juryman Last to Vote for Death," *NYT*, February 15, 1935.
[29] "Hauptmann Jurors Are Writing a Book," *NYT*, May 1, 1935.
[30] "Hauptmann Book to be Published," *NYT*, October 11, 1935.
[31] "Hauptmann Autobiography Sold," *NYT*, November 11, 1935.

> would waste time waiting for Mr. Wilentz to return from Florida. ... That suggestion is in keeping with his whole conduct of the case. ...
>
> He called Somers, Hier, Van Henke, and Streppone, and we had never heard of them. I objected strenuously to his calling Moses, but he insisted.[32]

Responding to Fisher's claims, Reilly said his decision to delay filing was based on "the gentlemanly practice of law" and would not harm Hauptmann's appeal in the least. Reilly went on to say, "Either Fisher gets out of this case or I get out. I am sick and tired of all this fooling around. I am tired of Fisher's double-crossing."[33] Anna Hauptmann arranged a peace conference among all the lawyers, and they arrived at a temporary resolution of their differences. The media naturally wanted to know if Reilly was still the lead counsel. When questioned on that issue, Pope responded, "Cut out your damned chiefs and seniors. We are four musketeers. One for all and all for one."[34] It was not long before the four musketeers became three.

When Hauptmann made his plea for donations, his wife agreed to become the face of the fundraising drive. She began to make speeches to different groups of German-American immigrants. They would charge admission to get into the speech, and then they would take up a collection at the conclusion of the speech. Anna Hauptmann raised several thousand dollars in this way. When donations to Hauptmann's appeal fund reached $12,000, Reilly presented Hauptmann with a bill for legal services in the amount of $25,000, saying the appeal fund would serve nicely to defray the costs of his services.[35]

---

[32] "Reilly and Fisher Break on Appeal," *NYT*, February 19, 1935.
[33] Ibid.
[34] "Hauptmann Wins Stay of Execution," *NYT*, February 22, 1935.
[35] "Reilly Asks $25,000 as Hauptmann Fee," *NYT*, March 31, 1935.

Reilly had already been compensated for his services. The Hearst newspaper group had agreed with Anna Hauptmann that they would pay Reilly's fee in return for her giving them a series of exclusive interviews.[36]

The Hauptmanns felt Reilly had gotten enough money from the newspaper deal. After speaking with her husband, Anna fired Reilly and named Fisher as lead counsel for the defense. As she was departing to go on a midwestern tour of fundraising events, she spoke to the media. "I saw Richard yesterday, and he agreed with me that Reilly should go." She went on to reveal that Hauptmann did not like Reilly and only kept him on the defense team because she insisted. [37] Reilly almost immediately announced that he intended to sue for his fee, saying "Whether Anna likes it or not, she is going to pay and pay through the nose."[38] Reilly took legal action to freeze the Hauptmann defense fund, claiming that Anna Hauptmann was wasting the fund and had no intention of paying legal fees from it.[39] Reilly employed a two front strategy, filing claims in both New York and New Jersey.[40] He could not have been happy when New Jersey Chancellor Malcolm Buchanan ruled on the suit. Buchanan refused to freeze the fund, found that Hauptmann owed Reilly nothing, and further found that Reilly probably owed Hauptmann $5,000 for money he obtained from the trust fund by "fraudulent and inequitable means." Buchanan's ruling was followed in short order by the ruling of Brooklyn Supreme Court Justice Charles C. Lockwood. Lockwood was less critical of Reilly, but Reilly was no more successful in New York

---

[36] Mark W. Falzini and James Davidson, New Jersey's Lindbergh Kidnapping and Trial (Charleston: Arcadia Publishing, 2012), 95.
[37] "Hauptmann Drops Reilly as Counsel," *NYT*, April 4, 1935.
[38] "Reilly Will Sue for $25,000 Fee," *NYT*, April 5, 1935.
[39] "Reilly Acts to Get Hauptmann Fund," *NYT*, May 5, 1935.
[40] "Reilly Balked in Hauptmann Suit," *NYT*, May 30, 1935.

than he was in New Jersey. Lockwood found that the money was donated to the fund for the purpose of pursuing an appeal and could not be used to pay previously existing legal fees.[41]

Anna Hauptmann wasn't the only person whom Reilly wanted to have "pay through the nose." He filed an ethics complaint asking the New Jersey Bar for a thorough investigation of Fisher's conduct in the Hauptmann case. Reilly alleged that Fisher had improperly tampered with the attorney-client relationship between himself and Hauptmann, and that as a result, Hauptmann had been duped into firing him. Reilly also complained that Fisher, in his capacity as the trustee for the appeals fund, had violated his fiduciary responsibilities by misappropriating the funds to his own use. The New Jersey Bar was not impressed by Reilly's complaint and refused to take any action against Fisher.[42] Reilly eventually abandoned his quest to get his hands on the Hauptmann appeal fund,[43] which had accomplished nothing other than distracting the attention of Hauptmann's lawyers from the task of prosecuting his appeal.

The first step in the appeal process was to try taking a writ of error to the Supreme Court, but they had to get permission from New Jersey Chancellor Luther A. Campbell to take the writ. Campbell denied the request, and the next step was to file a petition for writ of error to the Court of Errors and Appeals. Although appealing to the Supreme Court required the Chancellor's consent, appealing to the Court of Errors and Appeals did not.[44] Hauptmann's execution would be stayed until the resolution of the appeal. The Court of Errors and Appeals

---

41 "Reilly's Plea Denied," *NYT*, June 5, 1935.
42 "Reilly Plea Fails," *NYT*, April 28, 1935.
43 "Drops Hauptmann Suit," *NYT*, October 17, 1935.
44 "Hauptmann Wins First Appeal Move," *NYT*, February 20, 1935.

was a rather odd institution. It consisted of the Chancellor, six Supreme Court justices, and six part-time lay judges. The lay judges, who were appointed by the governor, did not have to be lawyers.[45]

The defense filed an Assignment of Errors in the Court of Errors and Appeals alleging 134 reasons that the conviction should be reversed. They divided these complaints into 18 groups:[46]

Group A: The court erred in overruling objections to certain questions asked of various prosecution witnesses on direct examination.

Group B: The court erred in refusing to strike certain portions of the testimony of various prosecution witnesses.

Group C: The court erred in sustaining objections to certain questions asked of prosecution witnesses on cross-examination.

Group D: The court erred in overruling objections to certain questions asked of various prosecution witnesses on redirect examination.

Group E: The court erred in sustaining objections to certain questions asked of various defense witnesses on direct examination.

Group F: The court erred in allowing the admission, over objection, of certain items of tangible evidence offered by the state.

Group G: The court erred in refusing to admit a photograph of the nursery window offered by the defense.

Group H: The court erred in refusing to allow certain questions asked of defense witnesses on redirect examination.

---

[45] "High Jersey Court Still Has Laymen," *NYT*, March 24, 1935.
[46] Transcript, 4567–4599.

Group I: The court erred in refusing to allow the witness Karl Henkel to testify that he believed his wife.

Group J: The court erred in admitting into evidence lines of testimony concerning hearsay statements by the defendant and other witnesses.

Group K: The court erred in refusing to strike the testimony of certain prosecution witnesses.

Group L: The court erred in refusing to allow certain questions asked on the direct examination of defense witness H. Norman Schwarzkopf.

Group M: The court erred in refusing to sustain objections to certain questions asked of defense witnesses on cross-examination.

Group N: The court erred in refusing to direct a verdict of acquittal at the close of the state's case and at the close of all the evidence.

Group O: The court erred in various ways when instructing the jury.

Group P: The court erred in refusing to give the jury certain instructions.

Group Q: The court erred in allowing the case to be tried in Hunterdon County rather than Mercer County, where the body of the victim was found.

Group R: The verdict of the jury was contrary to the weight of the evidence.

They later filed an amendment to the Assignment of Errors adding six additional complaints about the jury instructions to Group O.[47] The Assignment of Errors was disorganized and hard to follow, and most of the complaints had little or no merit. By the time they filed the appellate brief, they had revised and reorganized their complaints to 16 points, which the Court of Errors and Appeals dealt with in the order that they were presented.

---

[47] Transcript, 4789–4790.

See Appendix C for a summary of the defense contentions and the Court's rulings.

The three most serious defense contentions alleged that (1) there were improprieties in the summation by Wilentz, (2) there were improprieties in the jury instructions given by Justice Trenchard, and (3) that the jury verdict was contrary to the weight of the evidence. It appears that the defense might very well have won a new trial if they had objected to the comments Wilentz made in summation. The Court recognized that Wilentz had made many problematical arguments, but they held quite firmly that the defense did not properly preserve the error for appeal because they had not objected. The Court's ruling that Trenchard had properly instructed the jury may have been prompted in part because the New Jersey bench and bar had great respect for Trenchard's abilities. During his 35 years on the bench he never had a murder case reversed on appeal. [48] As to the third defense contention, the Court had this to say:

> Our conclusion is that the verdict is not only not contrary to the weight of the evidence, but one to which the evidence inescapably led. And discarding the testimony of the witness classified as irresponsible by the defendant, the result is the same. From three different and, in the main, unrelated, sources the proofs point unerringly to guilt, viz., (a) possession and use of the ransom money; (b) the handwriting of the ransom notes; and (c) the wood used in the construction of the ladder.
>
> (a) Bills totaling $14,600 were found hidden in defendant's home in the Bronx, New York, beneath the floor of the garage, and in the rafters of the dwelling house. In a hidden recess in one of the rafters contain-

---

[48] "T.W. Trenchard, Hauptmann Judge, Dies at Home in Trenton," *NYT*, July 24, 1942.

ing some of the bills was found a small revolver. On a board in a closet of the house was found, in defendant's handwriting, the address and telephone number of Condon. And we have the return of the sleeping suit by the man to whom the ransom money was eventually paid.

The explanation of the source of this money offered by defendant was incredible, and we find not the slightest evidence to corroborate it. The defendant's handling of the money makes clear his guilty connection with the enterprise. He was without funds before the payment of the ransom money, and in comparative poverty; he worked at his trade apparently, in the light of his subsequent conduct, because it was his only means of livelihood. After the payment of the money, he refrained from work entirely and speculated in Wall Street on a comparatively large scale. His actions thereafter are persuasive of guilt. It is clear his new found prosperity was evidenced long before he says he found the money claimed to have been left by Fisch. It is inconceivable that Fisch, if he had this money, would have left it in defendant's custody in the manner claimed, particularly when he was planning to leave for Germany on what seemed to be his last trip. He was afflicted with tuberculosis and died shortly after returning to his homeland. From the foregoing it is deducible, to a moral certainty beyond a reasonable doubt, that he collected the ransom money, and was therefore the kidnapper, particularly in view of—

(b) The identification of the handwriting on all the ransom notes, including the one left on the window sill of the nursery window, as that of Hauptmann. The peculiarities of expression and spelling common to all these notes and admittedly genuine writings by Hauptmann. It is likewise an inescapable inference that the writer of the ransom note on the window sill entered the nursery and perpetrated the crime.

Moreover, we have the chisel found at the scene of the crime. It was of a size that is ordinarily a part of a carpenter's tool chest but was missing from Hauptmann's set found in the Bronx home.

(c) Part of the wood used in the construction of the ladder was taken from Hauptmann's Bronx home. It is significant that long before Hauptmann's arrest, the wood, or part of it, was traced to a Bronx lumber yard near his home by the expert Koehler. And there was evidence that Hauptmann limped for some days after the kidnapping.

It is clear the ladder was used to reach the second story. Colonel Lindbergh heard the sound of breaking wood that evening, and the ladder was found broken. The witness Sweeny, by actual test, demonstrated that the entry of the second story window and the descent therefrom with the child could be accomplished with the ladder.

There is no significance in the selection by the kidnapper of the unlocked southeast window. The shutters, because of warping, could not be completely closed, and it is fair to assume that the intruder selected this unlocked window by pure chance, or when he found the other windows barred.

And the claim that entry was not made through this window had nothing to support it. Muddy footmarks were found on the window sill and nursery floor, and a suitcase placed on the floor under the window. Footprints were found outside the window.

The absence of defendant's fingerprints had no significance; it is clear that this self-confessed and apparently experienced criminal would naturally guard against the making of these tell-tale marks of his visit.

There was much more evidence tending to establish his guilt. It was a circumstantial case with the evidence pointing to guilt from so many directions as to leave no room for a reasonable doubt.[49]

---

[49] State v. Hauptmann, 115 N.J.L. 412, 420, 180 A. 809, 826–827 (Ct.Err. & App., 1935).

It is interesting that the Court's analysis completely ignored the testimony of those witnesses who said they saw Hauptmann in the vicinity of Lindbergh's home near the time of the abduction. Their assessment of the evidence coincided perfectly with the expressed opinions of jurors Charles Walton and Liscom Case—they ignored the shaky eyewitnesses and relied on the evidentiary triad of Ladder, Letters, and Loot.

Upon receiving word that the Court of Errors and Appeals had affirmed Hauptmann's conviction, the defense team petitioned the United States Supreme Court for a writ of certiorari to review the case. The Supreme Court gave them a laconic response: "Petition for writ of certiorari to the Court of Errors and Appeals of New Jersey denied."[50] On receiving news of the Supreme Court's refusal to hear Hauptmann's case, Wilentz took a death warrant to Justice Trenchard, who signed it and set the execution for the week of January 13, 1936.[51] In New Jersey at the time of the Hauptmann case, death warrants provided that an execution had to occur within a specific time period. If a higher court stayed the execution to review the case, a new death warrant had to be issued after the appeal was over.

One might think that the way was now clear for Hauptmann's execution. It was not. Governor Harold G. Hoffman had taken an interest in the case and had decided to take a hand in it as well. While the appeal was still pending, Hoffman had taken the unprecedented step of going to the prison and interviewing Hauptmann in his cell.[52] Shortly after the Supreme Court denied certiorari, Hoffman announced his intention to ask the New Jersey

---

[50] Hauptmann v. New Jersey, 296 U.S. 649 (1935).

[51] "Hauptmann Death is Fixed by Court for Week of January 13," *NYT*, December 14, 1935.

[52] "Gov. Hoffman Saw Hauptmann in Cell," *NYT*, December 6, 1035.

Court of Pardons to grant Hauptmann a personal interview.[53] Most members of the Court of Pardons were already thoroughly familiar with the case. It consisted of the Chancellor, the six lay judges of the Court of Errors and Appeals, and the Governor. Hoffman, unlike governors in other states, did not have the power to unilaterally grant a pardon. He did, however, have the power to prevent a pardon. If a majority of the Court of Pardons voted for clemency, he could effectively veto the decision by casting his vote against clemency.[54]

The Court of Pardons discussed Hauptmann's petition for clemency on December 30, 1935, when they formally met on another matter. At this time the Court decided that Hoffman would set the date of the hearing on Hauptmann, and that the Court would not allow either Hauptmann or his wife to appear before it.[55] As the time for the execution drew near without the setting of a hearing date for the Court of Pardons to meet on Hauptmann, Warden Mark O. Kimberling took it upon himself to delay the execution, which had been set for January 14, for "a few days." Without a reprieve from a higher authority, Kimberling was required to execute Hauptmann on or before January 17. Hoffman set the hearing on the petition for clemency for January 10, at 10:30 a.m.[56]

On the eve of the pardon hearing Hoffman announced that he had received a letter purportedly from J.J. Faulkner, the man who had deposited $2,980 in ransom gold certificates on May 1, 1933. Hoffman said he got the letter two weeks previously, and he had asked a handwriting expert to examine it. According to Hoffman, the examiner

---

[53] Waller, *Kidnap*, 513.

[54] "Court Discusses Hauptmann Plea," *NYT*, December 28, 1935.

[55] "Court Discusses Hauptmann Plea," *NYT*, December 31, 1935.

[56] "Hauptmann's Plea Set for Saturday," *NYT*, January 7, 1936.

had proclaimed the letter to be written by the same hand which had signed J.J. Faulkner's deposit slip for $2,980. In the letter "Faulkner" pled for clemency for Hauptmann because Hauptmann was innocent.[57] The Faulkner letter did not deter the Court of Pardons. After a hearing which lasted from 10:30 a.m. until 5:00 p.m., the Court unanimously voted to deny clemency.[58] After the clemency hearing handwriting examiner J. Vreeland Haring and his son, J. Howard Haring, revealed that they had examined the Faulkner letter. Both declared that it was most definitely not written by the man who signed the J.J. Faulkner deposit slip. They characterized the letter as "a bungling attempt" to forge the Faulkner signature and either a hoax or an effort to frustrate justice.[59]

Working furiously against the January 17 deadline, the defense team began a frenzied effort to forestall the execution. On January 14, at 4:00 p.m., Hauptmann's lawyers arrived in the chambers of Federal District Judge J. Warren Davis and presented him with a petition for a writ of habeas corpus. Davis called Wilentz, who immediately came to Davis's chambers, and Davis held a hearing that very afternoon. At the conclusion of the hearing Davis announced his ruling from the bench.[60] In denying the petition, Davis said:

> Gentlemen, we do not have here the question of guilt of the prisoner. He has been declared to be guilty of murder after a very long and careful and patient trial.... This case, in my judgment, was tried brilliantly on both sides by very capable, earnest and industrious

---

[57] "Gov. Hoffman Gets 'Faulkner' Letter," *NYT*, January 10, 1936.
[58] Craig Thompson, "Hauptmann Loses Plea before Court; Talk of Seizing Condon," *NYT*, January 12, 1936.
[59] "Faulkner Note Held Fake," *NYT*, January 12, 1935.
[60] Craig Thompson "Hauptmann Loses Plea for Federal Court Writ; Hoffman Still Undecided," *NYT*, January 15, 1936.

> counsel, and counsel for the defense are to be commended for their zeal, industry, [and] ability.... What is complained of here took place largely before the eyes of Justice Trenchard, who is one of the most conscientious, capable and distinguished gentlemen and jurists that we have in this State. Before I became United States Attorney and went on the bench I tried murder cases before him. He has been eminently fair, and I am persuaded was so in this trial.... So it seems to me that if I, upon this same evidence and upon these same facts, were to grant this writ of habeas corpus I would, perhaps not technically, but I would in effect, be overruling the Court of Errors and Appeals of this State and the Supreme Court of the United States. This would, it seems to me, be sheer, inexcusable, judicial egotism on my part.[61]

The defense team immediately took their case to the United States Supreme Court. Shortly after noon on January 16 they presented a petition for writ of habeas corpus to the Court as it sat hearing other matters. The Supreme Court recessed for lunch and apparently discussed the petition over the lunch hour. They returned from lunch four minutes late, and Chief Justice Hughes read their decision denying the writ. The Court then resumed proceedings in the case which they were hearing before lunch.[62]

While the defense frantically tried to stop the execution, Hoffman was not idle. He had previously floated the idea that he might grant Hauptmann a reprieve,[63] which would have the effect of delaying but not stopping the execution, and he immediately began talking about the

---

[61] "Ruling on Hauptmann Plea," *NYT*, January 15, 1936.

[62] Ex Parte Hauptmann, 297 U.S. 693 (1936); "Supreme Court Rejects Hauptmann's Plea in Decision Read by Chief Justice Hughs," *NYT*, January 17, 1936.

[63] "Hoffman Doubts Reprieve Powers," *NYT*, December 28, 1935.

possibility again. There was some question as to whether he had the legal authority to grant such a reprieve, but previous governors had occasionally granted reprieves without being challenged. In order to insure that he would not be challenged, Hoffman asked to meet with Wilentz and Hauck. The three met, and Hoffman convinced the two prosecutors to agree to a reprieve by arguing that it would give them more time to convince Hauptmann to confess and name his accomplices. Wilentz and Hauck agreed to a 30 day reprieve, and Wilentz agreed to wait another 30 days before asking Trenchard to sign another death warrant.[64]

Against the backdrop of a rising tide of public opposition to Hoffman's handling of the case,[65] Hoffman announced that he had hired criminologist Robert W. Hicks to investigate certain "problems" with the case against Hauptmann. Hicks told the press that he saw the following problems with the case:

(1) Discrepancies between the description of the Lindbergh baby and the body found in Mercer County.
(2) The possibility that one person could have committed the kidnapping and another could have extorted the money.
(3) The possibility that eyewitnesses had misidentified Hauptmann, who looked very similar to Robert Scanlan, a man who claimed to have been on the Lindbergh property the day of the kidnapping.
(4) The fact that the handwriting in the ransom notes bore a striking resemblance to Isidore Fisch's handwriting.[66]

---

[64] Waller, *Kidnap*, 527; Craig Thompson, "Hauptmann Gets a 30 Day Reprieve from Gov. Hoffman," *NYT*, January 17, 1936.
[65] Waller, *Kidnap*, 527; Craig Thompson "Hauptmann Gets a 30 Day Reprieve from Gov. Hoffman," *NYT*, January 17, 1936.
[66] "Hoffman Hires Detective" *NYT*, January 17, 1936.

Hicks was actually on the payroll of two private citizens who had taken an interest in the case—Evalyn McLean, who had gotten duped out of $100,000 when she hired con man Gaston Means to act as go-between in ransom negotiations with the kidnappers, and Paul G. Clancey, the editor of *American Astrology*.[67] Hicks rented Hauptmann's old apartment and began investigating the attic with the help of Arch W. Loney, a wood expert who had been a potential defense witness at the trial.[68]

The retaining of Hicks was not Hoffman's first effort to insert himself into the investigation of the kidnapping. Shortly after the kidnapping Colonel Schwarzkopf had declined an offer by Ellis Parker, a detective from neighboring Burlington County, to assist in the investigation. Parker, who enjoyed a reputation as "the American Sherlock Holmes" determined to investigate the case anyway and received assistance from Hoffman, who was then Commissioner of Motor Vehicles. Hoffman authorized his large staff of investigators to assist Parker in the investigation. When the United States Supreme Court refused to hear Hauptmann's final plea, Parker was still investigating the case with the assistance of Samuel Lockwood, an investigator with the Department of Motor Vehicles.[69]

After Wilentz and Hauck agreed not to contest Hoffman's temporary reprieve, the governor became strident in his demands that the New Jersey State Police reopen and reinvestigate the case. Neither Schwarzkopf nor Wilentz seemed receptive to the governor's efforts. Schwarzkopf declared that the case had never been closed, and that the NJSP investigated new evidence whenever it came to light.

---

[67] Fisher, *The Lindbergh Case*, 398.
[68] *Ibid,* 410.
[69] Craig Thompson, "Hoffman to Order New Investigation," *NYT*, January 19, 1936.

Both Wilentz and Schwarzkopf asserted that they would not allow the governor to dictate how they handled individual cases.[70] The friction between Hoffman and Schwarzkopf increased upon Hoffman's learning that Schwarzkopf had been following up on information uncovered by Hoffman's independent investigation.[71]

Just before the expiration of the stay, the defense team, being assured that Hauptmann could get his sentence commuted if he would confess and name his accomplices, made one last-ditch effort to get Hauptmann to confess. Sometimes a defense attorney finds it necessary to "cross-examine" his own client in an effort to either prepare the client to take the witness stand or to demonstrate for him the hopelessness of his defense and help him come to the realization that he should accept the government's magnanimous plea offer and get a lesser sentence. Such a cross-examination, if not done tactfully, can destroy attorney-client rapport. One way to avoid ruining the attorney-client relationship is to enlist the aid of a colleague to do the examination. The Hauptmann defense team enlisted another lawyer to perform the task. The lawyer they called on was Samuel Leibowitz, who had won fame for his successful defense in the infamous Scottsboro Boys Case. Leibowitz felt sure that he could get Hauptmann to confess. Fisher was just as certain that Leibowitz could do no such thing. Leibowitz had several meetings with Hauptmann on death row at the prison in Trenton.

The stay expired and Justice Trenchard dutifully reset Hauptmann's execution for the week of March 30, 1936.[72] Leibowitz made one last visit to Hauptmann. During this visit he cross-examined Hauptmann vigorously for 4 ½ hours in an effort to persuade him to

---

[70] Ibid.
[71] "Troopers Sifting Hoffman Inquiry," *NYT*, January 20, 1936.
[72] "Hauptmann Death Date Set," *NYT*, March 11, 1936.

confess and save his life. Hauptmann steadfastly refused. Leibowitz quit the defense team in disgust, and then he took an unusual step. He released a partial transcript of his cross-examination of Hauptmann. His publication of the cross-examination presents us with the dual mysteries of why he released the transcript and how he escaped punishment from the bar for revealing confidential communications with a client. Leibowitz arguably did a better cross-examination of Hauptmann than the one performed by Wilentz, but Leibowitz had the luxury of being unencumbered by the rules of evidence:

> [**Q:** What is your theory of how the kidnapping could have been done?]
>
> **A:** I never thought about a theory, I never tried to think how it could be done.
>
> **Q:** How do you think the baby was taken out of the nursery window?
>
> **A:** Not out the window. Down the stairs. Taken down the stairs.
>
> **Q:** Then why was the ladder there?
>
> **A:** Oh, in case it was needed.
>
> **Q:** Then you believe the baby was deliberately killed?
>
> **A:** Oh, no, it was an accident.
>
> **Q:** Listen, Hauptmann, come clean with me. You think the ladder wasn't used by the kidnappers. The only indication of accidental death was the fact that the ladder broke and the kidnapper and baby fell to the ground. If the baby had been carried down the stairway inside, how do you account for an accident?
>
> **A:** You are worse as Wilentz.
>
> **Q:** What would you have done in case of an accident?
>
> **A:** I would have dropped the baby and run like hell in my automobile.
>
> **Q:** What would you have done had you got the baby away?

A: I would have taken the baby to a farmhouse close by.

Q: How would you have collected the ransom if you left the baby dead? Would you have taken the sleeping suit?

A: I don't know. I guess that's what the kidnappers would have done.

Q: Suppose you are Isidor Fisch with the ransom money. What would you do if you knew that the police all over the world were looking for this money and that if you were caught in this city or on the high seas or in Germany, you would have been brought back and held for the Lindbergh murder?

A: I guess I would leave it in a safety deposit box.

Q: You wouldn't put it in a paper box and wrap it around with string and leave it with a friend would you? Not even if you knew you were going to die in Germany?

A: I guess I wouldn't do that. People who are sick like Fisch are never very sure they are going to die.

Q: Hauptmann, did you ever play the numbers game?

A: No.

Q: You know about it. You know there is about one chance in 600,000 of winning?

A: Yes.

Q: Did you know that there is about the same chance that more than one person will misspell the same word in fifteen different notes? In the ransom notes the word 'light was spelled "l-i-h-g-t." What do you think of that?

A: [No intelligible answer.][73]

The week before Hauptmann was scheduled to die in the electric chair, Hoffman called for a group inspection of the attic. Wilentz, Hauck, Koehler, and Bornmann

---

[73] "Hauptmann Is Resentenced to Die; Leibowitz Suddenly Quits the Case," *NYT*, February 20, 1936.

attended, as did Loney and Hoffman. The meeting began with an examination of the attic floorboards. The attic had a rough floor consisting of 27 boards, with one outside board having been cut short. Koehler had identified this board as the source of Rail 16. Loney pointed out several apparent anomalies which he felt called the identification of Rail 16 into question. For each anomaly Loney identified, Koehler had an answer.

FIGURE 9-1

LONEY'S CRITIQUE OF RAIL 16

LONEY'S ANOMALY	KOEHLER'S EXPLANATION
(1) The outside board was nailed down with more nails than the other boards.	Outside boards are usually nailed down with more nails than interior boards.
(2) The outside board was 1/16" thicker than the other boards.	Such minor variation frequently occurs with unfinished woodwork.
(3) The side of the attic with the cut board had 14 floorboards while the side of the attic without had only 13.	The number of boards is not significant with a partially covered attic floor.
(4) The outside board was cut square but Rail 16 was cut at an angle.	Rail 16 was cut a second time after it was removed from the attic. There is a 1 1/4" section missing between the outside board and Rail 16.

As a final demonstration, Rail 16 was laid down across the rafters and nails were inserted into the holes. The holes in the rafters matched the location and angle of the holes in Rail 16, but they did not accommodate the full length of the nails. Anthony Hauck, who was also present for the demonstration, said "There's something fishy here. Someone has tampered with those nail holes." The meeting degenerated into a heated confrontation, with Hoffman accusing Bornmann and Koehler of perjury. Finally carpenters were summoned to remove the rafters from the attic so they could be sent to the physics laboratory at Columbia University for a thorough examination.[74] At the lab the rafters were split to expose the full depth of the nail holes. Hauck described the examination:

> Koehler and Loney saw them open, disclosing the nail holes. They discovered in each one of them, part way down, a wooden plug or block. When these were removed, the nails fitted exactly with their heads flush with the floor. I said to the governor, "Now are you satisfied?" and the governor replied that he was satisfied that Bornmann and Koehler had told the truth when they said the nails fitted flush with the floor.[75]

The finger of suspicion pointed at Loney, the man who had rented Hauptmann's old apartment and gotten an excellent opportunity to tamper with the nail holes in the rafters, but an innocent interpretation was available. It was possible that the wood particles had simply accumulated in the holes over time, and the prosecutors were willing to give Loney the benefit of the doubt.

Hoffman may have been satisfied that Bornmann and Koehler were no perjurers, but he wasn't through meddling in the case. He floated the idea of a second stay so that the board evidence could be further studied. Neither Wilentz nor Hauck were agreeable to a second stay. Wilentz called the exercise in the attic ridiculous and nonsensical. He said that he didn't attend the examination at Columbia University and only went to the attic examination to give support to the officers whose integrity had been questioned. Hauck was less diplomatic. He accused Hoffman of being in league with the defense team and vowed to fight any further stay.[76] Hoffman, feeling the

---

[74] Fisher, *The Lindbergh Case*, 410–412.
[75] "Hoffman Attacks Ladder Evidence," *NYT*, March 27, 1936.
[76] *Ibid.*

heat of the negative public sentiment, announced that he was not going to order a second stay "unless a situation arose which the Attorney General would agree warranted asking the court for another extension." When asked what sort of situation would warrant such a move, he replied, "a confession, for instance."[77]

Hoffman proved to be either a prophet or someone with inside information, because within a few days of his pronouncement every member of the Court of Pardons received a 25 ½ page confession signed by a man named Paul Wendel. One member of the Court, who preferred to remain anonymous, accused Hoffman of sending copies of the letter to the members of the court.[78] Hoffman denied doing such a thing, but he called a meeting of the Court of Pardons to consider the confession. Hoffman said he did not want a pardon from the Court, merely a delay of a few months to complete his independent investigation of the Hauptmann case. Upon learning of the confession Wilentz demanded that the confessor be handed over to the proper authorities. Wendel was surrendered to Hunterdon County authorities, and Wilentz personally interrogated the man for 1 ½ hours. After the interrogation Wilentz informed the media:

> Paul H. Wendel is being held on a charge of embezzlement based on bench warrants issued in 1931. Wendel has signed a couple of statements saying he had been the kidnapper of the Lindbergh baby which he now repudiated, and claimed they had been issued under duress.
>
> This man repudiated those statements and is now reducing his repudiation to writing.... He says that on February 14 of this year he was taken into custody in

---

[77] "No New Reprieve," *NYT*, March 26, 1936.

[78] "Hoffman Summons Board of Pardons," *NYT*, March 29, 1936.

> New York by persons unknown to him. He was questioned there, he said, and made a statement under duress.
>
> He was then delivered, he said, to the home of Ellis Parker in Mount Holly, N.J., and has been detained since by Parker in the New Lisbon State Home for Mental Defectives under a guard. He said he gave Parker a statement similar to the one given in New York by him, but that in doing so he insisted to Mr. Parker that he had nothing to do with the crime.
>
> He said that Parker obtained the statement under duress and Parker told him that if he would make a confession he would certainly make $1,000,000. He said Parker told him that Wilentz and Hauck would be superseded by the Governor and that Howard Eastwood, Prosecutor of Burlington County, would take charge of the case and that in that event he would have nothing to fear.[79]

Wilentz said he had no charge against Wendel in the kidnapping, and he assumed that the Mercer County Prosecutor would look into the case. Wendel's claim of kidnapping and coercion was validated when Ellis Parker and his son were convicted of kidnapping under the newly enacted Federal kidnapping statute, ironically becoming the first men convicted under the law enacted in response to the Lindbergh kidnapping.[80]

In the confusion ensuing from the Wendel confession, Wilentz and Hauck made their positions clear. A further reprieve by Hoffman would be vigorously contested, but if either the Court of Pardons or Justice Trenchard ordered a stay, the prosecution would not contest it. The prosecution may have said it would not contest a stay by the Court of Pardons, but they fully intended to argue against such a decision by the Court. On March 30, 1936,

---

[79] *Ibid.*

[80] United States v. Parker, 103 F.2d 857 (3rd Cir., NJ, 1939).

at 11:00 a.m. the Court took up the Hauptmann matter again and held a lengthy hearing in which they heard from both sides. During the argument, Hauck became so distraught that he fainted. The Court retired to deliberate, and Wilentz, Schwarzkopf, and other members of the prosecution team gathered in the Attorney General's office to await the decision. When Albert B. Herman, the court clerk, emerged with the Court's written decision, he was mobbed by reporters and prevented from delivering the written decision until he read it for them: "The second application for clemency before the Court of Pardons of New Jersey by Bruno Richard Hauptmann, sentenced to death for the murder of Charles A. Lindbergh, Jr., March 1, 1932, today was denied." A scrum developed over possession of the written opinion, and Herman both lost the opinion and had his coat torn. Mercer County Prosecutor Erwin E. Marshall, who had taken over the case against Wendel from the Attorney General, announced that in light of the Court's ruling, he did not intend to present the case to the Mercer County grand jury.[81] The path was now clear for Hauptmann to be executed—but not quite.

The following evening 8,000 people gathered outside the prison at Trenton to await news that the execution had been carried out. They were dumbfounded to learn that the execution had been stayed another 48 hours. At first they refused to disperse, thinking the announcement was some sort of hoax, but they finally left when newsboys began to shout, "Extra! Hauptmann Reprieved!"[82] Warden Kimberling had caused the delay. He was worried about the possibility of the Mercer County grand jury indicting Wendel for the murder. Not wanting to get into the

---

[81] "Hauptmann's Plea Fails; 'No Stay' Says Hoffman of the Execution Tonight," *NYT*, March 31, 1936.

[82] "8,000 in the Crowd at Trenton Prison," *NYT*, April 1, 1936.

uncomfortable situation of executing a man for a murder that someone else may have committed, he notified Marshall that he had set the execution for 8:00 p.m. He requested Marshall to notify him immediately if the grand jury indicted Wendel. Moments before the execution was to be carried out, Kimberling received a telephone call from Allyne Freeman, the foreman of the Mercer County grand jury, asking a delay so that the grand jury could complete its investigation of Wendel. Since he was free to execute Hauptmann on any day during the week of March 31, he agreed to put the execution off for 48 hours. Hoffman immediately issued a statement that he had nothing to do with the reprieve, but there was room for suspicion that he had engineered the situation—Allyne Freeman was a personal friend and political ally of Hoffman.[83]

The actions of the Mercer County grand jury certainly belied the old saw that a grand jury is merely the tool of the prosecutor. Marshall went before the grand jury that morning expecting to present the grand jury with an embezzlement case against Wendel, but he received a shock when Freeman immediately invited him to leave the grand jury room. The grand jury then began taking testimony on the murder charge without the assistance of the prosecutor. It was only then that Marshall learned Wendel had been booked into the Mercer County jail on a charge of murder. The booking officer, a friend of Ellis Parker, had ignored his instructions to book Wendel on embezzlement charges. As Marshall fumed outside the hearing room and the grand jury took the testimony of Ellis Parker and his son, Wilentz rounded up witnesses in an effort to bring the grand jury to their senses. Soon Wendel's son and daughter were standing outside the grand jury room ready to testify that Parker had asked

---

[83] Russell B. Porter, "Hauptmann Gets a Stay for at Least 48 Hours at Grand Jury's Request," *NYT*, April 1, 1936.

them to falsely swear that Wendel had given them the Lindbergh child and he had died in their custody. Marshall sent Leo Rogers, one of his assistants, into the grand jury room to inform them of the new development. They agreed to hear from the two witnesses and asked Marshall to return to the grand jury room. As Wendel's children testified before the grand jury, Parker and his son hovered near the door trying to eavesdrop on the proceedings. Finally, at 7:58 p.m. the grand jury broke for the day and Freeman called Kimberling to ask for more time.[84]

While the grand jury was considering the possibility of indicting Wendel, Fisher was also busy. He brought a petition before Justice Trenchard asking a delay of the execution until the Wendel matter could be thoroughly investigated. Wilentz appeared to oppose the petition, but Hauck was too ill to attend following his collapse before the Court of Pardons. Wilentz opposed a stay arguing that Wendel's confession was "the meanest, vilest fraud ever perpetrated in this state." Wilentz capped off his argument by giving Trenchard a copy of the Wendel confession. Trenchard studied the paper intently and then pronounced his ruling:

> I am of the opinion that these papers do not justify a rule to show cause for a new trial and do not justify an arrest of execution.
>
> It seems plain to me that this confession is incredible on its face, and out of harmony with the known facts of the case. In such a case I do not think I have the authority to interfere with the orderly course of justice in this case and will therefore have to deny counsel their petition....[85]

---

[84] "Grand Jury Takes Case in Own Hands," *NYT*, April 1, 1936.
[85] *Ibid.*

The next day, with the *Trenton Times* calling for his impeachment, Hoffman again denied having anything to do with Kimberling's decision to delay the execution. He also denied a charge by Marshall that he had known about Wendel's confession for over a month. William F. Conkling, Hoffman's press aid, did admit that Hoffman had known for some time that Parker was investigating Wendel. During his interview Hoffman hinted that he might be willing to order another reprieve for Hauptmann based on the Wendel confession. When asked what he would do if Hoffman ordered such a reprieve, Kimberling replied, "I will seek legal advice."[86]

On April 1, Wendel sent a letter to the grand jury requesting that he be allowed to testify before them. He stipulated that he would waive immunity for his testimony and would agree that anything he said could be used against him in a prosecution for the murder of the Lindbergh child. He concluded his letter by stating, "This alleged confession is untrue and made up out of the whole cloth and I can demonstrate it to you if you give me the opportunity."[87] The grand jury gave Wendel that opportunity on the following day, and he testified before them for four hours. Wilentz also gave two hours of testimony, and Hoffman testified for an hour and a half. The grand jury then voted to drop the investigation, but their decision put the status of the case in a sort of legal limbo. Marshall explained the dilemma, "As it stands there is still a charge of murder against Wendel.... The grand jury's action did not serve to dismiss the charge of murder inasmuch as they did not vote to return a no true bill." Although the vote of the grand jury stood 18–5 to discontinue the investigation, Freeman apparently blocked efforts to vote a no true bill.

---

[86] "Execution of Hauptmann Set for Tomorrow Night; Further Delay Possible," *NYT*, April 2, 1936.
[87] "Grand Jury Delays Action on Wendel," *NYT*, April 2, 1936.

In justification Freeman said, "As long as I remain foreman no vote will ever be taken in any case where there still remains testimony."[88]

Meanwhile, Fisher was still working to delay the execution. The morning of April 3, the day set for the execution, Fisher fired off two telegrams. The first asked Hoffman to order another reprieve. Hoffman did not reply. The second asked Hauck to take the Wendel case before the Hunterdon County grand jury. Hauck replied that he could not do so because he had no formal complaint against Wendel. That afternoon Fisher wired Hauck saying that he had obtained an arrest warrant for Wendel charging him in Hunterdon County with the murder of the Lindbergh child. Hauck replied that he would take the case before the grand jury on its next regularly scheduled meeting date, which was well after the date set for Hauptmann's execution. Kimberling, in a quandary over what to do about the murder charges pending against Wendel, asked for legal advice. At 3:00 p.m. that afternoon, he got it. Wilentz sent him a letter stating that only three things could stop the execution: (1) a reprieve by the governor; (2) a stay from Justice Trenchard; or (3) a commutation of sentence from the Court of Pardons. Kimberling understood his duty. At 8:45 on the evening of April 3 Bruno Richard Hauptmann died in New Jersey's electric chair,[89] but the controversy over the case lives on to this day.

---

[88] Russell B. Porter, "Another Reprieve Hinted," *NYT*, April 3, 1936.
[89] Waller, *Kidnap*, 675–686.

Appendix

Appendix A
Timeline

November 26, 1899: Bruno Richard Hauptmann born.

February 4, 1902: Charles A. Lindbergh born.

October 10, 1925: Bruno Richard Hauptmann marries Anna Schoeffel.

May 20, 1927: Charles A. Lindbergh departs New York on historic trans-Atlantic flight.

May 21, 1927: Charles A. Lindbergh arrives in Paris on historic trans-Atlantic flight.

May 27, 1929: Charles A. Lindbergh marries Anne Morrow.

June 22, 1930: Charles A. Lindbergh, Jr. born.

October 16, 1930: Whateleys come to work for Lindberghs.

January or February, 1932: Hauptmann leaves job at National Lumber and Millwork Company, Bronx, NY.

February, 1932: Millard Whited sees stranger near Lindbergh's estate. Later identifies stranger as Hauptmann.

LEGEND: Undisputed facts and prosecution evidence; <u>Defense evidence</u>; *Rebuttal evidence by prosecution;* [Evidence available to, but not used by, the prosecution.]

February 27, 1932: Lindberghs leave Morrow estate in Englewood to go to Lindbergh estate at Hopewell.

February 28, 1932: Charles B. Rossiter sees man standing by car near Princeton airport. Later identifies the man as Hauptmann.

February 29, 1932: Lindberghs decide to stay at Hopewell rather than return to Englewood.

March, 1932: Hauptmann meets Isidor Fisch at Hunter's Island.

March 1, 1932, 1:25 a.m.: William Brevort Bolmer speaks to man driving green car near Princeton airport. There is a poor ladder attached to the car and a woman in the car. The man is not Hauptmann. *The man is not Fisch either.*

March 1, 1932, a.m.: Amandus Hochmuth sees a man driving a car containing a ladder. Hochmuth later identifies the driver as Bruno Hauptmann.

March 1, 1932, 11:30 p.m.: Ann Lindbergh telephones Bessie Gow to come to Hopewell from Englewood to help care for baby.

March 1, 1932, 1:30 p.m.: Bessie Gow arrives at Lindbergh estate at Hopewell.

March 1, 1932, 2:00–3:00 p.m.: Lou Harding sees two men and a woman in a car with a ladder strapped on it. They stop and ask him directions to the Lindbergh home.

March 1, 1932, p.m.: Benjamin Lupica sees man driving auto containing ladder near Lindbergh gatehouse. Says the man is not Hauptmann. *Says the man looked like Hauptmann.*

March 1, 1932, p.m.: Christian Fredericksen, Elvert Carlstrom, Louis Kiss, and others see Hauptmann in Fredericksen's bakery in the Bronx. Kiss later goes to Leo Singer's house and discusses Singer's new radio.

March 1, 1932, p.m.: *Arthur Larsen was in Dunellen N.J. with Elvert Carlstrom.*

March 1, 1932, 7:00 p.m.: *Violet Sharpe serves Elizabeth Morrow her supper before Sharpe goes on date with Ernest Miller.*

March 1, 1932, 7:30–8:45 p.m.: Anna Bonesteel sees Violet Sharpe near Alpine ferry. Doesn't see two men. Doesn't see baby.

March 1, 1932, 8:00 p.m.: *Ernest Miller picks up Violet Sharpe for date and takes her to Peanut Grill in Orangeburg.*

March 1, 1932, 8:00–10:00 p.m.: Lindbergh baby abducted.

March 1, 1932, 8:30 p.m.: Red Johnson telephones Bessie Gow at Lindbergh estate.

March 1, 1932, 8:30–11:45 p.m.: *Isidor Fisch at the home of Henry Jung in the Bronx.*

March 1, 1932, 10:00: *Ernest Miller returns Violet Sharpe to residence of Elizabeth Morrow.*

March 2, 1932, 12:00-12:30 a.m.: Peter Sommer sees two men on Weehawken ferry. Later sees them assisting a woman with a baby. Sommer later identifies Isidor Fisch as one of the men and Violet Sharpe as the lady.

March, 1932: Ella Achenbach sees Hauptmann shortly after the kidnapping. He is limping.

March 2, 1932: Millard Whited reports to authorities that he saw stranger near Lindbergh's estate.

March 2, 1932: Joseph Dutt accompanies Peter Sommer to police to report what Sommer saw on 3/1/1932.

March 2, 1932: Lou Harding reports seeing two men on March 1, 1932. *Harding does not report seeing ladder.*

March 2, 1932: Lindberghs publish request asking that kidnappers feed the child according to a special diet.

March 4, 1932: Second ransom note mailed near Borough Hall, Brooklyn.

March 5, 1932: Second ransom note received by Lindbergh.

March 7, 1932: Third ransom note mailed from Station D, NYC.

March 8, 1932: Dr. John Condon's offer to act as go-between in ransom delivery published in *Bronx Home News.*

March 8, 1932: *George Wilton takes photograph of ladder documenting the four cut nail holes in Rail 16.*

March 9, 1932: Fourth ransom note sent to Dr. Condon from Station T, NYC.

March 9, 1932: Condon receives letter, contacts Lindbergh, delivers letter to Hopewell.

March 10, 1932: Condon receives telephone call concerning ransom.

March 11, 1932: Condon publishes note to kidnappers in *Bronx Home News.*

March 12, 1932: Condon receives phone call asking if he was going to be home between 6:00 and 10:00 p.m.

March 12, 1932, p.m.: Cabdriver Joe Perrone receives $1.00 to take a letter to Dr. John Condon. Perrone later identifies Hauptmann as the person who gave him the dollar.

March 12, 1932, p.m.: Following directions, Dr. Condon finds sixth ransom note at frankfurter stand.

March 12, 1932, p.m.: Condon's first meeting with "Cemetery John" at Woodlawn Cemetery.

March 13, 1932: Frank Kelly meets Erastus Mead Hudson at Lindbergh home to process ladder for prints. Hudson notices only one nail hole in Rail 16.

March 13, 1932: Condon publishes note about money in *Bronx Home News.*

March 14, 1932: Condon repeats March 11 note in *Bronx Home News.*

March, 1932: Hildegarde Alexander sees a man "tailing" Condon. Later identifies the man as Hauptmann.

March 15, 1932: Condon repeats March 11 and 14 notes in *New York American.*

March 16, 1932: Condon publishes notes in *New York American* and *Bronx Home News.*

March 16, 1932: Condon receives laundered sleeping suit from Station E, Brooklyn.

March 17, 1932: Lindbergh given sleeping suit at Condon's home.

March 17, 1932: Condon puts note in *New York American* and *Bronx Home News.*

March 18, 1932: Condon puts note in *Bronx Home News*, "I accept."

March 19, 1932: Condon puts notes in *Bronx Home News* and *New York American.*

March 19, 1932: Eighth ransom note delivered to Station N, NYC.

March 20, 1932: Condon puts "urgent" note in *Bronx Home News.*

March 21, 1932: Condon puts note in *New York American* and *Bronx Home News.*

March 21, 1932: Condon receives eighth ransom note.

March 22, 1932: Condon puts note in *New York American* and *Bronx Home News.*

March 22, 1932: Henry "Red" Johnson eliminated as a suspect by NJSP.

March 23, 1932: Condon puts note in *New York American* and *Bronx Home News.*

March 23, 1932: Condon and Al Reich meet woman at Tuckahoe, N.Y.

March 24, 1932: Condon puts note in *New York American* and *Bronx Home News.*

March 25, 1932: Condon puts note in *New York American* and *Bronx Home News.*

March 26, 1932: Condon puts note in *New York American* and *Bronx Home News.*

March 27, 1932: Condon puts note in *Bronx Home News.*

March 28, 1932: Condon puts note in *New York American* and *Bronx Home News.*

March 29, 1932: [Hauptmann's electricity and gas cut off due to nonpayment of bill.]

March 29, 1932: Condon puts note in *New York American.*

March 29, 1932: Bessie Gow finds thumb guard near entrance to Lindbergh estate.

March 29, 1932: Ninth ransom note delivered to Station N, NYC.

March 30, 1932: Condon puts note in *New York American.*

March 30, 1932: Condon receives ninth ransom note.

March 31, 1932: Condon puts note in *New York American* and *Bronx Home News.*

April 1, 1932: Condon puts note in *New York American* and *Bronx Home News.*

April 1, 1932: Tenth ransom note sent to Condon from Fordham Station, Bronx.

April 1, 1932: Condon receives tenth ransom note.

April 2, 1932: Hauptmann's total known assets $4,941.40.

April 2, 1932: Condon note "Everything O.K." published in *New York American.*

April 2, 1932: Hauptmann does not report for work at Majestic Apartments.

April 2, 1932, p.m.: Condon receives eleventh ransom note from unidentified cab driver.

April 2, 1932, p.m.: Following directions, Condon finds twelfth ransom note at Bergen's Greenhouse.

April 2, 1932: Condon pays $50,000 to "Cemetery John"; receives "Boad Nellie" note.

April 2, 1932, p.m.: Philip Moses sees four men near St. Raymond's Cemetery.

April 2, 1932, 9:00–9:30 p.m.: *Isidor Fisch spends approximately one half hour at home of Ottilia Hoerber transacting business. He left around 9:00-9:30.*

April 2, 1932, 9:30–11:00 p.m.: Hauptmann and Hans Kloppenburg have a music night at Hauptmann's home. [In the dark, because the lights have been cut off.]

April 2, 1932, 9:30–10:00 p.m.: Benjamin Heier sees man resembling Isidor Fisch at St. Raymond's Cemetery.

April 2, 1932, 9:30–10:00 p.m.: *Joseph J. Farber has automobile accident with Benjamin Heier 8.5 miles away from St. Raymond's Cemetery.*

April 4, 1932: Hauptmann picks up tools at Majestic and leaves job.

April 4, 1932: [Hauptmann pays utility bill; service restored].

April 7 (?), 1932: First ransom bill detected at a bank near the Majestic Hotel.

May 1, 1932: Second ransom bill detected at Schrafft's Restaurant in Lower Broadway.

May, 1932: Albert S. Osborn enters the case as a handwriting examiner.

May 12, 1932: Body of Charles Lindbergh, Jr. discovered.

May 23, 1932: *Harold S. Betts examines the ladder and makes note of the four cut nail holes in Rail 16.*

May 25, 1932: Arthur Koehler enters the case.

June 10, 1932: Violet Sharpe commits suicide.

July, 1932: Gerta and Karl Henkel meet Hauptmann at Hunter's Island.

August, 1932: *Henkels introduce Hauptmann to Isidor Fisch.*

December, 1932: *Anna Hauptmann quits her job.*

May, 1933: Oscar Bruchman sees Isidor Fisch pay for a cab ride. Fisch has a roll of bills.

May 2, 1933: J.J. Faulkner exchanges $2980 worth of gold notes from ransom money.

May 3, 1933: Isidor Fisch gives Sam Streppone a shoebox sized package to hold for a few days.

August, 1933: Gustave Miller repairs leak at Hauptmann's apartment. Sees leak in closet.

August 2, 1933: Theron Main sees Isidor Fisch in a bank.

August 18, 1933: Theron Main sees Isidor Fisch with a number of gold notes.

August 19, 1933: Isidor Fisch books passage on a ship to Germany for 12/6/1933.

November, 1933: Hauptmann lends Isidor Fisch $2,000.

November 14, 1933: Isidor Fisch pays for ticket to Germany. Has big roll of bills.

November, 1933: Bertha Hoff sees Isidor Fisch with a bundle of money.

November 26, 1933: Five dollar ransom note passed at Loew's Sheridan Square Theater. Cashier Cecile Barr later identifies Hauptmann as the passer.

November 26, 1933: Birthday party for Hauptmann at his residence.

November 29, 1933: Arthur Koehler visits National Millwork and Lumber Company in the Bronx, NY.

December 2, 1933: Farewell party for Isidor Fisch at Hauptmann's home. Fisch gives Hauptmann shoebox.

December 6, 1933: Isidor Fisch leaves for Germany.

December 16, 1933: *Isidor Fisch arrives in Germany. He has $500 in his possession.*

March, 1934: Arthur Koehler sees the entire ladder for the first time.

March 29, 1934: Isidor Fisch dies in Germany.

June 25, 1934: Hauptmann wraps several stacks of gold notes in paper from the *New York Daily News.* They are later found hidden in his garage in two different places.

August, 1934: Hauptmann discovers ransom money in Fisch's shoebox.

September 6, 1934: Hauptmann wraps several stacks of gold notes in paper from the *New York Daily Mirror.* They are later found hidden in his garage in two different places.

September 15, 1934: Hauptmann buys gas at Warner-Quinlan gas station in the Bronx. Pays for it with a $10.00 gold certificate. Attendant writes his tag number on the bill.

September 18, 1934: Ransom bill bearing Hauptmann's license tag number discovered by bank teller. Bill traced back to Warner-Quinlan gas station. Attendant later identifies Hauptmann as passer of bill.

September 19, 1934: Hauptmann arrested $20.00 ransom bill found in his pocket.

September 19, 1934: Paper similar to that used for ransom notes found in Hauptmann's writing desk.

September 20, 1934: Detectives find $13,760 in ransom money in Hauptmann's garage. The money is wrapped in pages from the *New York Daily News* and the *New York Daily Mirror.*

September 21, 1934: Anna Hauptmann hires James Fawcett to defend Hauptmann in extradition proceedings.

September 24, 1934: Detectives find Condon's address and phone number written on board in Hauptmann's closet.

September 26, 1934: Detectives find $850 in ransom money concealed in block of wood in Hauptmann's garage.

September 26, 1934: Detectives find board missing from Hauptmann's attic.

October 9, 1934: Rail 16 nail holes matched to nail holes in Hauptmann's attic.

October 15, 1934: Hauptmann's extradition trial begins.

October 16, 1934: Hauptmann loses extradition trial. People ex rel. Hauptmann v Haney, 153 Misc. 61; 274 N.Y.S. 813 (Bronx County, 1934).

October 19, 1934: Hauptmann loses his appeal of the extradition trial. People ex rel. Hauptmann v. Haney, 242 A.D. 257; 274 N.Y.S. 824 (App.Div. 1934).

October 19, 1934: Hauptmann returned to New Jersey to stand trial for murder of Charles A. Lindbergh, Jr.

November 2, 1934: Hauptmann discharges Fawcett and hires Edward J. Reilly to defend him on charges of murder in New Jersey.

December, 1934: Arthur Koehler visits Bronx lumberyard second time.

December 19, 1934: Hauptmann files suit to compel Fawcett to turn over his files to Reilly.

December 31, 1934: Trial court gives Fawcett a lien in the amount of $ 4,221.57 on Hauptmann's file and rules that he can keep the file until the lien is satisfied.

January 2, 1935: Hauptmann's murder trial begins.

January 18, 1935: Appellate court orders Fawcett to turn his files on Hauptmann over to Reilly, Hauptmann's trial attorney. In re Petition of Hauptmann, 243 A.D. 616; 277 N.Y.S. 631 (App.Div. 1935).

February 13, 1935: Hauptmann convicted of murder, sentenced to death.

February 13, 1935: Foreman Charles Walton announces "No one will ever learn from us what went on in that jury room."

February 14, 1935: In a jailhouse interview, Hauptmann proclaims his innocence and asks for financial aid to prosecute his appeal.

February 15, 1935: Hauptmann signs pauper's affidavit seeking state payment for the transcript of the trial testimony.

February 19, 1935: Trenchard accepts pauper's oath and orders state to pay for transcript, stays execution date to accommodate appeal.

February 19, 1935: Petition for writ of error to Supreme Court denied by chancellor of Oyer and Terminer (trial) court.

February 19, 1935: Mark O. Kimberling's appointment as warden of prison in Trenton approved by New Jersey Senate.

February 21, 1935: Writ of error to Court of Errors and Appeals to review Hauptmann's conviction obtained & served on Kimberling.

February 23-24, 1935: Two $10.00 Lindbergh ransom bills passed at East Boston airport.

February 27, 1935: Anna Hauptmann makes first public appearance asking for donations to defense fund.

March 28, 1935: Defense moves to continue case until October term of Court of Errors and Appeals. Wilentz objects. Delay granted until May term, but not October term. Hearing set for June 20.

March 29, 1935: Reilly presents bill for $25,000 to Hauptmann and his wife.

April 3, 1935: Anna Hauptmann dismisses Reilly as counsel for Hauptmann. Reilly sues for $25,000. Later gets court order tying up defense funds until his bill paid.

April 17, 1935: Reilly writes NJ Bar asking for invest-tigation of Fisher's conduct in defense of Hauptmann.

April 27, 1935: President of NJ Bar rejects Reilly's request for investigation of Fisher.

April 29, 1935: Egbert Rosencrans sues to enjoin Jersey Law Publications Society from selling copies of official transcript to general public. Suit filed on behalf of Hauptmann and Somerset Publishing Co.

April 30, 1935: Hauptmann loses petition to enjoin publication.

May 2, 1935: Defense requests permission to take depositions in support of appeal to show disorder surrounding trial. Request denied. Defense request to include prosecution summations in record granted.

May 4, 1935: Reilly obtains order tying up defense fund.

May 16, 1935: New Jersey Law Printers sues Hauptmann over cost of printing transcript.

May 18, 1935: Wilentz gets permission to include Reilly's summation in record on appeal.

May 21, 1935: Record on appeal filed with Court of Errors and Appeals.

May 29, 1935: New Jersey Chancellor Malcolm Buchanan refuses to freeze Hauptmann's defense fund, finds that Reilly is owed nothing by Hauptmann, and finds that Reilly probably owes Hauptmann $5,000 for money he obtained from trust fund by "fraudulent and inequitable means."

June 4, 1935: Brooklyn New York Supreme Court Justice Charles C. Lockwood refuses to appoint receiver to handle Hauptmann defense fund, finding that the money was donated for the appeal, and therefore, unavailable for use to pay previously existing attorneys fees.

June 18, 1935: New Jersey Supreme Court rules that suit by Fawcett's assignee to recover attorney's fees may go to trial. Matera v. Hauptmann, 13 N.J. Misc. 483; 179 A. 626 (1935).

June 20, 1935: Oral arguments held before New Jersey Court of Errors and Appeals.

July 5, 1035: Hauptmann files supplemental brief with Court of Errors and Appeals.

October 9, 1935: Court of Errors and Appeals releases its opinion affirming Hauptmann's conviction.

October 10, 1935: Warden Kimberling releases Hauptmann's autobiography.

October 15, 1935: Hauptmann obtains stay for appeal to Supreme Court.

October 16, 1935: Reilly drops suit for legal fees from Hauptmann.

October 18?, 1935: Governor Harold Hoffman meets secretly with Hauptmann on death row.

October 30, 1935: Hauptmann autobiography sold for low figure to New York newspaper.

December 5, 1935: Hoffman announces his intention to ask Court of Pardons to grant Hauptmann a personal interview.

December 9, 1935: U.S. Supreme Court denies certiorari in Hauptmann's appeal. Hauptmann v. New Jersey, 296 U.S. 649; 56 S. Ct. 310; 80 L. Ed. 461(1935).

December 13, 1935: Trenchard signs Hauptmann's death warrant and sets his execution for the week of January 13.

December 23, 1935: Fisher files Hauptmann's appeal before Court of Pardons.

December 24?, 1935: Hoffman receives letter from "J.J. Faulkner."

January 11, 1936: Court of Pardons hears Hauptmann's case. He is not present. Court denies clemency.

January 14, 1936, 2:00 p.m.: Hauptmann's lawyers arrive in Trenton to present habeas corpus petition to Federal District Judge J. Warren Davis. Hauptmann signs petition.

January 14, 1936, after 4:00 p.m.: Hauptmann's lawyers arrive in Judge Davis's chambers to present writ. Davis calls Wilentz on phone. Wilentz comes to Judge's chambers. Hearing held in courtroom. Davis immediately rules from the bench and denies petition. Refuses defense request for stay.

January 16, 1936, shortly after 12:00 Noon: Application for leave to file petition for writ of habeas corpus delivered to justices as they sit in court hearing another case.

January 16, 1936, 2:00 p.m.: Supreme Court breaks for half hour lunch.

January 16, 1936, 2:34 p.m.: Supreme Court returns from lunch 4 minutes late, Chief Justice Hughes reads order denying application for leave to file petition for writ of habeas corpus. Arguments resume in case they were hearing before lunch. Ex Parte Hauptmann, 297 U.S. 693; 56 S. Ct. 385; 80 L. Ed. 985 (1936).

January 16, 1936: Anna Hauptmann meets with Hoffman. Hoffman later meets with Wilentz and Hauck. They agree to a 30 day stay of execution.

January 17, 1936: *Trenton Times* runs editorial entitled "Impeach Hoffman."

January 21, 1936: Robert Hicks rents Hauptmann's old apartment, begins investigation of attic with Arch Loney.

January 29, 1936: Hoffman orders NJSP to conduct new investigation of case; asks for weekly reports.

February 13, 1936: Sam Leibowitz has first meeting with Hauptmann.

February 14, 1936: Ellis Parker, Sr., Ellis Parker, Jr., Murray Bleefeld, Harry Weiss, and Martin Schlossman kidnap Paul Wendel in an attempt to coerce him to confess to the kidnapping and murder of the Lindbergh child.

February 17, 1936: Trenchard resentences Hauptmann; sets execution for week beginning March 30.

February 19, 1936: Leibowitz "cross-examines" Hauptmann in an unsuccessful effort to get him to confess.

February 24, 1936: After torture, Wendel confesses to the murder.

March 1, 1936: Hicks moves out of Hauptmann's old apartment, concluding his involvement in the investigation of attic. Loney continues investigation.

March 7, 1936: Loney tells Hoffman he can prove that Rail 16 did not come from attic.

March 26, 1936: Hoffman witnesses test of nail holes in attic. The nails do not fit. Rafters sent to Columbia University where they are examined and found to contain wood debris. After removal of debris, the nails fit.

March 27, 1936: Pardon board receives Wendel "confession."

March 29, 1936: Wendel surrendered to authorities, questioned by Wilentz and Hauck, repudiates confession.

March 29, 1936: Hoffman calls meeting of Court of Pardons to consider reprieve.

March 30, 1936: Court of Pardons refuses reprieve. Hoffman agrees.

March 31, 1936: Trenchard denies stay of execution, finds confession incredible.

March 31, 1936: Scheduled date of execution. Execution to occur at 8:00 p.m.

March 31, 1936, 1:30 p.m.: Mercer County grand jury foreman, Allyne Freeman, excuses Mercer County Prosecutor and begins grand jury investigation of Wendel for murder of Lindbergh baby.

March 31, 1936, 7:55 p.m.: Freeman calls Warden Mark Kimberling and says grand jury requests a 48 hour delay of execution so they can conclude their investigation. Kimberling agrees.

March 31, 1936, 8:00 p.m.: Scheduled date and time of execution.

April 1, 1936: Grand jury receives letter from Wendel volunteering to waive immunity and testify in his own defense.

April 2, 1936, 9:00 a.m.: Grand jury reconvenes to hear testimony from Wendel, Hoffman, and Wilentz. Grand jury invites Marshall to return to the hearing. Marshall accepts.

April 2, 1936, 12:00 midnight: Grand jury votes to discontinue investigation of Wendel.

April 3, 1936, a.m.: Fisher sends two wires: (1) a plea to governor for executive reprieve, and (2) a request to Hauck to have the Hunterdon County grand jury consider kidnapping charges against Wendel. Hoffman does not reply. Hauck replies that he has no formal complaint against Wendel. Fisher obtains a warrant against Wendel for kidnapping.

April 3, 1936, p.m.: Fisher wires Hauck asking that the case be put before the grand jury. Hauck replies that he will present it before the next regularly scheduled session of the grand jury.

April 3, 1936, 7:30 p.m.: Hoffman phones Kimberling and says there will be no more delays.

April 3, 1936, 8:45 p.m.: Hauptmann executed.

APPENDIX B
Proof Modules

ARREST (ARR)

Arac, Benjamin—Stenographer. Hauptmann's admission that writing on board was his.

Bruckman, Henry D.—N.Y.P.D. Found board in Hauptmann's closet bearing Condon's address and phone number.

Cashman, James M.—N.Y.P.D. Found Hauptmann's tool chest.

Cramer, Anselm—N.Y.P.D. Search of garage. Finding ransom money.

Eichin, Henry—Engineer. Map of Bronx.

Enkler, Charles F. W.—N.Y.P.D. Search of garage. Finding ransom money.

Fink, Barney L.—New York Telephone Company. Identified Condon's phone number.

Petrosino, James Paul—New York Police Department (N.Y.P.D.) Search of Hauptmann's garage. Finding ransom money.

Seery, William F.—F.B.I. Identifying Hauptmann's tag number on bill. Arrest of Hauptmann.

Sisk, Thomas H.—F.B.I. Arrest of Hauptmann. Recovery of ransom bill from him.

Tobin, Maurice W.—N.Y.P.D. Identifying money found in garage.

Wallace, John—N.J.S.P. Circumstances of Hauptmann's arrest.

AUTOPSY (AUT)

Allen, William J.—Discovery of body of Lindbergh baby.

Dormer, Elmira—No children missing from St. Michael's Orphanage in March of 1932.

Gow, Bessie Mowat—Identification of body of Charles A. Lindbergh, Jr.

Lindbergh, Sr., Charles A.—Identification of body of Charles A. Lindbergh, Jr.

Mitchell, M.D., Charles H.—M.E. Conducted autopsy.

Swayze, Walter H.—Coroner. Recovery of body. Delivery to morgue.

Walsh, Harry W.—Jersey City Police. Recovery of body.

Wilson, Orville—Discovery of body of Lindbergh baby.

Zapolsky, Andrew—N.J.S.P. Recovery of body.

CORRESPONDENCE (COR)

Condon, John F.—Delivered ransom to Cemetery John.

Lindbergh, Sr., Charles A.—Receipt of various ransom notes.

Perrone, Joseph Anthony—Took ransom note from Hauptmann to Condon.

O'Brien, James J.—Perrone showed him Hauptmann's letter to Condon.

Gaglio, P. Milton—Drove Condon to Lindbergh home.

Rosenhain, Max—Went with Condon to Lindbergh home.

Reich, Alfred J.—Drove Condon to first meeting with Cemetery John.

Breckinridge, Henry—Receipt of ransom letters from Hauptmann.

Alexander, Hildegarde Olga—Saw Hauptmann tailing Condon at subway station.

Lyons, John A.—N.Y.P.D. Finding paper similar to ransom notes in Hauptmann's writing desk.

DELIVERY (DEL)

Lindbergh, Sr., Charles A.—Delivery of ransom money to Hauptmann.

Condon, John F.—Delivered ransom to Cemetery John.

Breckinridge, Henry—Worked with Condon during negotiations. At Condon's home when message came for delivery of ransom.

Hacker, Myra Condon—At Condon's home when message came for delivery of ransom.

Wilson, Frank J.—I.R.S. Special agent involved in preparing ransom bills.

DISAPPEARANCE (DIS)

Achenbach, Ella—Saw Hauptmann limping shortly after May 1, 1932.

Bornmann, Lewis J.—N.J.S.P. Responding officer.

DeGaetano, Nuncio—N.J.S.P. Responding officer.

Gow, Bessie Mowat—Nurse to Lindbergh baby.

Hochmuth, Amandus—Lindbergh neighbor. Saw Hauptmann driving with ladder on day of disappearance.

Kelly, Frank A.—N.J.S.P. Responding officer, fingerprint technician.

Lamb, John J.—N.J.S.P. Responding officer.

Lindbergh, Anne Morrow—Mother of victim.

Lindbergh, Sr., Charles A.—Father of victim.

Maish, Morton Clemmer—Identified thumb guard found on grounds of Lindbergh home.

Roberts, Walter E.—Surveyor. Layout of Lindbergh

home & surrounding area.

Rossiter, Charles B.—Saw Hauptmann near Princeton Airport on Saturday before kidnapping.

Whateley, Elsie—Maid to Lindberghs.

Whited, Millard—Saw Hauptmann around Lindbergh premises before kidnapping.

Williamson, Charles E.—Hopewell Police Department. Responding officer.

Wolf, Joseph—New Jersey State Police (N.J.S.P.) Responding officer.

FINANCES (FIN)

Biedrich, Jr., Herman—Banker. Hauptmann's banking transactions.

Burkard, Joseph H.—Lawyer. Prepared mortgage for Hauptmann.

Frank, William E.—Treasury Dept. Summary of Hauptmann's finances.

Morton, Edward F.—Timekeeper, Majestic Apartments. Hauptmann did not work April 2, 1932. Quit shortly thereafter.

Mulligan, William—Stockbroker. Hauptmann's stock dealings.

Trister, Harry—Banker. Hauptmann's banking transactions.

HANDWRITING EXAMINATION (HAN)

Cassidy, Harry M.—Handwriting examiner. Connected Hauptmann to ransom notes.

Finn, James J.—N.Y.P.D. Collected known standards from Hauptmann.

Horn, William F.—N.J.S.P. Collected known standards from Hauptmann.

Osborn, Albert D.—Handwriting examiner. Connected Hauptmann to ransom notes.

Osborn, Albert S.—Handwriting examiner. Connected Hauptmann to ransom notes.

Ritchie, Thomas J.—N.J.S.P. Collected known standards from Hauptmann.

Schwarzkopf, H. Norman—N.J.S.P. Collected known standards from Hauptmann.

Sellers, Clark—Handwriting examiner. Connected Hauptmann to ransom notes.

Souder, Wilmer T.—Handwriting examiner. Connected Hauptmann to ransom notes.

Stein, Elbridge W.—Handwriting examiner. Connected Hauptmann to ransom notes.

Tyrrell, John F.—Handwriting examiner. Connected Hauptmann to ransom notes.

Walter, Herbert J.—Handwriting examiner. Connected Hauptmann to ransom notes.

LADDER (LAD)

Bornmann, Lewis J.—N.J.S.P.Chain of custody on ladder. Matching Rail 16 to Hauptmann's attic. Nail holes.

Cramer, Anselm—N.Y.P.D. Corroborating Bornmann re nail holes.

Dorn, Joseph Jennings—Sawmill owner. Milled Rails 12 & 13.

Enkler, Charles F. W.—N.Y.P.D. Corroborating Bornmann re nail holes.

Hirsch, David—Hauptmann worked for National Lumber and Millwork Company, Bronx, NY in 1931 & early 1932. Hauptmann bought lumber from yard on December 29, 1931.

Hochmuth, Amandus—Lindbergh neighbor. Saw Hauptmann driving with ladder on day of disappearance.

Keith, Stanley R.—Metallurgist. Chain of custody on ladder.

Koehler, Arthur—Wood expert. Connects Ladder to Hauptmann. Chain of custody on ladder.

Miller, Lawrence—Visits to National Lumber and Millwork Company, Bronx, NY by Arthur Koehler in 1933 and December of 1934.

Rauch, Max—Hauptmann's landlord. Missing board from attic.

Schluter, William M.—Sawmill bookkeeper. Books show Rails 12 & 13 sent to National Lumber and Millwork Company, Bronx, NY.

Sweeny, John J.—Newark Police. experimented with ladder.

RANSOM MONEY (RAN)

Barr, Cecile M.—Sells Hauptmann a movie ticket on November 26, 1933. Hauptmann pays with $5.00 ransom bill.

Bartow, Francis D.—Preparation of ransom money for delivery.

Bowen, Daniel R.—Preparation of ransom money for delivery.

Cody, William M.—Corn Exchange Bank. Took Cecile Barr's ransom bill in deposit.

Cragin, Stuart W.—Preparation of ransom money for delivery.

Echtermauer, William—Preparation of ransom money for delivery.

Finn, James J.—N.Y.P.D. Chain of custody on Cecile Barr's ransom bill.

Helmich John—Preparation of ransom money for delivery.

Hinton, Longstreet—Preparation of ransom money for delivery.

Lyle, Walter—Gas station attendant. Wrote Hauptmann's license plate number on ransom bill.

Lyons, John Joseph—Gas station attendant. Saw Hauptmann pass ransom bill.

Manville, Jr., Hiram E.—Preparation of ransom money for delivery.

Ozmec, Miran John—Corn Exchange Bank. Receipt of ransom bill from gas station. Inspection of ransom bill from gas station.

Reynolds, Stephen C.—Preparation of ransom money for delivery.

Schneider, Henry E.—Preparation of ransom money for delivery.

Seery, William F.—F.B.I. Recovery of ransom bill from Corn Exchange Bank.

Strong, William R.—Corn Exchange Bank. Receipt of ransom bill from gas station.

DEFENSE CASE (DEF)

Bolmer, William Brevoort—Gas station attendant. At 1:15 a.m. on March 1, 1932 saw man in green car with a poor ladder. This was near the Princeton airport. There was a woman with him. The man was neither Hauptmann nor Isidor Fisch.

Bonesteel, Anna—Saw Violet Sharpe near Alpine, N.J. ferry on March 1, 1932. She had no baby.

Bruchmann, Oscar John—In May of 1933 Isidor Fisch took a cab ride and paid for it from a roll of bills.

Carlstrom, Elvert—Saw Hauptmann in Fredrickson's bakery on evening of March 1, 1932.

DeBisschop, Charles—Lumberman. Not qualified as an expert. Rail 16 did not come from the attic board.

Diehl, William—Character witness. Millard Whited has bad reputation for truthfulness.

Dutt, Joseph—On March 2, 1932 went with Peter Sommer to police to report what Sommer saw.

Fredericksen, Christian—Baker in Bronx. Hauptmann was at his bakery on March 1, 1932.

Fredericksen, Kate—Hauptmann was at her husband's bakery on March 1, 1932.

Harding, Lou—Saw two men and a woman in car with ladder on March 1, 1932. They asked directions to Lindbergh home.

Hauptmann, Anna—Wife of defendant. Alibis for pertinent dates.

Hauptmann, Bruno Richard—Defendant. General denial. Alibis for pertinent dates. Explanation of ransom money.

Heier, Benjamin—Saw man resembling Isidor Fisch at St. Raymond's Cemetery between 9:30–10:00 p.m. on April 2, 1932.

Henkel, Gerta—Met Hauptmann at Hunter's Island in July of 1932. Fisch met Hauptmann at Hunter's Island also.

Henkel, Karl—Introduced Hauptmann to Fisch in July or August of 1932.

Heyne, Hilda—Attended Isidor Fisch's going away party on December 2, 1933.

Heyne, Otto—Attended Isidor Fisch's going away party on December 2, 1933.

Hile, Augusta—Loaned $4350 to Isidor Fisch. He never paid it back.

Hoff, Bertha—In October or November of 1933 Isidor Fisch came to her house with Alfred Budreau. Fisch had a bundle of money.

Hudson, Erastus Mead—Fingerprint expert. Used silver nitrate method to raise more than 500 identifiable prints from Ladder. Hauptmann's prints should have been on the ladder. Only two nail holes in Rail 16 and only one of them was square.

Joerg, Carl Herman—On March 2, 1932 went with Peter Sommer to police to report what Sommer saw.

Kelly, Frank A.—N.J.S.P. Fingerprinting ladder. Fingerprinting baby's bedroom. Finding no prints.

Kiss, Louis—Saw Hauptmann in Fredrickson's bakery on evening of March 1, 1932 and later went to home of Leo Singer and discussed Singer's new radio.

Kloeppenburg, Hans—Attended birthday party for Hauptmann on November 26, 1933. Attended Fisch's going away party.

Kubler, Louis—N.J.S.P. Present for examination of ladder by Dr. Erastus Hudson.

Lenz, George E. J.—Character witness. Millard Whited has bad reputation for truthfulness.

Lupica, Sebastian Benjamin—Saw man resembling Hauptmann driving car with ladder in it near Lindbergh home on March 1, 1932.

Main, Theron J.—On August 2, 1933 saw Isidor Fisch in a bank. On August 3, 1933 saw Fisch in possession of a number of gold notes.

Manley, Walter—Saw Hauptmann in Fredrickson's bakery on evening of March 1, 1932.

Mielke, Ewald—Lumberman. Rail 16 did not come from the attic board.

Miller, Gustave—Plumber. In August 1933 did repair work at Hauptmann's and saw leak in closet.

Moses, Philip—Taxi driver. Saw four men near St. Raymond's Cemetery on April 2, 1932.

Muller, Maria—At November 26, 1933 birthday party for Hauptmann.

Orr, Hugh—Architect. Can't measure marks on solids unless you measure them in three dimensions.

Schussler, Victor—Lived in same house as Hauptmann. Attended Isidor Fisch's going away party. Lost a chisel after Hauptmann arrested.

Schwarzkopf, H. Norman—N.J.S.P. Building of duplicate ladder. Experimentation with it

Seal, Stanley—Wood worker. Planes make different marks on wood if you hold them differently.

Seykora, John E.—F.B.I. Interviewed John Condon re his return to the cemetery and discovery of footprint.

Sisk, Thomas H.—Testimony re footprint found at grave in St. Raymond's Cemetery.

Sjostrom, E. Paul—N.J.S.P. Custodian of photos of fingerprints raised from the Ladder.

Snook, Russell H.—N.J.S.P. Fingerprints on ladder.

Sommer, Peter H.—Saw two men on Weehawken ferry on evening of March 1, 1932. One resembled Isidor Fisch. Later saw them assisting Violet Sharp with a baby.

Steinweg, George—Received payment from Isidor Fisch for ticket to Germany. Fisch had a lot of money.

Streppone, Sam—On May 14, 1933 Isidor Fisch gave him a shoebox-sized package to hold for a few days.

Tartell, Joseph T.—Bought movie tickets from Cecile Barr. She couldn't recognize him.

Trendley, John M.—Handwriting examiner. Hauptmann didn't write the ransom notes.

Uhlig, Henry—Went to Germany with Fisch. Fisch bought Uhlig's ticket.

Van Henke, August—Saw Hauptmann near Fredricksen's bakery on evening of March 1, 1932.

Vetterle, Paul—At Hauptmann's birthday party on November 26, 1933.

Whithead, William—Character witness. Millard Whited has bad reputation for truthfulness.

Wollenberg, Louise—At December 2, 1933 going away party for Isidor Fisch.

Wollenberg, Otto—At December 2, 1933 going away party for Isidor Fisch.

REBUTTAL (REB)

Betts, Harold S.—Saw and made a record of the four nail holes in Rail 16 on May 23, 1932.

Bornmann, Lewis J.—Pulled eight nails out of the attic board.

Budreau, Alfred—Never went to Bertha Hoff's house with Isidor Fisch. Doesn't even know Isidor Fisch.

Christiansen, Oscar Hilbert—Account book shows that Elvert Carlstrom was working for him on March 1, 1932.

Farber, Joseph J.—On evening of March 1, 1932 had an automobile accident with Benjamin Heier approximately 8 ½ miles away from St. Raymond's Cemetery.

Fisch, Henna—When Isidor Fisch arrived in Germany, he had approximately $500.00 and nothing more.

Haring, J. Vreeland—Handwriting examiner. Hauptmann wrote the ransom notes. Did not call.

Hoerber, Ottilia—Isidor Fisch was at her house transacting business for a half hour on the evening of April 2, 1932. He left around 9:00-9:30.

Johnson, Elmer—Went to Peanut Grill with Ernest Miller and Violet Sharpe on evening of March 1, 1932.

Jung, Erna—Isidor Fisch at her home in the Bronx from 7:30 to 11:45.

Jung, Henry—Isidor Fisch at his home on the night of March 1, 1932.

Keith, Stanley R.—Metallurgist. Matching nails on ladder to nails in Hauptmann's garage. Did not call.

Koehler, Arthur—The two boards which Charles DeBisschop said came from two different trees were once part of the same board.

Kohl, Selma—Isidor Fisch's landlady. Fisch lived in the cheapest room available. He had very few clothes.

Konietzko, William—On March 2, 1932 Lou Harding reported seeing two men in a car. Harding did not mention a ladder being in the car.

Larsen, Arthur—On the night of March 1, 1932. Larsen was in Dunellen N.J. with Elvert Carlstrom working on job for Oscar Christiansen.

Levenson, Joseph O.—On the evening of March 1, 1932 he was at the home of Henry Jung in the Bronx. While there he, Jung, and Isidor Fisch transacted business.

Marshall, George—Night watchman at Morrow residence. Violet Sharpe left the residence around 8:30 and returned around 11:00 p.m.

Miller, Ernest—Met Violet Sharpe at 8:00 p.m. on March 1, 1932 at Morrow residence and went to Orangeburg to the Peanut Grill. Got her home around 10:30–11:00 p.m.

Minners, Catherine—Went to Peanut Grill with Ernest Miller and Violet Sharpe on evening of March 1, 1932.

Morrow, Elizabeth—Violet Sharpe served Morrow supper at 7:00. Did not see her after 7:45. Sharpe returned around 11:00.

O'Ryan, John F.—Hauptmann did not tell him where the ransom money was hidden until after it had been discovered by searchers.

Priest, George Madison—Translator. Translated Hauptmann's letter to the Fisches re Isidor's death.

Singer, Leo—Louis Kiss came to his home and they discussed Singer's new radio, but Singer didn't get the radio until March 10, 1932.

Wilton, George G.—Before Erastus Hudson fingerprinted the ladder, this witness took a photo of Rail 16 showing that there were four nail holes in it.

APPENDIX C

Points on Appeal

POINT I. "[T]he summation of the attorney-general violated the legal and constitutional rights of the defendant."

RULING: "[W]e find no legal error properly raised. Throughout the lengthy summation it was at one juncture, and one only, that defense counsel interposed with an objection that the state counsel was going outside the evidence. We shall return to this presently. With that exception the four lawyers representing defendant and employed by him, said nothing by way of protest." [1]

POINT I-A: "[T]he attorney-general argued with, and bullied the defendant and other witnesses on cross-examination."

RULING: "So far as the defendant himself is concerned, a rigid cross-examination was fully warranted. The state's direct case against him was strong, and as already noted, the main defense was denial of any participation in the crime, or presence at the scene. Defendant had admitted false statements in the New York proceedings; he assumed an evasive attitude on cross-examination; he admitted a series of crimes, convictions and criminal escapes in Germany, two unsuccessful attempts, and a

---

[1] New Jersey v. Hauptmann, 115 N.J.L. 412, 420, 180 A. 809, 816 (Ct.Err. & App. 1935).

third successful attempt to make unlawful entry into this country." [2]

POINT II: "[T]here was a material variance in the theory of the state and the proofs."

RULING: "The variance, if such there was, made, and could have made no difference in the defense, which was that the defendant was not there." [3]

POINT III: [The prosecutor's summation violated public policy.]

RULING: [This merely restates Points I and II.] "We deem Point III therefore to be without substance." [4]

POINT IV: "The defendant's constitutional rights under the fourteenth amendment of the constitution of the United States were contravened by the summation and material variance of theory."

RULING: "we conclude that there was no such infringement of the federal constitution." [5]

POINT V: "The venue was improperly laid in Hunterdon county instead of Mercer county."

RULING: "It was not necessary to show death in Hunterdon; proof of a felonious striking in that county, causing death wherever that occurred, was sufficient; and

---

[2] Id.
[3] Id at 816.
[4] Id at 817.
[5] Id.

we consider that of such striking there was sufficient proof, even though of a circumstantial character." [6]

POINT VI: "There was no proof of the common law crime of burglary, and the court erroneously charged the statutory crime."

RULING: [The Court disagreed, finding that there was indeed proof of common law burglary, and that the judge's instructions were sufficient to cover the common law crime.] [7]

POINT VII: "[T]here was no evidence of intent to steal [the sleeping suit because it was returned], and the court erroneously charged the jury [on that point]."

RULING: [The suit was returned in order to facilitate the extortion of $50,000.] "It was [therefore] well within the province of the jury to infer that if Condon had refused to go on with the preliminaries, the sleeping suit would never have been delivered. In that situation, the larceny was established." [8]

POINT VIII: "[T]he burglary, if any, was complete in Hunterdon county and separable from the murder presumed to have been committed in Mercer county."

RULING: "As to the argument that the crime of burglary is complete when there is a nocturnal breaking and entering with intent, that is doubtless true for the purposes of a conviction of burglary; but we think it not

---

[6] Id at 818.
[7] Id.
[8] Id.

applicable to a homicide in the commission of a burglary."[9]

POINT IX: [Reasserts that error was committed when Wilentz changed the theory of culpability for murder.]

RULING: "We have already said, and repeat, that the alternative theory of homicide suggested in the summing up by the attorney-general was not adopted by the court, nor submitted to the jury. Consequently this point is without substance.[10]

POINT X: "The court by its charge impaired a free verdict and impressed upon the jury his conclusions as to the evidence...."

RULING: "The right of the trial judge to give the jury the benefit of his individual view of the evidence, so long as he is careful to avoid controlling them by a binding instruction, is settled in the state beyond peradventure."[11]

POINT X-A: "The court by its charge ... imposed upon the defendant an unauthorized rule as to reasonable doubt."

RULING: "[T]he criticism appears to be utterly and absolutely unwarranted."[12]

POINT XI: [The court erred in refusing to give a jury instruction on expert testimony requested by the defense.]

RULING: "We find no error in the refusal...."[13]

---

[9] Id at 820.
[10] Id.
[11] Id at 821.
[12] Id at 822.

POINT XII: [The court erred in refusing to give several additional jury instructions requested by the defense.]

RULING: [The Court examines and rejects each complaint.] [14]

POINT XIII: [The court erred in refusing to allow Joseph T. Tartell to testify on behalf of the defendant.]

RULING: "We think that this was wholly irrelevant and properly excluded." [15]

POINT XIV: [The court erred in refusing to strike the testimony of Frank A. Kelly that he saw ladder marks under the nursery window.]

RULING: "Assuming the technical impropriety of the statement that they were 'ladder marks,' the other testimony put the jury in a position to form their own conclusion, and they had the ladder in evidence." [16]

POINT XIV-A: [Complained about the refusal to strike the testimony of Morton Clemmer Maish about the rust-resistant qualities of the thumb guard.]

RULING: "[After the witness had been released and had returned home to Wyoming] counsel for the first time moved to strike the testimony out. The court denied the motion on the merits. It is sufficient to say that it came too late. Moreover, the motion made the next day was to strike out the Maish testimony *in toto*. Part of it was

---

[13] Id at 823.
[14] Id at 824.
[15] Id.
[16] Id at 825.

clearly competent; and for that reason also the motion was properly denied." [17]

POINT XV: [The court erred in admitting the ladder into evidence.]

RULING: "All of the changes that had been made were described and had been accounted for. As an exhibit, the ladder was sufficiently identified, and its history was sufficiently shown to justify its admission. The claim that it was not brought home to the defendant is without substance." [18]

POINT XVI: "[T]he verdict was against the weight of evidence."

RULING: "[T]he verdict is not only not contrary to the weight of the evidence, but one to which the evidence inescapably led." [19]

---

[17] Id.
[18] Id.
[19] Id at 826.

Table of Cases

Addis v. Rushmore, 74 N.J.L. 649, 65 A. 1036 (Ct.Err. & App. 1907).

Banks v. Dretke, 540 U.S. 668 (2004).

Brady v. Maryland, 373 U.S. 83 (1963).

Castner v. Sliker, 33 N.J.L. 507 (Ct. Err. & App., 1869).

Coleman v. Public Service Coordinated Transport, 120 N.J.L. 384, 199 A. 772, 773 (Sup.Ct. 1938).

Daughtrey v. State, 325 So.2d 456 (1st DCA), *cert. denied* 336 So.2d 600 (Fla., 1976).

Ex Parte Hauptmann, 297 U.S. 693 (1936).

Hauptmann v. New Jersey, 296 U.S. 649 (1935).

Magnuson v. State, 187 Wis 122, 203 N.W. 749 (1925).

Morgan v. State, 464 So.2d 1306 (4th DCA Fla., 1985).

People *ex rel.* Hauptmann v. Hanley, 153 Misc. 61, 274 N.Y.S. 813 (New York Sup.Ct., Bronx County), *affirmed* 242 App.Div. 257 (New York Ct.App., 1934).

State v. Beigenwald, 106 N.J. 13, 524 A.2d 130 (1987).

State v. Branning, 271 Kan. 877, 887, 26 P.3d 673, 680 (2001).

State v. De Paola, 5 N.J. 1, 73 A.2d 564 (1950).

State v. Hauptmann, 115 N.J.L. 412, 180 A. 809 (Ct.Err. & App., 1935) *cert.denied*, 296 U.S. 649 (1935).

State v. Jones, 115 N.J.L. 257, 179 A. 320 (Ct.Err. & App. 1935).

State v. Kaplan, 115 N.J.L. 374, 180 A. 423 (Sup.Ct. 1935).

State v. Lafferty, 749 P.2d 1239 (Utah, 1988).

State v. Overton, 85 N.J.L. 287, 88 A.2d 689, 691 (Ct.Err. & App., 1913).

State v. Sands, 76 N.J. 127, 386 A.2d 378 (1978).

State v. Swint, 328 N.J.Super. 236, 745 A.2d 570 (2000).

State v. Warady, 77 N.J.L. 348, 349, 72 A. 37 (Sup.Ct., 1909).

United States v. Parker, 103 F.2d 857 (3rd Cir., NJ, 1939).

Bibliography

Ahlgren, Gregory, and Stephen Monier. *Crime of the Century: The Lindbergh Kidnapping Hoax*. Boston: Branden Books, 1993.

Aristotle, *Poetics and Rhetoric*. Translated by W. Rhys Roberts. New York: Barnes and Noble Books, 2005.

Berg, A. Scott. *Lindbergh*. New York: Berkley Publishing Group, 1999.

Clark, Ronald, George R. Dekle Sr., and William S. Bailey. *Cross-Examination Handbook: Persuasion, Strategies, and Techniques*. Frederick MD: Wolters-Kluwer, 2014.

Cahill Jr., Richard T. *Hauptmann's Ladder: A Step-by-Step Analysis of the Lindbergh Kidnapping*. Kent, Ohio: Kent State University Press, 2014.

Clausewitz, Carl von. *On War*. Translated by J.J. Graham. London: N. Trubner and Company, 1873. [https://archive.org/details/onwartrbyjjgrah00claugoog]

Cook, William A. *The Lindbergh Baby Kidnapping*. Mechanicsburg, Pa.: Sunbury Press, 2014.

Corbett, Edward P.J., and Robert J. Connors, *Classical Rhetoric for the Modern Student*. New York: Oxford University Press, 1999.

Dekle, Sr., George R. *The Last Murder: The Investigation, Prosecution, and Execution of Ted Bundy*. Santa Barbara: Praeger, 2011.

Demaris, Ovid. *The Lindbergh Kidnapping Case: The True Story of the Crime that Shocked the World*. Derby, Conn.: Monarch Books, 1961.

Falzini, Mark W., and James Davidson. *New Jersey's Lindbergh Kidnapping and Trial.* Charleston, SC: Arcadia Publishing, 2012.

Falzini, Mark W. *Their Fifteen Minutes: Biographical Sketches of the Lindbergh Case.* Bloomington, IN: iUniverse, 2008.

Fisher, Jim. *The Lindbergh Case.* New Brunswick, N.J.: Rutgers University Press, 1994.

Foldes, Michael, Diana Bean, and Chuck Haupt. *Sleeping Dogs: A True Story of the Lindbergh Baby Kidnapping.* Amazon Digital Services, Inc.: Michael Foldes, 2012.

Gardner, Lloyd C. *The Case That Never Dies: The Lindbergh Kidnapping.* Princeton: Rutgers University Press, 2004.

Graham, Shirley A. "Anatomy of the Lindbergh Kidnapping," *Journal of Forensic Science,* Vol. 42, No. 3. 368-377. May, 1997.

Haring, J. Vreeland. The *Hand of Hauptmann: The Handwriting Expert Tells the Story of the Lindbergh Case.* Plainfield, NJ: The Hamer Publishing Company, 1937.

Holden, Henry M. *Famous Cases of the FBI: The Lindbergh Baby Kidnapping.* Amazon Digital Services, Inc.: Blackhawk Publishing, 2012.

Keith, Stanley R. "Identification of the Lindbergh Ladder Nails." *The Iron Age.* 16-22, 71. October 17, 1935.

Kennedy, Ludovic. *The Airman and the Carpenter: The Lindbergh Kidnapping and the Framing of Richard Hauptmann.* New York: Viking Penguin, Inc., 1985.

Kinney, Thomas D., and Kenneth R. Broda. "The Pathologist's Assistant." *Human Pathology* 5, no. 5 (1974): 503-505.

Koehler, Arthur. "Technique Used in Tracing the Lindbergh Kidnapping Ladder." *The Journal of Criminal Law and Criminology,* Vol. 27, No. 5. 356-365. 1937.

Lantham, Richard A. *A Handlist of Rhetorical Terms*, 2nd ed. Berkley: University of California Press, 1991.

Moore, Brooke Noel, and Richard Parker. *Critical Thinking*, 7th ed. New York: McGraw Hill, 2003.

O'Brien, P.J. *The Lindberghs: The Story of a Distinguished Family*. International Press, 1935.

Quintilian. *The Orator's Education*, Vol 2. Translated by Donald A. Russell. Cambridge: Harvard University Press, 2001.

Rhetorica ad Herennium. Translated by Harry Caplan. Cambridge: Harvard University Press, 1999.

Scaduto, Anthony. *Scapegoat: The Lonesome Death of Bruno Richard Hauptmann*. G. P. Putnam's Sons, New York 1976.

Schrager, Adam J. *The Sixteenth Rail: The Evidence, the Scientist, and the Lindbergh Kidnapping*. Golden CO: Fulcrum, 2013.

Sellers, Clark. "The Handwriting Evidence against Hauptmann." *Journal of Criminal Law and Criminology*, Vol. 27, No. 6. 874-886. Mar. - Apr., 1937.

Transcript of Trial, *State of New Jersey v. Bruno Richard Hauptmann*. Hunterdon County Oyer and Terminer Court, 1934. [http://heinonline.org/HOL/Index?index=trials/abzf&collection=trials]

Waller, George. *Kidnap: The Shocking Story of the Lindbergh Case*. New York: Pocket Books, 1962.

Westcott, Edward Noyes. *David Harum: A Story of American Life*. New York: D. Appleton and Company, 1899.

Zorn, Robert. *Cemetery John: The Undiscovered Mastermind of the Lindbergh Kidnapping*. New York: The Overlook Press, 2012.

Index